# FLOYD CLYMER'S BOOK OF THE SOLEX CARBURETOR

## INTRODUCTION

Welcome to the world of digital publishing ~ the book you now hold in your hand, while unchanged from the original publication, was printed using the latest state of the art digital technology. The advent of print-on-demand has forever changed the publishing process, never has information been so accessible and it is our hope that this book serves your informational needs for years to come. If this is your first exposure to digital publishing, we hope that you are pleased with the results. Many more titles of interest to the classic automobile and motorcycle enthusiast, collector and restorer are available via our website at **www.VelocePress.com.** We hope that you find this title as interesting as we do.

## NOTE FROM THE PUBLISHER

The information presented is true and complete to the best of our knowledge. All recommendations are made without any guarantees on the part of the author or the publisher, who also disclaim all liability incurred with the use of this information.

## TRADEMARKS

We recognize that some words, model names and designations, for example, mentioned herein are the property of the trademark holder. We use them for identification purposes only. This is not an official publication.

## INFORMATION ON THE USE OF THIS PUBLICATION

In today's information age we are constantly subject to changes in common practice, new technology, availability of improved materials and increased awareness of chemical toxicity. As such, it is advised that the user consult with an experienced professional prior to undertaking any procedure described herein. While every care has been taken to ensure correctness of information, it is obviously not possible to guarantee complete freedom from errors or omissions or to accept liability arising from such errors or omissions. Therefore, any individual that uses the information contained within, or elects to perform or participate in do-it-yourself repairs or modifications acknowledges that there is a risk factor involved and that the publisher or its associates cannot be held responsible for personal injury or property damage resulting from the use of the information or the outcome of such procedures.

It is important that the reader recognizes that any instructions may refer to either the right-hand or left-hand sides of the vehicle or the components and that the directions are followed carefully. One final word of advice, this publication is intended to be used as a reference guide, and when in doubt the reader should consult with a qualified technician.

# CONTENTS

Compiled and updated from the **Floyd Clymer** book, 'Handbook of Imported Carburetors & Fuel Injection', this publication focuses on the SOLEX series of carburetors. Specifically, the **C 32 PAIA-7, 32 PAIA-4, 44 PHH, B 32, PBI-5, 32 PBI, 40 PBIC (or 40 PICB), 40 PI, 22 ICBT, 28 IBT, 32 PIBT, 32 PDIST, 32 DISTA, B 32 PAIA, 32 PAIA-4, 26 VFI, 26 VFIS, 28 PCI, 28 PICT (or 28 PICT I), 30 PICT, 32 PHN, 32 PDSIT.**

It is important for the reader to remember that the data was extracted from a book that was published in the mid 1960's, so the information it contains is relevant to that date. However, as this series of **Solex** carburetors was in production for more than 20 years after the publication date, much of the information it contains is applicable to those same carburetors that were fitted to later makes and models of automobiles. Therefore, while some minor differences in mounting and linkage may occur, the same adjustment and tuning data can be applied.

Consequently, for the sake of simplification, this book focuses on six major UK and European manufacturers that utilized **Solex** carburetors including Alfa Romeo, Jaguar, Mercedes-Benz, Renault, Sunbeam and Volkswagen. In addition, there are a number of different models included in the index under each of those manufacturers that identifies some, but certainly not all, makes and models that utilize the same, or similar, carburetors.

The book is split into two main sections; the first section includes an overview of design and operational information, overhaul and adjustments, the second section focuses, in detail, on the installation of the various **Solex** carburetors identified above.

While there are certainly many other technical books that deal with current range of **Solex** carburetors, including those manufactured under license by Mikuni, detailed information on the earlier carburetors is more difficult to find. Consequently, we believe this book is an important addition to any automotive enthusiast's library.

# INDEX

The different SOLEX carburetors covered in this publication are listed below. In addition, examples of the manufacturers and the vehicles that utilize those carburetors are also identified.

However, it should be noted that many of these carburetors were also installed on other automobile makes and models. Therefore, while there may be some minor differences in mounting and linkage, the same maintenance and adjustment data can be applied. For example, the *Mercedes-Benz 190 SL uses a 44 PHH SOLEX which is also used by Alfa Romeo.

| | | |
|---|---|---|
| SOLEX (General) - Operation, overhaul & adjustments | | Page 1 |
| C 32 PAIA-7<br>32 PAIA-4<br>44 PHH | Alfa Romeo<br>Giulia 1600TI<br>2600 Sedan, Spider & Sprint | Page 55 |
| B 32<br>PBI-5 | Jaguar 2.4 | Page 85 |
| 44 PHH | Mercedes-Benz 190 SL<br>(* See note above) | Page 76 |
| 32 PBI<br>40 PBIC (or 40 PICB) | Porsche 356 | Page 95 |
| 40 PI | Porsche 911 | Page 108 |
| 22 ICBT<br>28 IBT<br>32 PIBT<br>32 PDIST<br>32 DISTA | Renault<br>4CV, Dauphine<br>Caravelle & Speciale<br>1130<br>R8 | Page 118 |
| B 32 PAIA<br>32 PAIA-4 | Sunbeam<br>Alpine III, IV & Rapier IV | Page 124 |
| 26 VFI<br>26 VFIS<br>28 PCI<br>28 PICT (or 28 PICT I)<br>30 PICT | Volkswagen<br>Beetle 1100, 1200 & 1300<br><br>Transporter 1200 & 1500<br>Beetle 1300, 1500 & Karmann Ghia | Page 153 |
| 32 PHN<br>32 PDSIT | Volkswagen<br>1500, 1500S & 1600 | Page 170 |

## IMPORTANT INFORMATION – PLEASE READ

Please note that for the sake of accuracy, the predominance of the information in this publication was translated exactly as it was presented in the original Solex French language factory manuals.

Consequently, some of the phrasing, grammar, punctuation and word usage may be subtly different from that commonly used in the English language. However, the information, as presented, is readily understandable.

In addition, while we have done our best to identify any anomalies and errors that may have occurred during the translation process, we are certain that we will have missed one or two and we request your indulgence in ignoring them.

Finally, as the original factory documents were supplied to authorized dealers and repair facilities that were expected to be familiar with Solex products, they were written with little regard to their use by an enthusiastic amateur. Therefore, to better assist the novice reader, wherever practical, illustrations that relate to a particular segment of text have been referenced and those appropriate text sections have also been identified.

# SOLEX CARBURETORS

Solex carburetors are identified by numerals and letters which relate to throttle bore size and type. The 28 PCI, for example is a 28 mm downdraft, where the letter I signifies a single-port downdraft. A 40 PHH, is a 40 mm dual side-draft, or horizontal port type, and a 40 PII is a dual downdraft of the same size. Other letters in the designation indicate various functions and adjuncts. Similarly, each variable part in the Solex is numbered and identified by a system which enables the mechanic to substitute intelligently. A full explanation of these parts and their identification is included in the following discussion of Solexes.

All Solex carburetors are fitted to the engine in accordance with the principles outlined here. When replacing another type of carburetor with a Solex or when using a Solex of a type not originally fitted, be sure that these methods are employed.

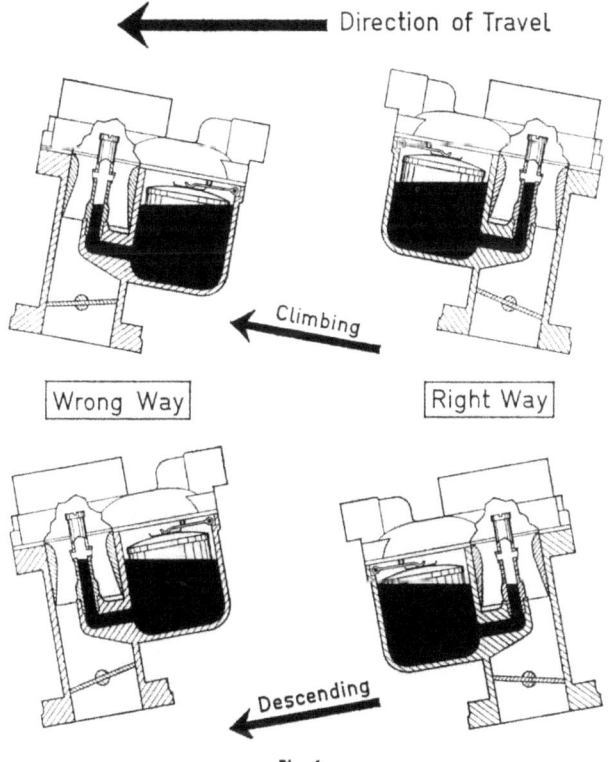

Fig. 4

Position of the Float Chamber

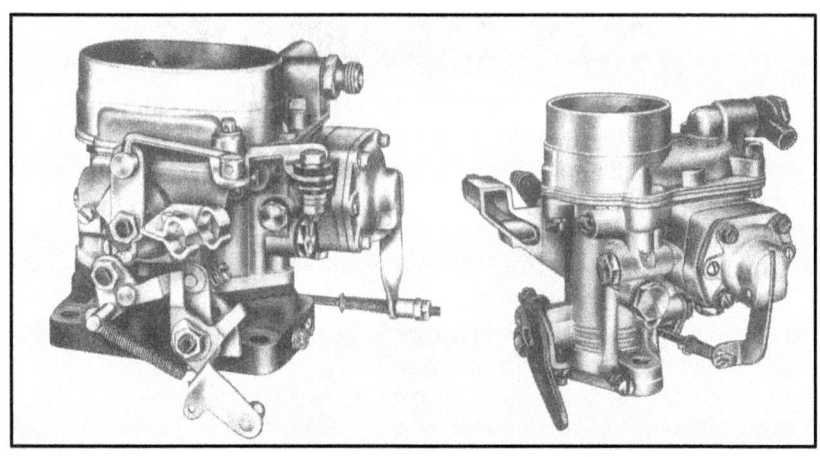

Type 32 PAITA (Downdraught Compound Carburetor)   Type 32 PICB (Downdraught Carburetor)

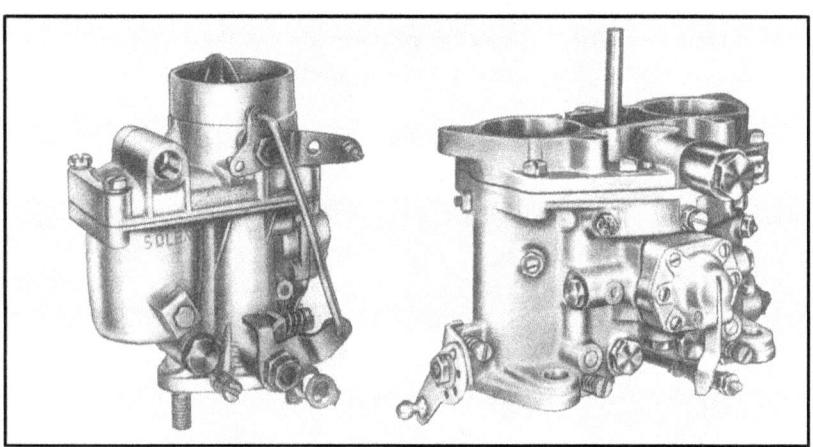

Type 28 PCI (Downdraught Carburetor)   Type 40 PII-4 (Dual-port Downdraught Carburetor)

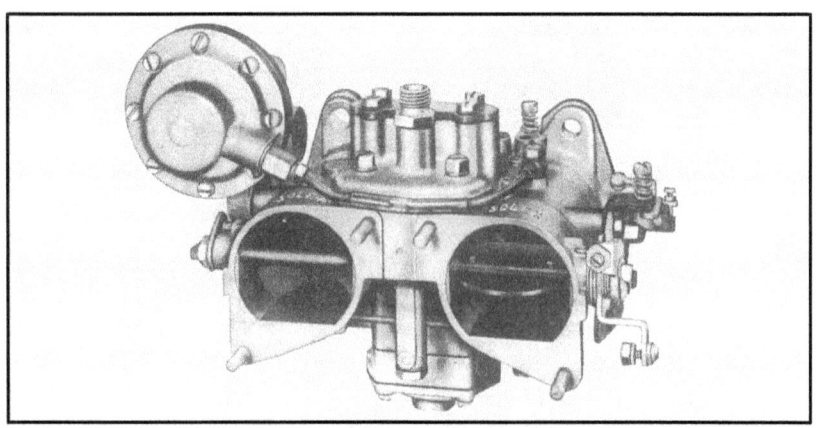

Type 44 PHH (Horizontal Compound Carburetor)

## THE FITTING OF CARBURETORS

The carburetor should be fitted with the float chamber forward to avoid fuel starvation when accelerating or climbing (Fig. 4).

Flange gaskets should not be thicker than 1 m/m as thicker or soft gaskets may cause the flange to warp.

The carburetor securing nuts should be tightened evenly to prevent distortion or breakage of the flange. Where possible shakeproof washers should be used.

When fitting the throttle control linkage it is essential to ensure that there is no play in the controls and no tension on the levers. Make sure that the throttle butterfly opens and closes completely.

Keep the control operation in mind when fitting the controls if the throttle lever is connected to the control rod with a ball joint. When fitting the controls avoid angles which can cause the controls to stick or slip out of position.

When fitting multiple carburetors it is suggested that the controls are arranged as shown in **Fig. 5** as with this method tuning

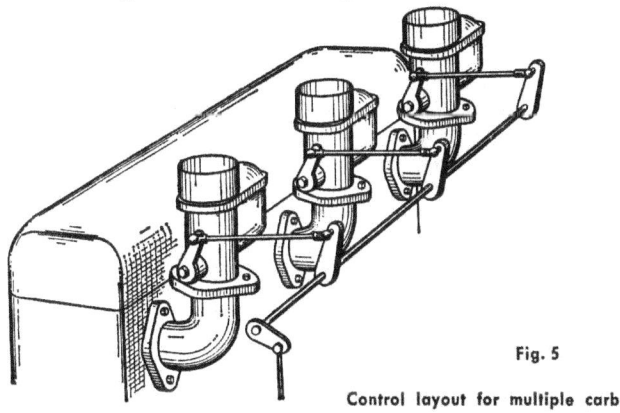

Fig. 5
Control layout for multiple carburetors

is simplified and the controls are unlikely to stick. It is not advisable to connect the throtle spindles in a direct line, i.e. end to end, and to operate them from one end, as with this method it is practically impossible to get the throttle butterflies to open and close simultaneously. The length of the operating spindle is such that it is liable to twist.

All SOLEX carburetors consist of several circuits each of which has a specific function and its own adjustable parts. These circuits are:
1. The Float System
2. The Starter System

3. The Idling System
4. The Main Jet Circuit
5. The Accelerator Pump and
6. The Enrichment Device.

## THE FLOAT SYSTEM

The Float System regulates the fuel level in the carburetor (**Fig. 6**).

The fuel must be maintained at a constant level, it is fixed for all carburetors for a fuel pump pressure equal to 1-2 metres of water and for fuel with a specific gravity of 0.730.

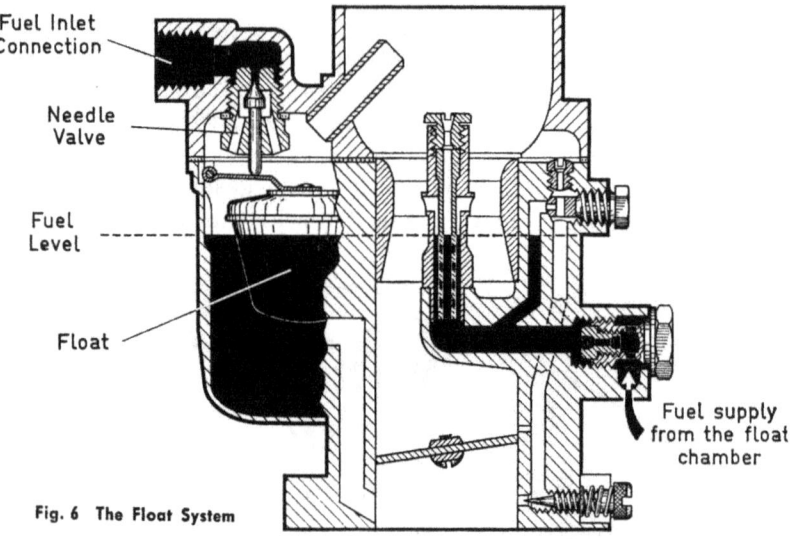

Fig. 6 The Float System

For higher fuel pump pressures a smaller needle valve must be used.

Variations in the specific gravity of the fuel and the pump pressure can be compensated for by the use of washers of different thickness under the needle valve.

## THE STARTER SYSTEM

There are two principle arrangements of the starter system: the Starter Disc Valve and the Strangler.

### A. THE STARTER DISC VALVE

The starting circuit with disc valve (**Fig. 7**) ensures instant starting with a cold engine, idling when cold and a smooth transfer.

It has two adjustable parts, the starter fuel jet **Gs** and the starter air jet **Ga**.

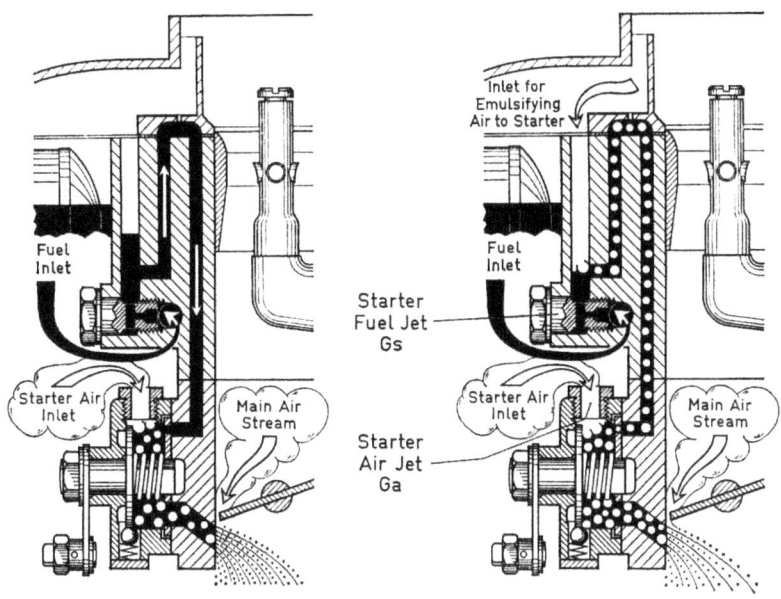

Fig. 7 Operation of the Starter Disc Valve
a) Phase 1    b) Phase 2

The starting device should be used only when the engine is cold and has not reached its normal working temperature.

As soon as the engine is warm the starting device should be put out of action, to prevent the excessive use of fuel. The starting device should not be used when attempting to start a hot or warm engine.

When operating the starting device the throttle butterfly must be kept closed in the idling position.

The starting device may be operated automatically or manually. Only the second method will be described in the following text.

Dependent upon the carburetor type there are several versions of the starter disc valve.

a) **Simple Starter**

Operation of the starter control causes the rotation of the disc valve which has only one drilling for a rich starting mixture **(Fig. 8)**.

In this version the starter control must be pulled out completely (Starter in operation) or returned fully home (Starter out of action). The starter control must never be used in an intermediate position.

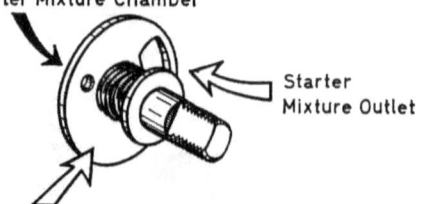

Fuel inlet to the Starter Mixture Chamber

Starter Mixture Outlet

Air Inlet through Starter Air Jet Ga

**Fig. 8** Disc Valve of a simple Starter

**b) Bi-Starter**

The disc valve of the bi-starter has two different drillings, one for a rich starting mixture the other for a weaker starting mixture (**Fig. 9**).

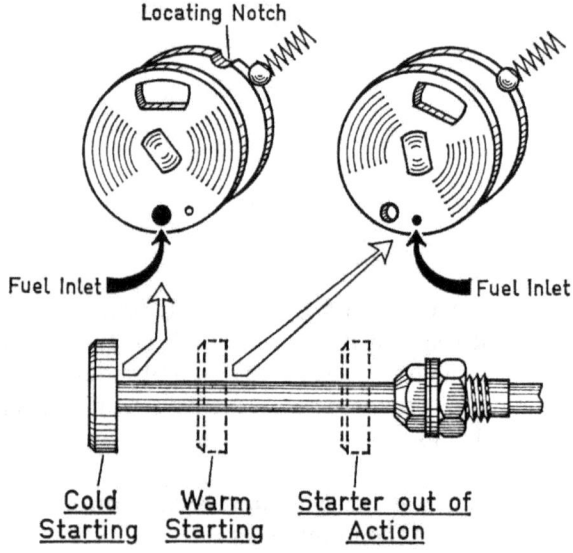

Locating Notch

Fuel Inlet — Fuel Inlet

Cold Starting | Warm Starting | Starter out of Action

**Fig. 9** Disc Valve and Starter Control of a Bi-Starter

This type has three positions:
Starter control fully pulled out = Cold starting
Starter control halfway out = Warm starting
Starter control pushed home = Starter out of action.

In the cold starting position the mixture is very rich to ensure instant starting of the cold engine. In the warm starting position, located by a notch on the disc valve and thus indicated on the movement of the starter control, the starting mixture is substantially weakened due to the small transfer drilling. This position should be used as soon as the engine warms up after a short time in the cold starting position or when a warm engine has to be restarted.

Dependent on the size of the carburetor, the bi-starter is made in three sizes (small, medium and large). The larger size differs from the other types by the addition of a permanent air vent of 3 m/m in diameter, so that a small starter air jet **Ga** can be used. The line inserted on **Fig. 10** shows approximately the correct size of the starter fuel jet **Gs** and the starter air jet **Ga** in relation to the total capaciy of he engine. In exceptional circumstances it will be found by experiment, that the size of the starter fuel jet **Gs** varies from the size indicated theoretically.

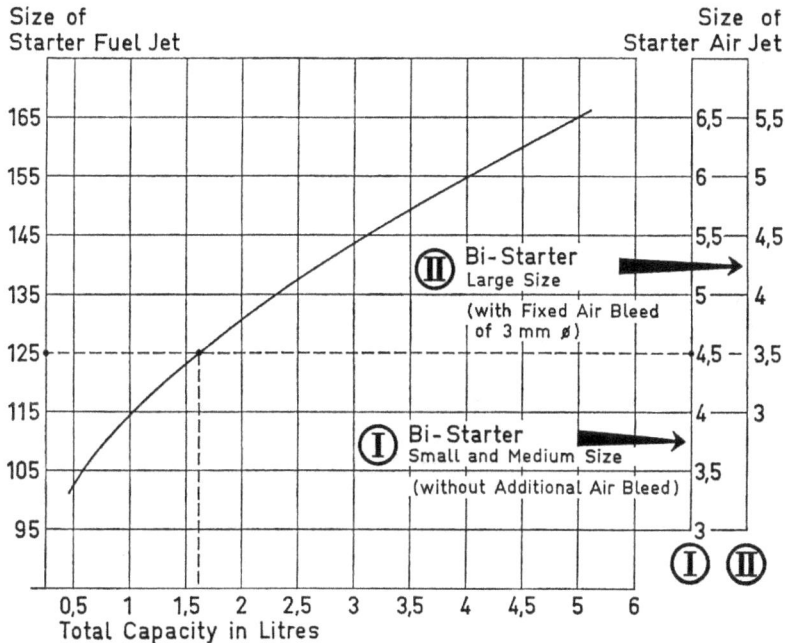

Fig. 10 Approximate sizes of jets for bi-starter in relation to total capacity

## c) Progressive Starter

The progressive starter differs from those previously described as there are no definite starter valve positions and the weakening of the starter mixture is spread over the whole movement of the starter. When the starter control is pulled out fully the richest mixture is delivered. As the starter conrol is pushed home the mixture is progressively weakened until, when the control is fully home, the starter is completely out of action.

In the progressive starter the formation of the starting mixture commences in the starter valve which has various shaped cavities on the inner face. In these cavities, fuel metered by the

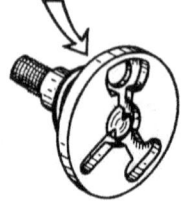

Air intake through a calibrated hole in the starter valve

**Fig. 11**

Starter Valve of a progressive starter

starter fuel jet **Gs**, or rather a preformed emulsion of fuel and air drawn from the additional air intake to the starter valve mix with air entering through a calibrated hole in the starter valve (**Fig. 12a**). In this type the calibrated hole in the starter valve replaces the starter air jet **Ga**. Rotation of the starter valve gradually reduces the size of the orifice through which the fuel passes resulting in a progressive weakening of the starter mixture similar to the warm running position of the bi-starter.

The progressive starter has an air valve which opens and closes the intake for the additional air supply.

It also has a channel between the cavity in the starter valve and the mixing chamber of the carburetor. Through this channel, known as the "quick drive away channel" additional fuel is delivered when the vehicle is driven away and the throttle butterfly opened with the starter still in operation (**Fig. 12b**). Thus a greater flexibility is given when driving away with a cold engine.

### B. THE STRANGLER (CHOKE)

The strangler is the simplest form of starting device. It consists of a butterfly, simple in operation, which closes the air intake to the carburetor.

In contrast to the starter disc valve, when the strangler is operated the throttle butterfly must be slightly opened. This is ensured by mechanical linkage between the strangler lever and the throttle lever (**Fig. 13**).

When starting the engine depression, acting on the main jet system through the open throttle butterfly, causes the discharge of fuel.

The start takes place in the same effective manner as with the starter disc valve, but the adjustment of the mixture strength in the warming-up period depends on the experience of the driver in operating the starter control.

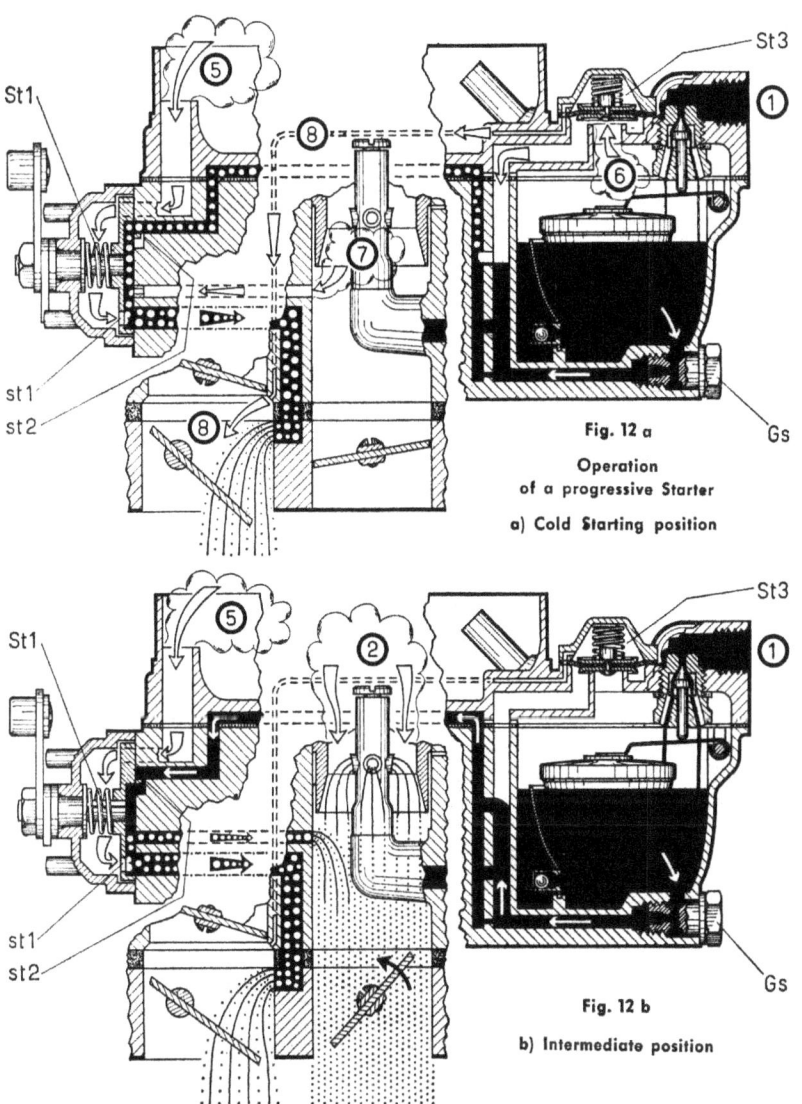

**Fig. 12 a**
Operation
of a progressive Starter
a) Cold Starting position

**Fig. 12 b**
b) Intermediate position

| | |
|---|---|
| Gs | Starter Fuel Jet |
| St 1 | Starter disc Valve |
| St 3 | Starter air valve |
| st 1 | Calibrated hole in starter valve |
| st 2 | Starter progression orifice |

| | |
|---|---|
| 1 | Fuel Inlet |
| 2 | Main air stream |
| 5 | Starter air inlet |
| 6 | Additional air intake to starter valve |
| 7 | Additional air intake to starter mixing chamber |
| 8 | Depression acts |

There are two types of strangler: the strangler with air valve and the semi-automatic strangler.

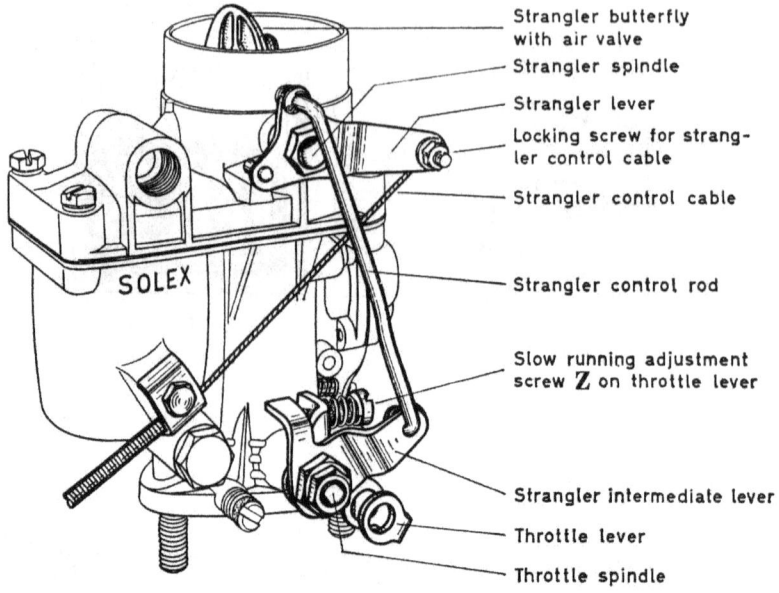

Fig. 13 Linkage between the strangler lever and the throttle lever

a) **Strangler Butterfly with Air Valve (Fig. 14)**

In this type the offset strangler butterfly has a spring loaded air valve on the larger side, which opens as soon as the engine starts and it is subjected to depression. This allows the air for the starting mixture to enter the mixture chamber.

The strangler butterfly remains in the closed position.

b) **Semi-Automatic Strangler (Fig. 15)**

In this type the air for the starting mixture passes the strangler butterfly. The strangler butterfly, which is offset on a freely moving spindle, flutters rapidly its movement being determined by depression on one side and by the strangler butterfly on the other.

## THE IDLING SYSTEM

### A. IDLING WITH MIXTURE CONTROL (Fig. 16)

The idling system consists of four adjustable parts: the pilot jet **g**, the pilot jet air bleed **u**, the volume control screw **W** which controls the output of the pilot jet and the slow running adjustment screw **Z** controlling the idling speed.

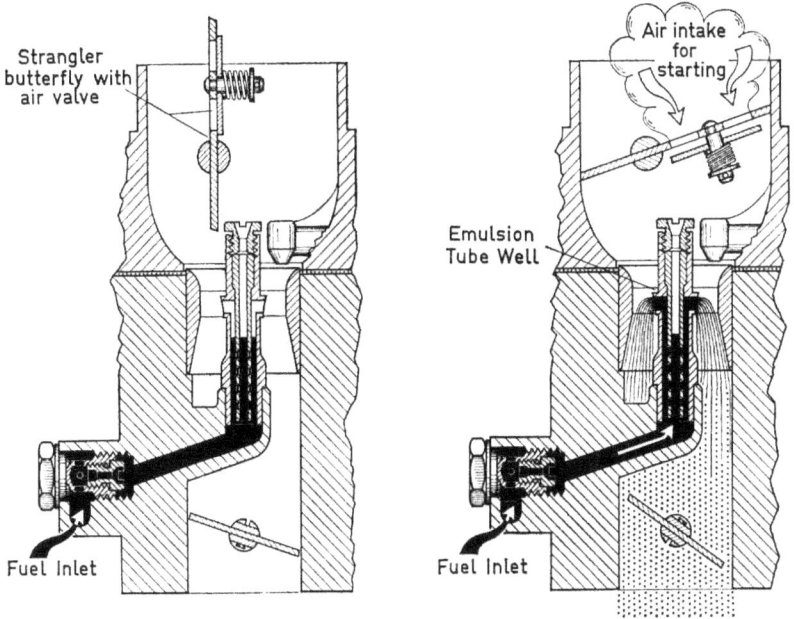

**Fig. 14 Strangler Butterfly with Air Valve**

a) Normal position            b) Starting position

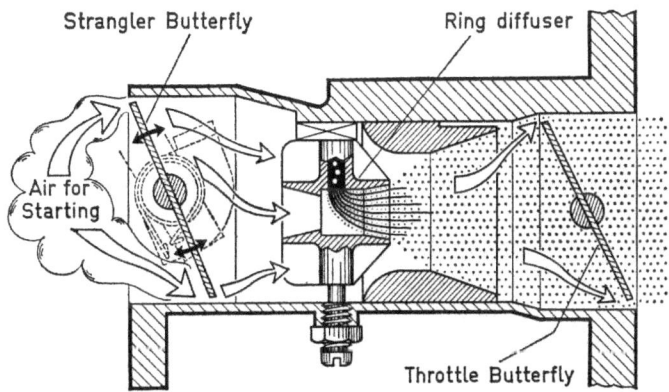

**Fig. 15 Semi-Automatic Strangler**

Great attention must be given to the correct adjustment of the idling. Even wih the best carburetors incorrect adjustment of the idling can cause trouble in operation. We therefore advise that great care should be taken in making the idling adjustment.

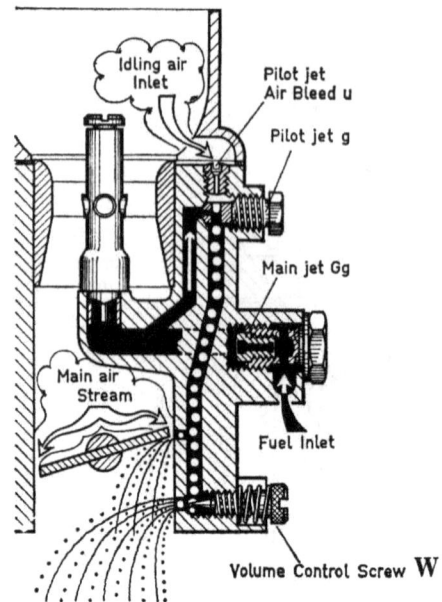

Fig. 16 Idling with mixture control

Check the condition of the plugs and make sure that plug gaps (0.6-0.8 m/m — follow the manufacturers specification) are correct before adjusting the idling.

When adjusting the idling of simple carburetors proceed as follows:
1. Let the engine reach its normal working temperature.
2. Screw in the slow running adjustment screw **Z** to increase idling speed slightly.
3. Unscrew the volume control screw **W** until the engine commences to run unevenly (to "hunt") then screw in slowly until the engine runs evenly.
4. Slowly unscrew the slow running adjustment screw **Z** until the idling speed returns to normal.
5. If the engine is then "hunting" slightly, screw in the volume control screw **W** a little more.

When adjusting the idling of dual port carburetors proceed as follows:
1. Let the engine reach its normal working temperature then switch off.
2. Screw both volume control screws **W** in fully then unscrew each one complete turn.
3. Start engine.
4. Adjust slow running adjustment screw **Z** to give correct

idling speed.

5. If the engine commences to "hunt" (mixture too rich), screw both volume controls **W** in slightly, and by an equal amount.

6. If the engine commences to "stagger" (mixture too lean), unscrew both volume control screws **W** by an equal amount.

**NOTE:**
Unscrewing the volume control screw **W** makes the idling mixture richer, screwing it in makes the mixture weaker. The volume control screw **W** should never be screwed in too tightly.

The "normal" idling speed is generally considered to be approximately 500 r.p.m. We recommend that, with modern engines, the idling speed should never be set at slower speeds; on the contrary with some engines the speed may be increased. If the slow running is set too slow it is frequently the cause of stalling.

A revolution counter simplifies the adjustment and enables the idling to be adjusted very accurately and we strongly recommend its use.

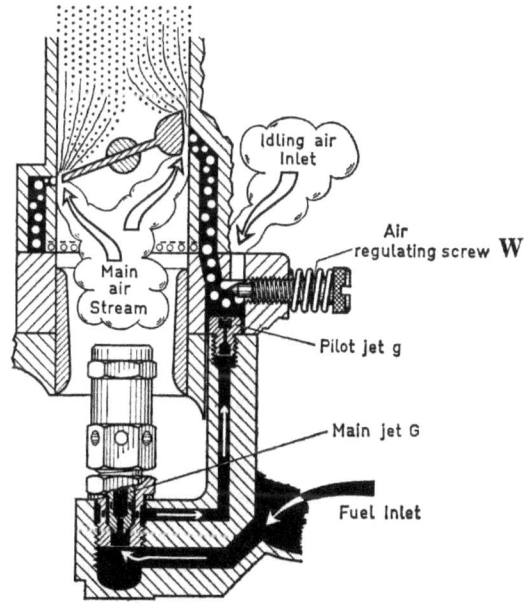

Fig. 17 Idling with air control

### B. IDLING WITH AIR CONTROL (Fig. 17)

Some of the updraft and horizontal carburetors of the older BF type have idling with air control. This idling system incorporates three adjustable parts: the pilot jet **g**, the air regulating screw **W** and the slow running adjustment screw **Z** (**Fig. 13**).

When adjusting the idling of these carburetors proceed as follows:
1. Let the engine reach its normal working temperature.
2. Screw in the slow running adjustment screw **Z** to increase idling speed slightly.
3. Screw in the air regulating screw **W** until the engine commences to run unevenly (to "hunt") then unscrew slowly until the engine runs evenly.
4. Unscrew the slow running adjustment screw **Z** slowly until the idling speed returns to normal (in this case 400-500 r.p.m.).

**NOTE:**

Unscrewing the air regulating screw **W** weakens the idling mixture, screwing it in makes it richer. The air regulating screw should never be screwed in too tightly.

**C. MISCELLANEOUS**

a) **By-pass Orifices**

The drillings in the throttle chamber close to the throttle butterfly, are known as the "by-passes." There may be one or more of these orifices which are connected with the idling system.

The purpose of the by-pass is to ensure a smooth transfer from the idling to the normal driving position, i.e. to the main jet circuit.

The position of by-pass drilling or drillings may be varied. Not every new carburetor is therefore suitable for a given engine — the position of the by-pass needs careful checking to see which gives the best transfer.

If, after fitting a new carburetor the transfer proves unsatisfactory due to a flat-spot when accelerating slowly, the throttle butterfly should, if possible be located on the flat-spot. This can be done by adjustment of the slow running screw. The carburetor should then be removed and the position of the by-pass in relation to the edge of the throttle butterfly determined.

A flat-spot usually occurs when accelerating if either:
a) the throttle butterfly has passed the by-pass orifice and the main jet has yet started to operate (**Fig. 18a**) or
b) if to the contrary, the throttle butterfly has not yet reached the by-pass orifice (**Fig. 18b**).

In the following we shall endeavor to explain how the by-pass and the throttle butterfly edge may be brought closer together or further separated.

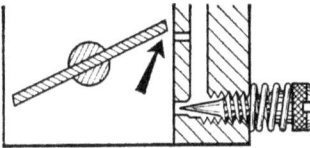
a) The throttle butterfly has passed the "by-pass" orifice.

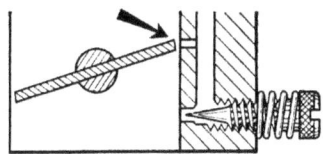
b) The throttle butterfly has not reached the "by-pass" orifice.

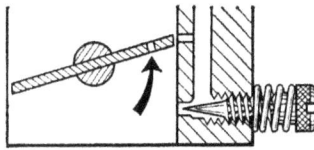
c) A hole in the throttle butterfly causes the "by-pass" orifice to discharge slower.

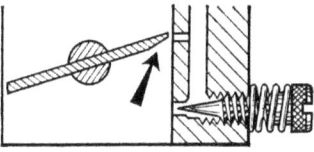
d) A bevelled edge on the throttle butterfly causes the "by-pass" orifice to discharge earlier.

Fig. 18 Throttle butterfly and by-pass orifices

If the by-pass orifice is desired to operate only with a wider opening of the throttle butterfly a hole drilled in the edge of the throttle butterfly should prove satisfactory. This enables he throttle butterfly to be closed slightly more when idling (**Fig. 18c**). This arrangement is a satisfactory remedy in case a).

If the by-pass orifice is intended to operate with a smaller throttle butterfly opening a small amount should be filed off the lower edge of the throttle butterfly on the side nearest the by-pass. This brings the edge of the throttle butterfly nearer to the by-pass (**Fig. 18d**). In this manner it is possible to help in case b).

### b) Mono-jet and Bi-jet Idling

In the majority of carburetor types, fuel for idling is taken after passing through the main jet and, so to speak, controlled by the main jet (see **Fig. 23**).

This arrangement results in a small amount of air entering through the slow running system as the engine speed increases under normal working conditions affecting the formation of the mixture. This arrangement is known as a "mono-jet" system as the formation of the mixture is effected entirely through the main jet, it is also described as a dependent idling system.

With an independent idling system the fuel for idling is taken before it passes through the main jet (see **Fig. 24**). In this case the idling system is completely independent and under normal operation always affects the formation of the mixture, therefore very careful adjustment of idling setting is required. This is known as the "bi-jet" system.

On the same engine the main jet will always be smaller with a "bi-jet" system than with a "mono-jet" system.

## THE MAIN JET CIRCUIT

On all modern carburetors there are four adjustable parts for normal operation as follows (**Fig. 19**): the choke tube (venturi) **K**, the main jet **Gg**, the air correction jet **a** and the emulsion tube **s**.

On carburetors of the older BF type there are only two adjustable parts for normal operation which are (**Fig. 20**): the choke tube **K** and the main jet **G**.

### A. SELECTION OF THE CHOKE TUBE (VENTURI) K

After the size of the carburetor has been determined, the correct choke tube **K** has to be selected.

When a test bench is available, the choke tube to select is that which gives power output 3-4% lower than that obtainable with larger choke tubes. This ensures a good performance from most normal engines.

To obtain the best performance over the whole revolution range it is necessary to select the choke tube which only just gives the highest output. When experimenting on the test bench main jets, large enough to ensure that there is no loss of power through weakness, should be used. Heavy fuel consumption should also be avoided although the effect of too rich a mixture is relatively unimportant.

If no test bench is available, the diameter of the choke tube can be calculated as follows, to arrive at a starting point:

After determination of the size of carburetor multiply the result by 0.8.

In the example mentioned before, a four cylinder engine with a capacity of 1200 $cm^3$ with peak revolutions of 4500 r.p.m. the diameter of the carburetor was calculated as 30 m/m. The size of the choke tube, to serve as a starting point for tuning, should have a diameter $30 \times 0.8 = 24$ m/m.

Usually this will be about the best size for the choke tube. Starting with this size, it is necessary to find by road test the smallest choke tube size which gives the maximum speed.

The choke tubes are different for various sizes and types of carburetor.

### B. SELECTION OF THE MAIN JET Gg AND THE AIR CORRECTION JET a

The following rule of thumb can be used to decide the main jet size:

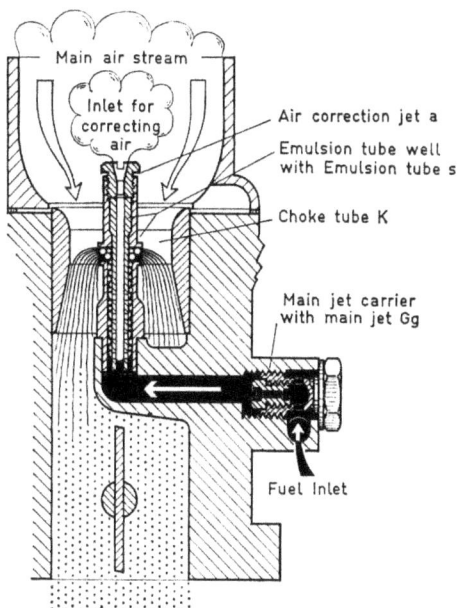

Fig. 19 Main jet circuit of a downdraught carburetor

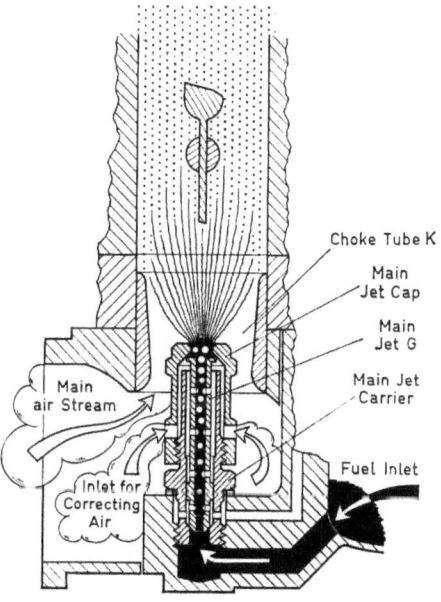

Fig. 20 Main jet circuit of a updraught carburetor

1. The size of the main jet **Gg** is approximately five times the size of the choke tube.

Example: Choke tube **K** = 24 m/m
Main jet **Gg** = 24 × 5 = 120

2. The size of the air correction jet **a** is approximately equal to the size of the main jet **Gg** + 60.

Example: Main jet **Gg** = 120
Air correction jet **a** = 120 + 60 = 180

The affect of the main jet **Gg** and the air correction jet **a** are shown on **Figs. 21 and 22**.

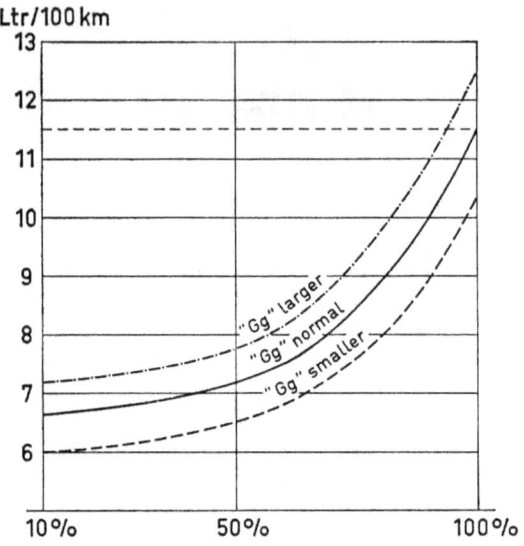

Fig. 21  Diagram of the affect of the main jet Gg

The curves on **Fig. 21** show the affect of the main jet **Gg**. It will be seen that a change of main jets affects the fuel consumption throughout the range, but the consumption curve is shifted approximately parallel to itself. Increasing or decreasing the size of the main jet affects the fuel consumption by approximately the same amount at both high and low engine speeds.

The curves on **Fig. 22** show the affect of the air correction jet **a**. They show that, as opposed to the main jet **Gg** a change of the air correction jet **a**, has a greater affect at high engine speeds than at low speeds. Increasing or decreasing the air correction jet **a** results in the curves getting further apart as the engine speed increases. The smaller the air correction jet is, the greater the affect of the depression upon it and consequently the enrichening of the mixture. As already stated this affect increases with the engine speed.

## C. SELECTION OF THE EMULSION TUBE s

Although the emulsion tube is an adjustable part its affect is small and it is difficult to give general directions for the selection of the correct emulsion tube.

It is best to use the emulsion tube indicated in the settings list or spare parts list for the particular carburetor. In emergency a sandard emulsion tube can also be used (i.e. No. "0" or No. "10").

It is advisable never to change the emulsion tube of a carburetor until after trying to eliminate minor faults which are often difficult to locate (i.e. minor flat-spots when accelerating).

Sometimes when accelerating a so-called "rich flat-spot," resembling a "gulp" occurs, caused by too much fuel. This can be due either to the accelerator pump or the main jet circuit.

With pump type carburetors the setting of the pump should be changed as described in detail on pg. 24.

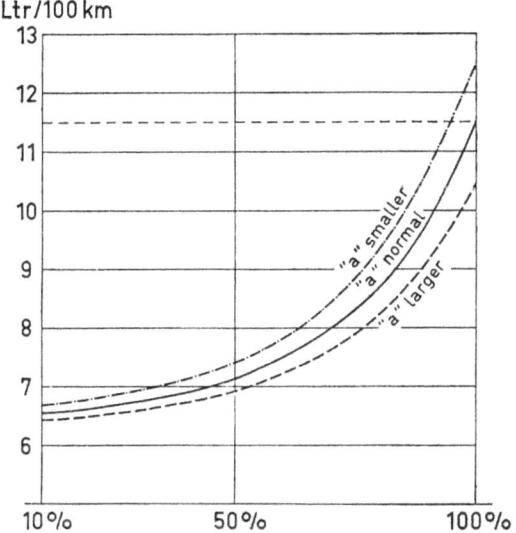

Fig. 22 Diagram of the affect of the air correction jet a

If the carburetor has no pump, an emulsion tube with large holes and the bottom sealed by a plug, can be tried.

On carburetors which feed only one or two cylinders, as is usual on racing cars, short emulsion tubes should be used.

## D. JET ASSEMBLIES

The layout of the adjustable parts of the various carburetor types are known as the jet assembly. Although the working principles are the same for all carburetors, the adjustable parts are differently arranged owing to the type of carburetor and its development. The differences are mainly in the way in which the correctional air is supplied and in the arrangement of the main jet.

### a) Jet Assembly No. 12 (Fig. 23)

This assembly is used on the updraft and horizontal carburetors of the older BF types. It consists of the jet carrier, the main jet **G** and the jet cap **A**.

The main jet **G** and the emulsion tube **s** are combined in one part which is marked with two numbers (i.e. $110 \times 51$). The first number indicates the size of the calibrated drilling, while the second indicates the position and size of the emulsion holes drilled in the side of the jet.

The emulsion holes control the automatic weakening of the mixture by the correctional air which is calibrated by the drillings in the side of the main jet cap **A**.

The sequence of the combined main jet and emulsion tubes is as follows: 51 - 56 - 52 - 58 - 53 - 54

For example if a size 120 main jet is used with all the foregoing emulsion tubes the addition of correctional air or the weakening increases in the order given above.

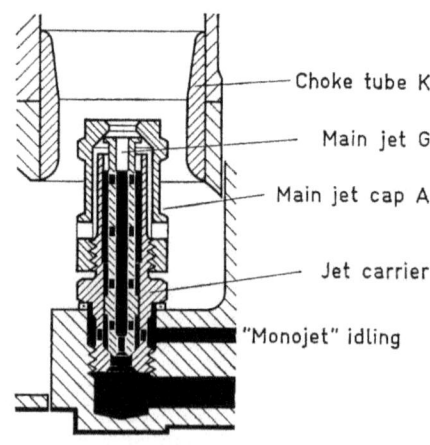

Fig. 23 Assembly No. 12

### b) Jet Assembly No. 8 (Fig. 24)

This assembly is found on many carburetors of the older BF types and is used mostly on two stroke engines.

In construction it is similar to assembly 12, if differs however, in that it has a "bi-jet" or independent idling system. As ex-

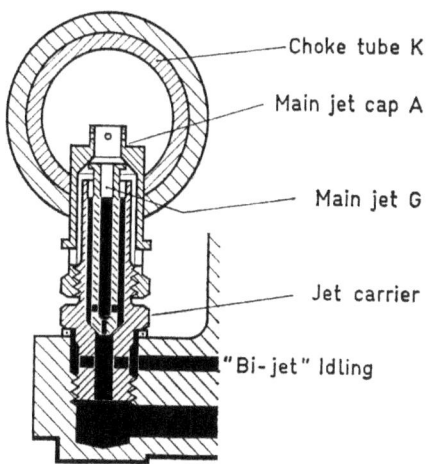

Fig. 24 Assembly No. 8

plained, this means that the fuel for idling is taken before it passes through the main jet while in assembly 12 it is taken after passing through the main jet.

The main jet **G** for this assembly is indicated with the letter "F" coupled with the size (i.e. $105 \times F$), and characterizes the emulsion tube which has only two emulsion holes.

c) **Jet Assembly No. 21 (Fig. 25)**

This assembly is found on the majority of modern downdraft carburetors.

It consists of an emulsion tube well with emulsion tube s, air correction jet **a** and the main jet carrier **Y** with the main jet **Gg**.

In this type, the emulsion tube is located in the emulsion tube well and in a simple way is held in place by the screwed in air correction jet. Dismantling and cleaning are therefore simplified.

d) **Jet Assembly No. 22 (Fig. 26)**

This assembly is used on modern carburetors of the horizontal type.

It consists of a discharge nozzle, the emulsion tube s, the air correct jet **a** and the main jet carrier **Y** with the main jet **Gg**.

It differs from assembly 21 essentially in that the air correction jet is no longer located in the middle of the main air intake, but above it, and that the emulsion tube crosses the choke tube diagonally. This facilitates dismounting and cleaning.

e) **New jet Assemblies (Figs. 27 and 28)**

In horizontal and downdraft carburetors of the latest models

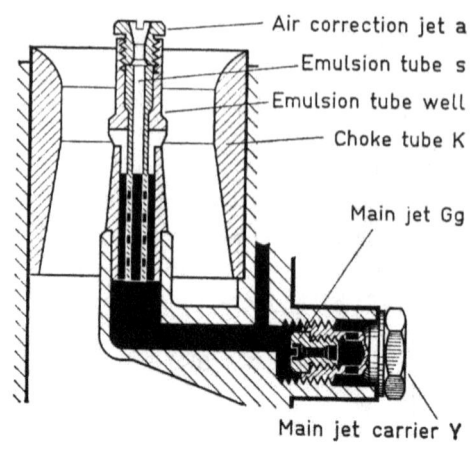

Fig. 25 Assembly No. 21

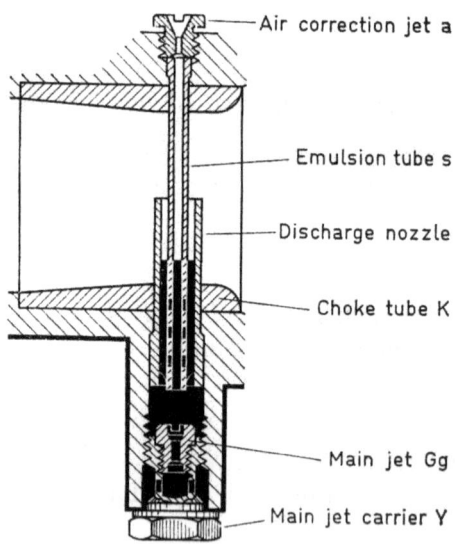

Fig. 26 Assembly No. 22

the emulsion tube and air correction jet are no longer located centrally in the choke tube, but at the side in a cylindrical well situated in the float chamber of the carburetor which is supplied with fuel through the main jet (i.e. types 44 PHH and 40 PII). This application can also be found in the secondary barrel of compound downdraft carburetors (type 32 PAITA).

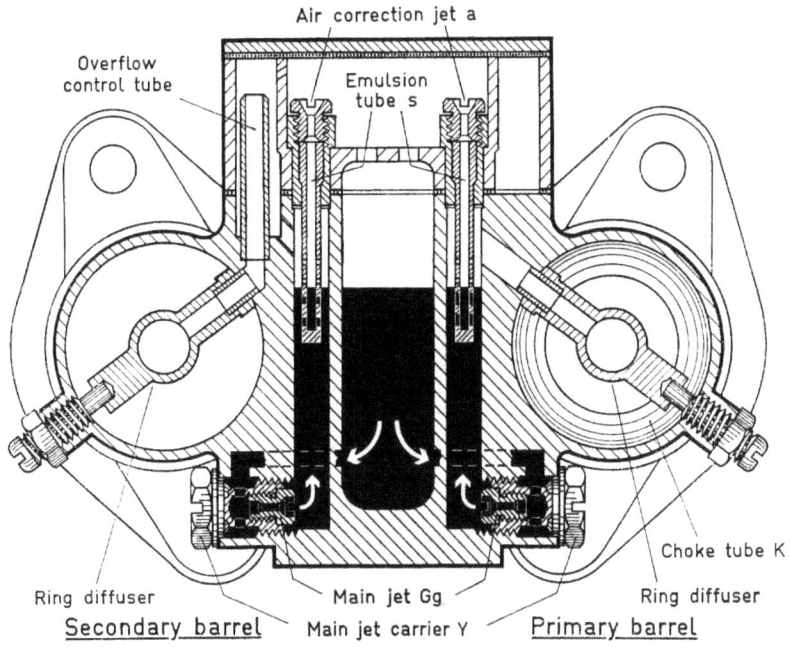

Fig. 27 Jet assembly of the 44 PHH carburetor

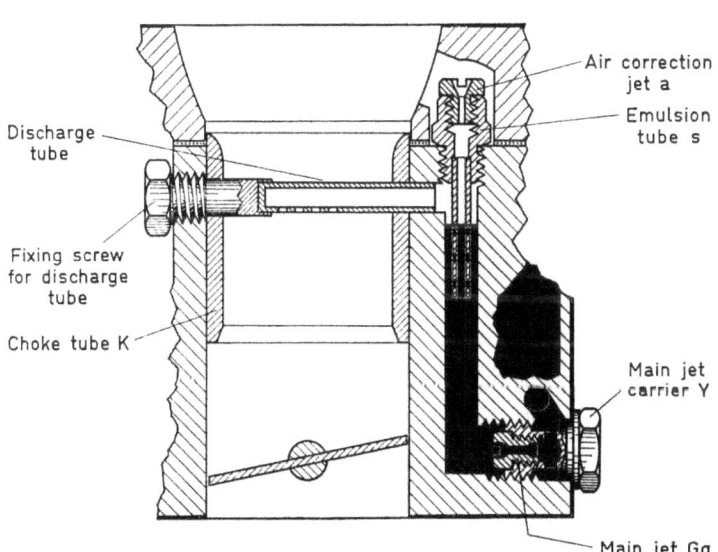

Fig. 28 Jet assembly of the 40 PII carburetor

The fuel mixture is discharged through a connection between the emulsion tube well and the choke tube. This connection may be a simple tube (mixture discharge tube) or it may be a ring diffuser.

## THE ACCELERATOR PUMP

Generally accelerator pumps are needed for acceleration, and give the greatest advantage the longer the induction manifolds are, the greater the diameter of the induction manifold or respectively the choke tube in relation to the capacity of one cylinder.

Accelerator Pumps are generally mechanically operated (**Fig. 29**). On older types of carburetors pneumatic pumps are also

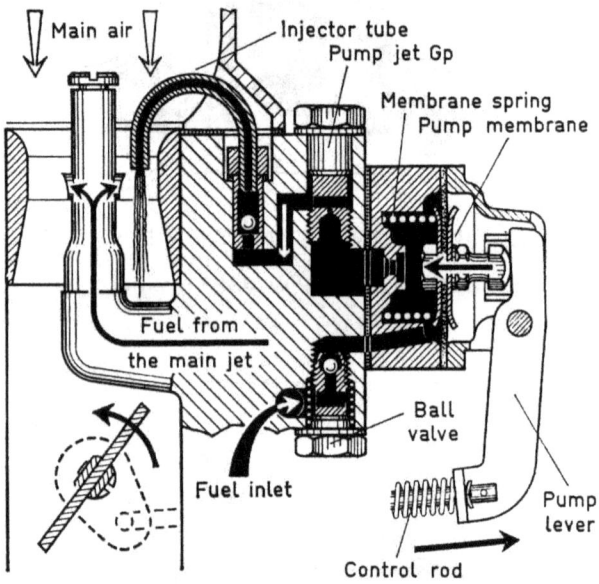

Fig. 29 Mechanically operated accelerator pump

found (**Fig. 30**). In the first case the pump is connected to the throttle spindle by a control rod; in the second case it is operated by depression.

On all accelerator pumps on Solex carburetors, the amount of fuel injected and the duration of the injection can be adjusted.

The quantity of fuel injected by mechanical pumps is controlled by the adjustment of the length of the control rod. The control rod, between the intermediate lever on the throttle spindle and the pump lever, has three holes and a split pin for securing the pump lever. Each of these holes corresponds with

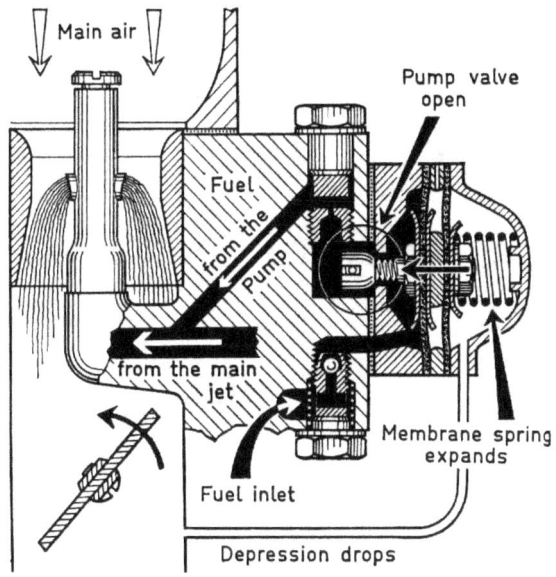

Fig. 30 Depression operated accelerator pump

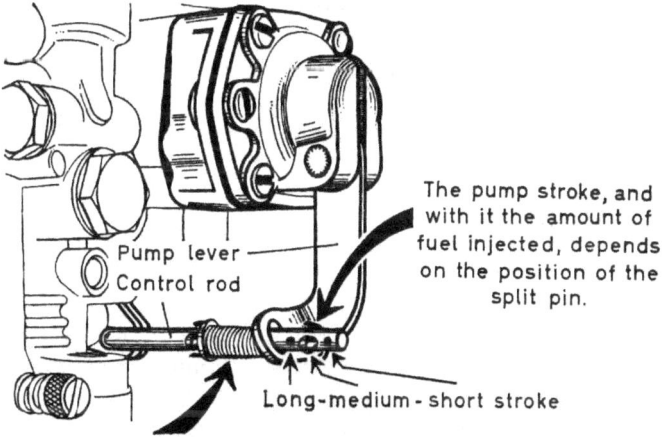

Fig. 31 Adjustment of the quantity of fuel injected with three holes and a split pin

a different length of pump stroke and therefore the injection of a different amount of fuel (**Fig. 31**). Instead of the holes and split pin, the pump lever may also be secured with an adjusting nut and a lock nut (**Fig. 32**).

With depression operated pumps the amount of fuel dis-

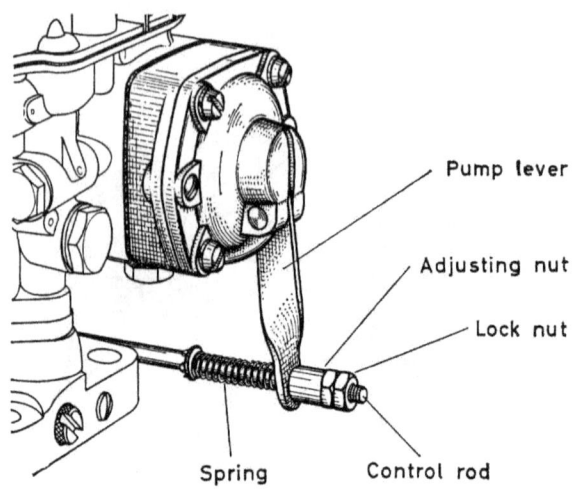

**Fig. 32** Adjustment of the quantity of fuel injected with adjusting nut

charged is determined by the position of the pump valve on the pump membrane spindle.

The duration of the injection depends upon the size of the pump jet **Gp**, which regulates the quantity of fuel which can pass through in a given time. It will be clear that the smaller the jet, the longer the fuel will take to flow through it. The size of the pump jet is generally a third of the size of the main jet (Main jet Gg = 180, Pump jet = 60). It must not be smaller than size 35.

Mechanically operated accelerator pumps are made, according to the carburetor model, in three basic types and a few special ones:

The measurement between the fixing screws of the first type is 27 m/m. The identification number "7" marks this type which is used on downdraft carburetors with a diameter of 32 m/m (except dual port and compound carburetors).

The measurement between the fixing screws of the second type is 35 m/m. This type carries the identification number "8" and is used on downdraft carburetors with a diameter of 35 and 40 m/m also on compound carburetors with diameters of 32 and 44 m/m.

The distance between the fixing screws of the third type is the same, it differs in that a ball valve is fitted in the lower pump body, which in the other types is located in the carburetor body, and that, after drilling and tapping there is the possibility of using an economy jet that is marked with the number "9" and is used on dual port carburetors with a diameter of 30 or 32 m/m.

The 28 PCI carburetor has a special version of the mechanical pump, reduced in size (**Fig. 33**). It has not variable pump jet but a fixed calibrated orifice for the fuel.

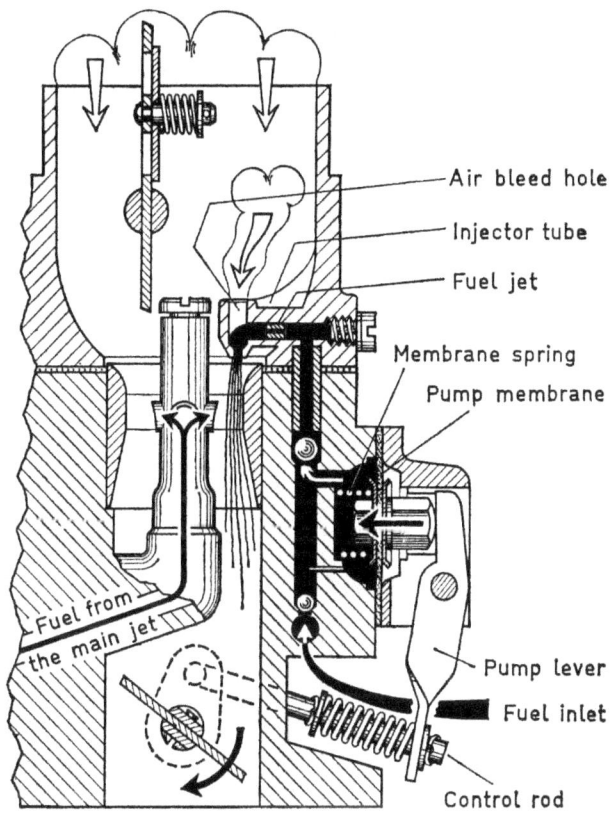

Fig. 33 Accelerator pump of the 28 PCI carburetor

When the throttle butterfly is opened the pump lever exerts pressure on the membrane. The pump pressure injects additional fuel into the mixing chamber through the injector tube.

Exceptionally the 40 PII-4 differs from the foregoing basic principles because this dual port carburetor is fitted with an accelerator pump with the identification number "7". This small accelerator pump is sufficient, as this type of carburetor is used

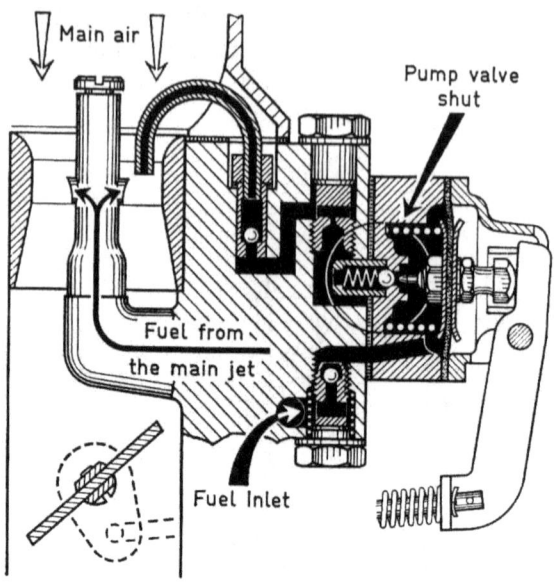

Fig. 34 "Rich" pump with ball valve (pump 73)

a) Part Load

The pump valve is closed when the throttle butterfly is in the part load position. Additional fuel cannot be discharged.

especially on racing and sports cars on which each mixing chamber feeds one cylinder only by the shortest way.

In mechanical pumps the full load enrichment and weakening devices are combined. The additional markings of the pump indicate immediately when such a device is incorporated with the pump and if so, of which type it is.

1. If the pump has neither of these devices ("neutral" pump), the number "2" is placed after the identification number (pump types 72, 82 and 92).

2. If the pump has a full load enrichment device ("rich" pump), the number "3" is added to the identifying number (pump types 73, 83, 93).

3. If the pump has a device for full load weakening ("weak" pump), the number "4" is placed after the identification number (pump types 74, 84, 94).

Pumps for downdraft compound carburetors are also marked with the number "1" (pump types 821, 831 and 841).

The enrichening or weakening devices may have either ball or disc valves **(Figs. 34 to 36)**.

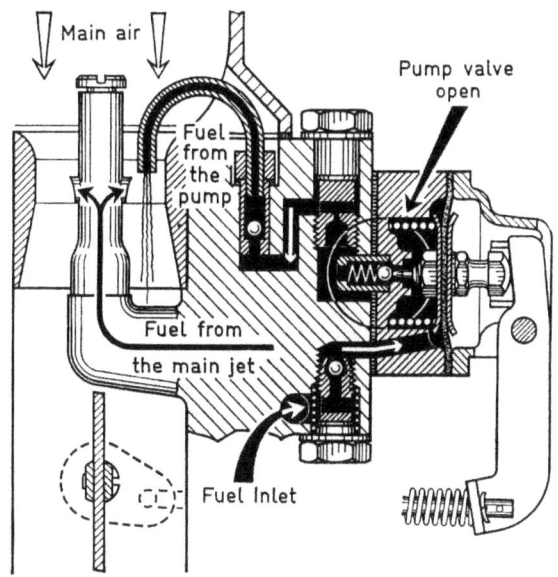

b) Full Load

When the throttle butterfly is in the full load position the pump valve is opened. Additional fuel is discharged to enrichen the mixture.

The following general directions can be given for the application of these devices:
1. Pumps with the final number "2" ("neutral" pump) are recommended for all carburetors feeding normal four cylinder engines.
2. Pumps with the final number "3" ("rich" pump) are especially suited for carburetors feeding four cylinder sports cars; normal six or eight cylinder engines, or supercharged engines.
3. Pumps with the final number "4" ("weak" pump) are suitable for use on carburetors feeding only one, two or three cylinders.

The fuel from the carburetor pump is normally discharged into the mixing chamber through one injector tube (with dual port carburetors two injector tubes or a duel injector tube are used). In exceptional cases the injector tube takes the form of a nozzle cast into the float chamber cover (i.e. carburetor type 28 PCI).

There are two types of injector tubes:
a) the "high" injector with its mouth at the level of the correction jet,

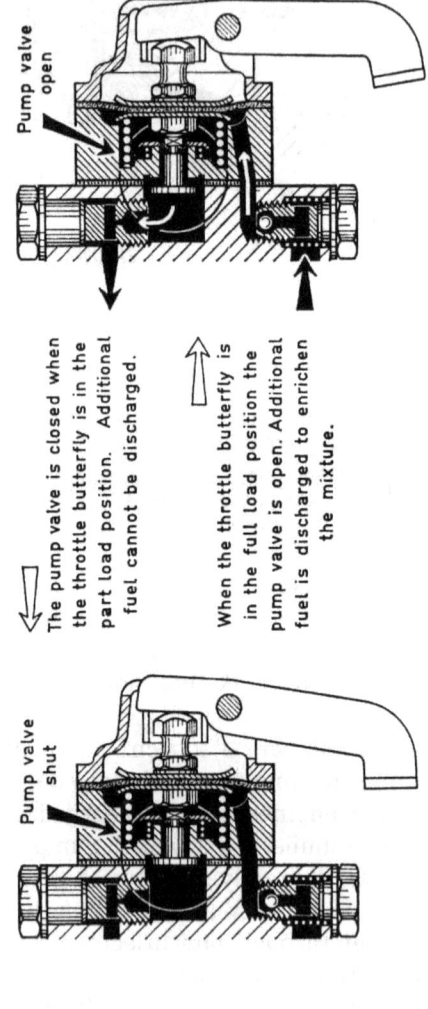

Pump valve open

⇦ The pump valve is closed when the throttle butterfly is in the part load position. Additional fuel cannot be discharged.

⇧ When the throttle butterfly is in the full load position the pump valve is open. Additional fuel is discharged to enrichen the mixture.

Pump valve shut

Fig. 35 "Rich" pump with disc valve (pump 83)

a) Part Load  b) Full Load

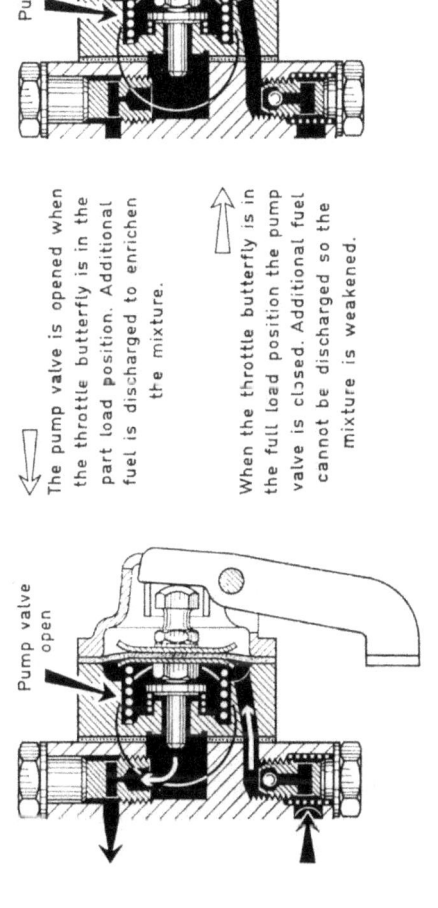

Pump valve shut

The pump valve is opened when the throttle butterfly is in the part load position. Additional fuel is discharged to enrichen the mixture.

When the throttle butterfly is in the full load position the pump valve is closed. Additional fuel cannot be discharged so the mixture is weakened.

Pump valve open

Fig. 36 "Weak" pump with disc valve (pump 84)

a) Part Load     b) Full Load

b) the "low" injector with its mouth in the venturi throat.

The mouth of the "low" injector lies in the area of greatest depression, which is not so in the case of the "high" injector.

The following directions can be given for their use:
1. It is recommended that "high" injectors should be used with pumps with the final number "2" ("neutral" pumps).
2. When pumps with the final number "3" ("rich" pumps) or "4" ("weak" pumps) are used it is better to use "low" injectors.

## THE ENRICHMENT DEVICE

The enrichment device is a new development for automatically enrichening the fuel air mixture in the higher engine speed range.

The enrichment device is connected with the main jet circuit (**Fig. 37**). Both are placed in cylindrical wells in the float chamber of the carburetor. The first well is supplied with fuel by the main jet **Gg** and contains the emulsion tube **s** and the air correction jet **a**. The fuel/air mixture is discharged through a ring diffuser. The second well is supplied with fuel by the enrichment device fuel jet and is closed at the top by an air jet. It is connected by a cross channel in a bridge to the inside of the emulsion tube in the main jet circuit.

When the engine is working under part load or at full load at low engine speeds only the main jet circuit operates. As the depression increases further it is transmitted through the cross channel in the bridge to the enrichment device. Additional fuel/air mixture is discharged, the amount increasing progressively as the engine speed rises.

The size of the air correction jet **a** (main jet circuit) in relation to the size of the enrichment device air jet determines the additional quantity of fuel.

Instead of specified enrichment jets the flow of fuel and the entry of air into the enrichment device well may be controlled by calibrated drillings (i.e. carburetor type 40 PII-4).

A simplified enrichment device is to be found in the 32 PICB-1 carburetor. An enrichment device tube, located in the float chamber cover is connected with a well in the float chamber into which the fuel is free to flow. The mouth of the rather large calibrated enrichment device tube is approximately on a level with the rim of the float chamber cover, therefore in a zone of comparatively reduced depression. The depression at this point is only great enough to cause additional fuel to be delivered by the enrichment device tube at high engine speeds.

The main jet circuit with fuel enrichment permits fine adjustment and accurate calibration of the fuel supply for the

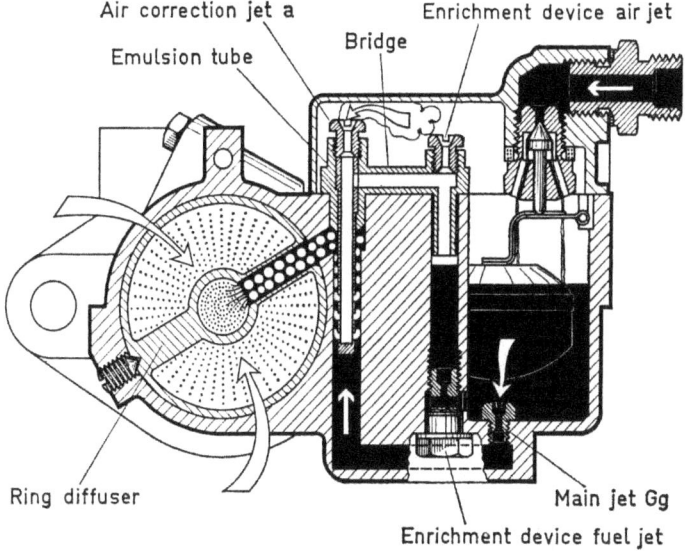

Fig. 37 Operation of the enrichment device of the 44 HR carburetor
a) full throttle at low engine speeds

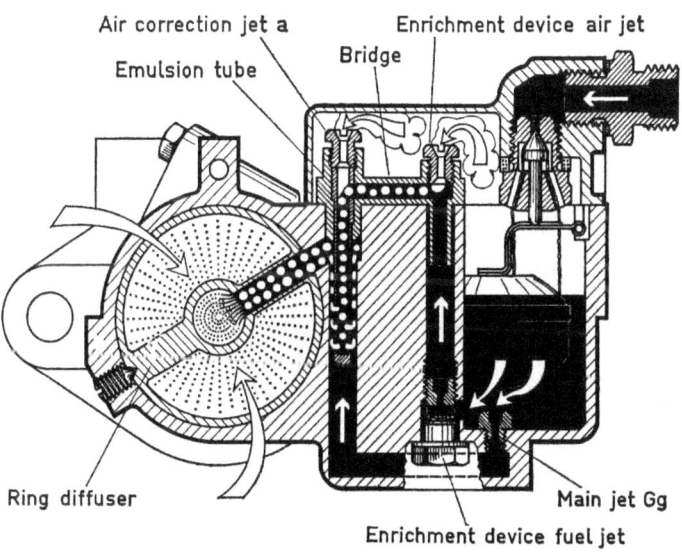

b) full throttle at high engine speeds

engine taking into account the desired economy and the maximum performance when required.

## TUNING THE CARBURETOR

It must be determined if the carburetor feeds:
1. a normal four cylinder engine
2. a four cylinder sports engine, six or eight cylinder engines or a supercharged engine
3. one, two or three cylinders.

### 1. A CARBURETOR FOR NORMAL 4 CYLINDER ENGINES

It is first necessary to determine the size choke tube **K** which gives the greatest performance (in no circumstances should this be too large, rather a little too small).

During the necessary experiments a slightly larger main jet **Gg** than the calculated size should be used. In the case of the air correction jet **a,** calculated in relation to the main jet, the opposite applies so that there is no danger of part of the performance being lost through over-weakening of the mixture.

When the size of choke tube has been decided, the main jet **Gg** should be reduced until the engine no longer reaches the performance first achieved, keeping the air correction jet the same size.

Then the main jet should be increased and the size which just gives the best performance should be fitted. In this way the first correct point on the consumption curve is determined. On **Fig. 38** such a curve is shown and this point is marked "A".

It is possible that this setting is not suitable for all working conditions. Especially at ¾ load the curve may lie as shown by the top broken line ("**Gg** and **a** as selected"). It can be assumed that at part load the best fuel consumption is not being obtained. To determine whether this is correct it is necessary to check the consumption at the so-called "part load point," which is at a speed equivalent to 75% of the maximum speed of the vehicle. This is marked "B" on the diagram.

When a test bench is available tests should be taken at a point equivalent to 75% of the peak revolutions and also at an output equal to half the maximum performance. At these speeds the main jet should again be reduced without changing the air correction jet.

If the vehicle still runs well, the main jet should again be reduced until the performance is adversely affected (uneven running, ocasional back firing in the carburetor, loss of power). The main jet finally used, that which gives the lowest consumption at 75% of the peak revolutions, should not be changed.

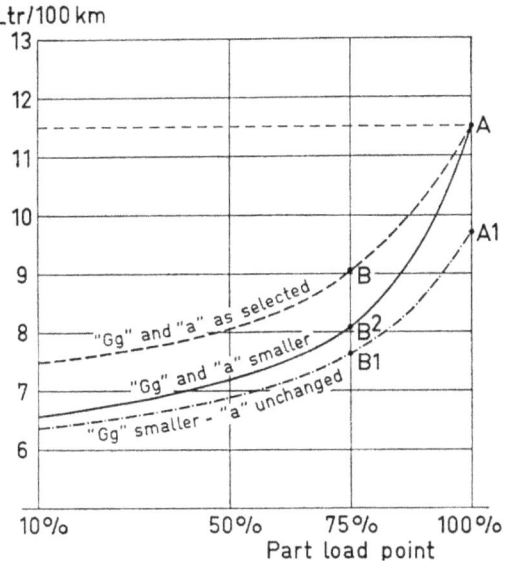

Fig. 38 Consumption curve of a vehicle on a level road

The consumption now lies at point "B1" on the lower broken curve on the Chart ("**Gg** smaller, a unchanged"). This curve lays "parallel" to the upper broken line, to which reference has already been made in the section dealing with the selection of the main jet (**Fig. 21**). Owing to this change point "A" (upper curve) has now moved to point "A1" (lower curve) indicating that the mixture is too weak at full load operation. The use of a smaller correction jet than that which has been used in the first tests will richen the mixture under full load. This results in points "A1" and "B1" rising to "A" and "B2" respectively and a final consumption curve as indicated by the continuous line on the diagram.

If at the commencement of the tests the reverse effect is apparent and at part load the mixture is too weak it is necessary to work in the reverse direction and begin by increasing the main jet until the correct part throttle operation is obtained. Then the air correction jet should be increased until the correct mixture strength for maximum performance is reached.

On most engines acceleration can be improved by an accelerator pump. As the Solex carburetor, with the correct setting, will provide a trouble free fuel/air mixture for full load and part load operation, suitably as a whole for all four cylinder touring engines, a simple accelerator pump, without additional enrichment or weakening devices can be used. Therefore "neu-

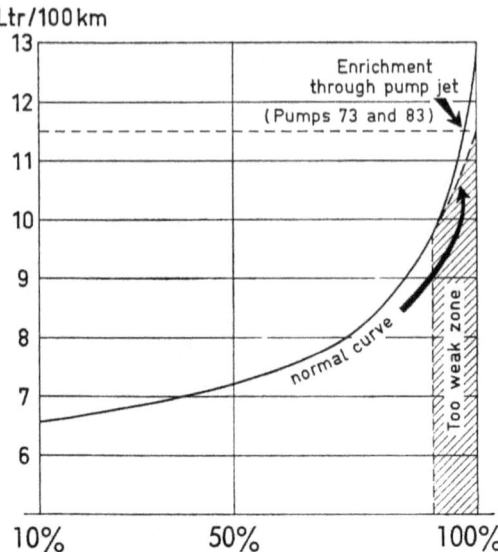

**Fig. 39** Consumption curve of a vehicle on a level road with enrichment through the pump jet

tral" pumps with the indicating number ending in "2" should be used in conjunction with a "high" injector tube. As the mouth of the tube will not be in the area of greatest depression the fuel discharged from the tube will be nil or negligible.

## 2. A CARBURETOR FOR 4 CYLINDER SPORTS ENGINES, FOR 6 OR 8 CYLINDER ENGINES OR FOR SUPERCHARGED ENGINES

In these cases the above procedure cannot be used as the engine requires a very different mixture composition between full load and part load (**Fig. 39**). It is therefore advisable to procede as follows:

As described at the beginning of the previous section, the size of the choke tube **K** should first be decided and then a test should be taken at the "part load point" (75% of the maximum speed). This will result in a main jet $Gg$ and an air correction jet **a** being determined which will give correct running with the lowest consumption.

It is absolutely essential to use an accelerator pump in these tests with full load enrichment ("rich" pump with the indicating number ending in "3") which allows an additional fuel system to come into operation when the throttle butterfly has nearly fully opened. It is also essential to use a "low" injector tube, the mouth of which is in the area of greatest depression at the discharge orifices of the emulsion tube well.

Using this arrangement tests must be made to attain the highest speed of the vehicle and to determine the smallest pump jet which will give this speed.

Without the fuel supplied through the "low" injector tube and calibrated by the pump jet **Gp** it is not possible to reach the highest speed. It is essential to select the correct size of pump jet **Gp** if the maximum speed is to be reached.

Subsequently it has to be ascertained that a good acceleration is assured by the thus determined pump jet **Gp** within the entire speed range. It will be remembered that the quantity of fuel which is injected can be adjusted as described in detail on pg. 24.

## 3. A CARBURETOR FOR 1, 2 OR 3 CYLINDERS

This arrangement is usually found on sports or racing car engines or when several carburetors are used on one engine.

It is generally found—as opposed to that in the previous section—that the fuel/air mixture is too weak at part throttle operation **(Fig. 40)**.

In this case basically an accelerator pump with full load weakening ("weak" pump with indicating number ending in "4") should be used with a "low" pump injector.

The same tuning procedure as described in detail on pg. 24 should be used during which a blank pump jet (without drilling) should be fitted.

However, in this manner the setting determined, has a small main jet **Gg** and a small air correction jet **a**. The vehicle should then be driven at 75% of its maximum speed which will give the

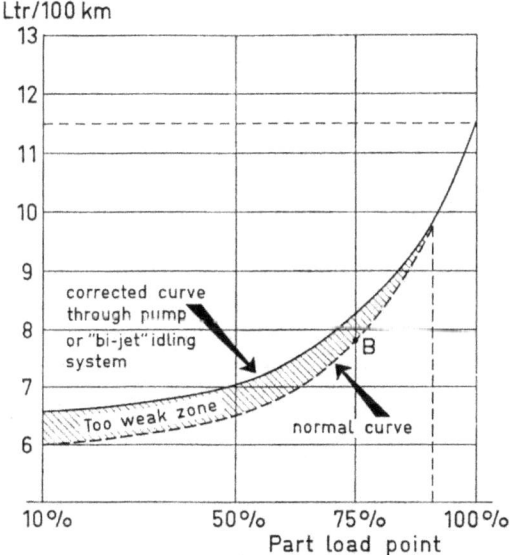

Fig. 40 Influence of the "weak" pump or of a "bi-jet" idling system

point "B" on the broken curve in **Fig. 40**.

If the mixture is too weak the blank pump jet should be replaced by a pump jet **Gp** the size of which is to be suitable to give normal running—always at 75% of maximum speed.

However, if the engine runs well at the part load point the setting should be left as determined and a "neutral" pump (with indicating number ending in "2"), in conjunction with a "high" injector tube, should be fitted with which the acceleration is satisfactory without enrichment correction.

Sometimes carburetors with "bi-jet" idling systems are also used, with which a correct curve can be obtained without the necissity of using a "weak" pump. This is particularly advantageous in the case of a simple carburetor or if for some reason the accelerator pump does not function satisfactorily. The "bi-jet" idling system gives approximately the same results as a "weak" pump. It has however fewer possibilities of adjustment as it is really independent on the idling setting.

Only a few types of carburetors and mainly carburetors for racing cars have "bi-jet" idling systems.

## ALTITUDE CORRECTOR

At great heights (over 1200-1500 m / 3600-4500 ft), the carburetion of vehicle engines presents a problem which can be helped by the Solex altitude corrector, as long as there is sufficient space for fitting this device.

As the height increases the mixture gets richer and this is counteracted by the altitude corrector **(Fig. 41)**, the flow through the main jet **Gg** being reduced by a needle which is operated by a barometric capsule.

The altitude corrector is fitted in place of the main jet carrier. The normal main jet **Gg** is screwed in, in the same way as into the main jet carrier. The fuel flows to the main jet through four large oblique drillings and one small one. The fuel flow through the larger drillings is controlled by the needle connected to the pressure capsule. When the pressure capsule expands under the influence of the decreasing atmospheric pressure, the needle progressively reduces the flow of the fuel to the main jet.

The setting of the altitude corrector is dependent upon the size of the main jet for which it is determined. The size of the main jet should not be changed later, neither should the setting of the altitude corrector be altered. For this reason the adjusting nut, which determines the setting of the altitude capsule in relation to the needle is fitted with a locking washer.

When ordering an altitude corrector it is necessary to quote

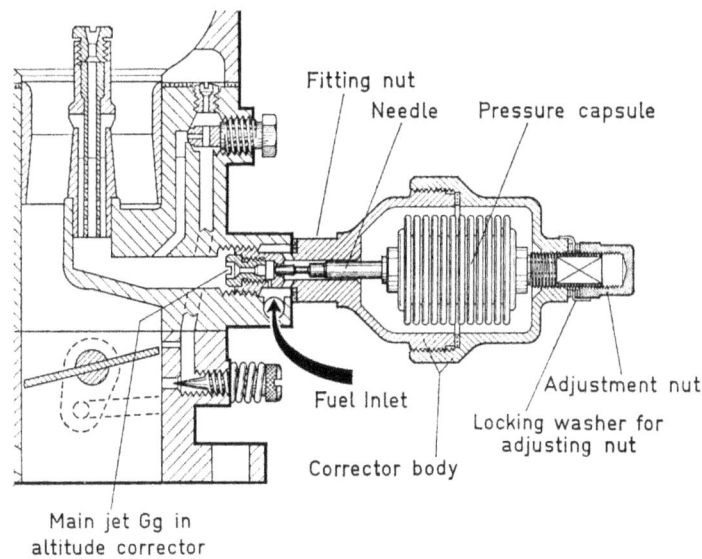

Fig. 41 SOLEX Altitude Corrector

the engine type, the type of carburetor and the size of the main jet **Gg** in use.

## DEPRESSION OPERATED IGNITION ADVANCE

Most Solex carburetors are provided with a threaded drilling, for the connection of a tube for the adjustment of the ignition by vacuum.

This provision can only be used if the distributor is fitted with a vacuum operated adjusting device.

The threaded drilling is normally sealed with a screw plug. It is only necessary to remove it to fit the vacuum tube to the distributor.

## AUTOMATIC STARTER (HOT AIR)

### 1. MODEL BICT - Fig 42

**a) Description**

In the BICT model, a rotating starter disc valve **1** is connected by a spindle **2** to the bimetallic spring **3** which is enclosed in a watertight and thermally sealed body. One end of the spring **3** is fixed to the body in such a way that a rise in temperature allows the spring to expand and turn the disc valve in a rotary movement. To ensure that the spring is heated, the body is connected by an external tube **5** to a refractory U shaped tube **6** dropping right into the hot exhaust gases and joined to atmos-

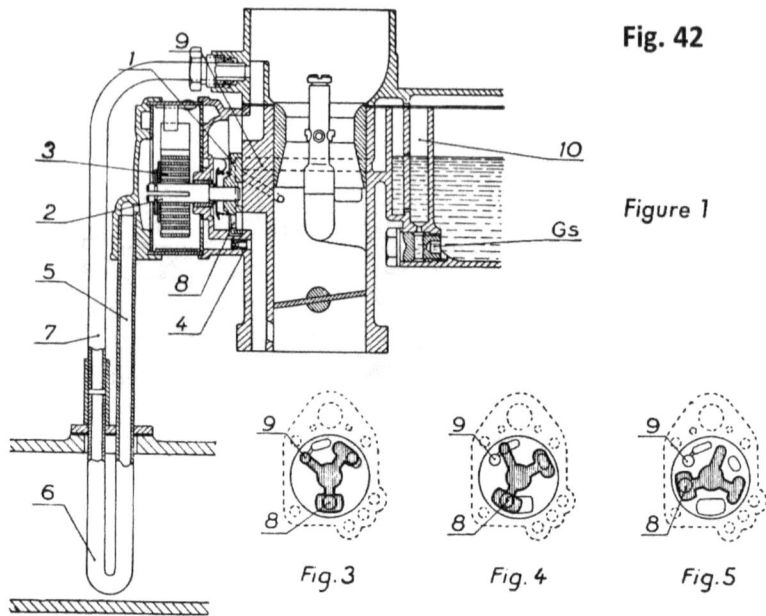

Fig. 42

phere by a filter **7**. The casing is at another point, connected by a channel **4** to the inlet manifold. Thus, the predominant vacuum in the inlet manifold draws in the air by a drilling **7**. This air is heated in the tube **6** and transmitted to the spring **3** before entering the engine. The disc valve has different inlets and a communication **8** with the general air inlet of the carburetor. This communication forms the starter air jet.

The fuel is fed through a channel **9** which draws the fuel from a well **10** fed by the starter fuel jet **Gs**. This well **10** is vented at the top into the float chamber which is under a constant level.

**b) Operation**

When the engine is cold, before it is started, the ports are in the positions of **Figs. 1 and 3**, that is to say the disc valve ports are in direct communication with the equivalent ports provided on the face on which the disc valve rests.

At the time of starting, when driven by the starter motor, the engine turns, the fuel is fed via the channel **9** and the air by the orifice **8**.

When the engine is running and the spring is warmed by the passage of hot air, the disc valve begins to turn, first taking the position of **Fig. 4** where only one port of the disc valve (shaded) is opposite the ports on the face, thus causing a progressive weaking of the mixture, this action continues until the disc valve ports do not communicate with the ports on the face (**Fig. 5**). At this point the choke is completely out of action and the engine is idling. Finally, when the disc valve is in the position of **Fig. 5,** a light spring becomes fixed in a slot of the spindle 2 to keep the disc valve **1** out of action. in order that this spring releases itself from the slot so that the disc valve can take up its working position again, it is necessary to considerably lower the temperature at which the spring is operative. This device aims at avoiding a too rapid or premature return to action of the choke when the engine cools slightly during a brief halt.

## 2. MODEL ICBT - Fig. 43

### a) Description

In the ICBT carburetor, the function of the Autostarter is similar to that of the BICT but it has an additional device, for certain engines, to obtain an improved restart when the Autostarter is still in action.

In the ICBT, the fuel is delivered by a channel **9** which draws the fuel from a well **10** fed by the starter fuel jet **Gs**. This well **10** opens at the top into a circular well **11** the center of which is connected with the inside of the float chamber by the channel **12**. The orifice of this channel **12** can be closed by a membrane valve which is subject to the vacuum of the manifold through the tube **13**, in such a way that, at rest or with a weak vacuum predominant in the manifold, the passage between the chamber **11** and the channel **12** is closed, and that, at high vacuum, this channel is open.

### b) Operation

When the engine is cold, the ports are in the positions of **Figs. 1 and 3,** that is to say, the communication between **11** and **12** is closed and the disc valve ports are in direct communication with the equivalent ports provided on the face on which the disc valve rests.

When the engine is running the depression acting in the channel **13** withdraws the membrane and frees the communication between **12, 11** and **10**, which has the primary effect of weakening the mixture to stop the engine "hunting" through excess fuel. Then as the spring is warmed by the hot air, the disc valve begins to turn, first taking the position of **Fig. 4**, where only one port of the disc valve (shaded) communicates with the ports on the face, thus causing a progressive weakening of the mixture and this continues until the disc valve ports do not communicate with any of the ports on the face (**Fig. 5**). At this moment, the starter is completely out of action and the engine is idling.

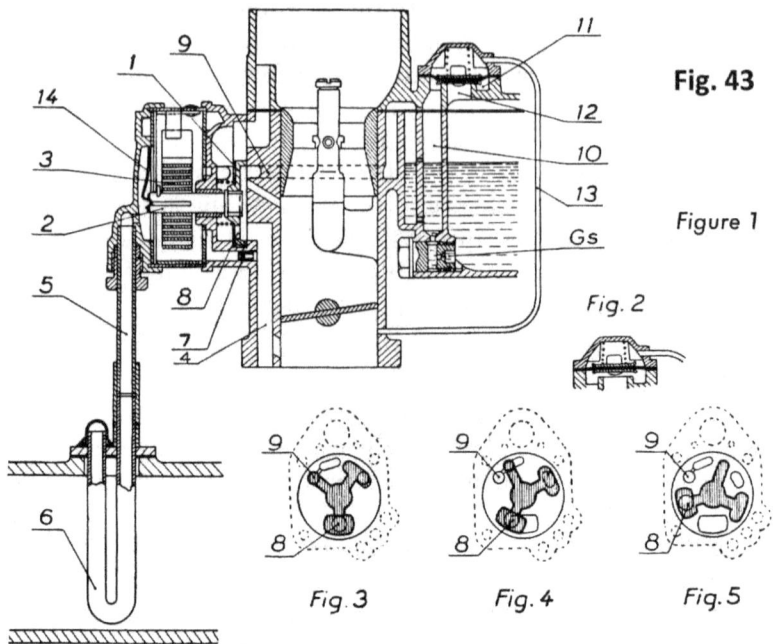

Fig. 43

Figure 1

Fig. 2

Fig. 3   Fig. 4   Fig. 5

When running on the starter, the accelerator is pressed, the vacuum in the manifold becomes very weak, the membrane closes the communication between **11** and **12** again thus providing a momentary richening of the mixture to ensure drive away.

The working of the ICBT model is thus exactly the same as that of the BICT.

However, the device retaining the disc valve **1** in the "out of action" position is different; the two small springs acting on the flats of the spindle are replaced, in this model, by a light spring **14** riveted to the Autostarter cover, the end of which fits into a slot provided in the spindle **2**.

### 3. MODEL IBT - Fig. 44
a) **Description**

The IBT model is similar in its working principle to the ICBT with however the following differences: The mixture is fed through a channel **23** which draws the fuel from a well **30** fed by the **Gs**. This well opens at its top into the constant level float chamber through a drilling **16**. The mixture is fed into the engine through a tube **17** the air by the **Ga 8**.

A piston **18** determines the size of the mixture passage according to the working conditions. The spring **19** which helps

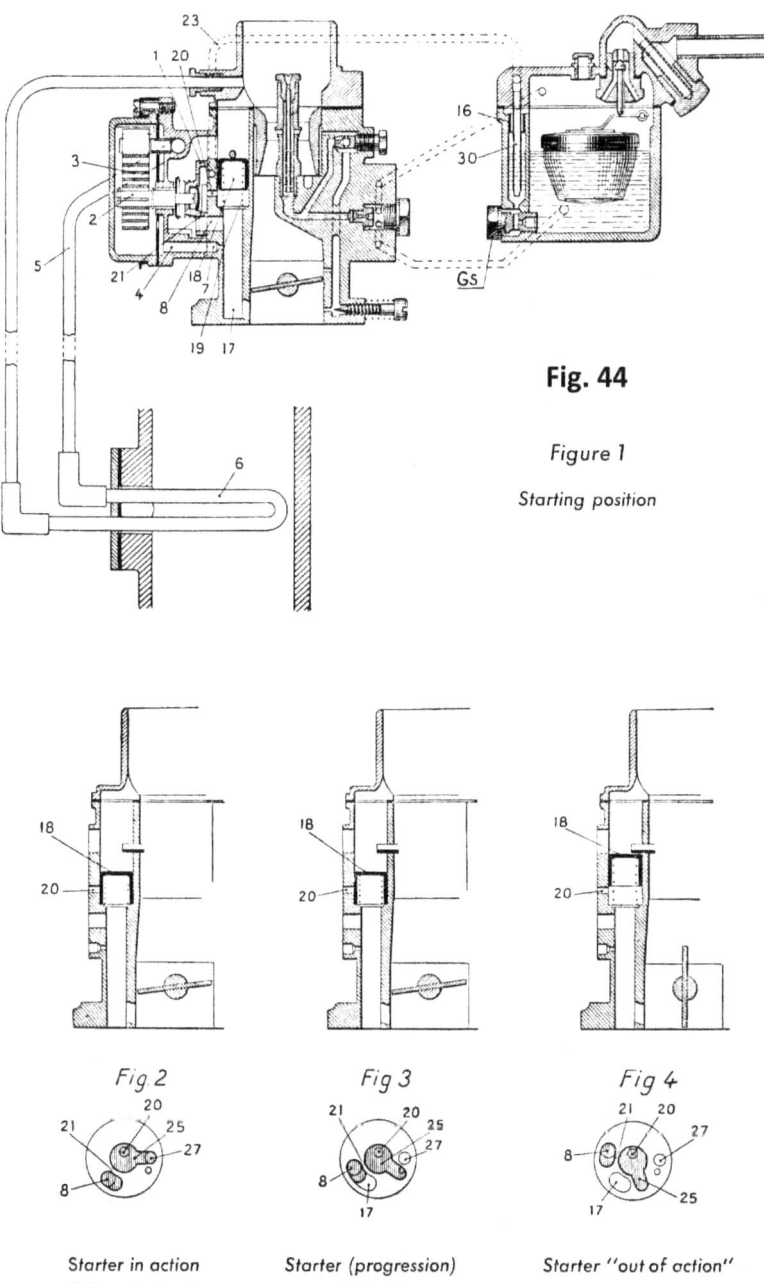

**Fig. 44**

*Figure 1*

*Starting position*

*Fig. 2*

Starter in action
(after starting)

*Fig 3*

Starter (progression)
(Idling)

*Fig 4*

Starter "out of action"

this piston in its high position is calibrated in such a way that, with weak vacuum in the inlet manifold the piston **18** remains in its high position and uncovers the channel **20**.

On the other hand, with high vacuum, the piston **18** is drawn away and the passage between the disc valve ports **25** and the underside of the butterfly is closed except through the drilling **21**.

### b) Operation

In cold weather and when the engine is cold, the piston occupies the position (**Fig. 1**) and the disc valve the **Fig. 2** position, that is to say, the disc valve ports **25** are in direct communication with the equivalent ports on the face on which the disc valve rests.

At the time of starting, when the engine turns, driven by the starter motor, the vacuum in the inlet manifold is relatively weak. The piston **18** keeps high position (**Fig. 1**) and the fuel passes through the channels **23** and **20**, when the air is fed through the orifice **8**; the mixture is then very rich. On the other hand, when the engine is running, the vacuum becomes high, the piston **18** is withdrawn (**Fig. 2**) and the fuel only comes through the orifice **21** which has the effect of weakening the mixture.

As the spring is warmed by the passage of hot air, the disc valve begins to turn, first taking the position of **Fig. 3** where only one of the ports of the disc valve (shaded) communicates with the orifices on the face, thus causing a weakening of the mixture. After acceleration, the butterfly is open or partly open, the vacuum in the inlet manifold becomes weak, the piston **18** rises again (**Fig. 4**) and the passage of fuel through the large channel **20** is unrestricted. This increase in diameter with a subsequent increase in mixture volume helps in assisting with a smooth 'drive away'.

As long as the choke is not cut off, the action of the spring continues until the disc valve ports do not communicate any more with the ports on the face (**Fig. 4**) and, at this moment the starter is completely out of action.

### 4. SETTING AND DISMOUNTING

The setting of the Autostarter is fixed at the time of fitting in the workshop and it is carried out with the help of a thermometer and a special setting pointer. The setting of the Autostarter consists essentially in calibration of the spring after it has been warmed up to the surrounding temperature. It is therefore, absolutely inadvisable to separate the spring from the starter body. On the other hand, if, after a certain working time, it is suitable to carry out a check or a change of the Autostarter, the following operations may be carried out.

**a) ICBT Model (Fig. 45)**
(1) Unscrew the biconical joint.
(2) Unscrew the two fixing screws on the cover.
(3) Take off the Autostarter cover.
(4) Remove the casing and its insulation.
(5) Take off the body of the Autostarter by removing the 4 fixing screws.

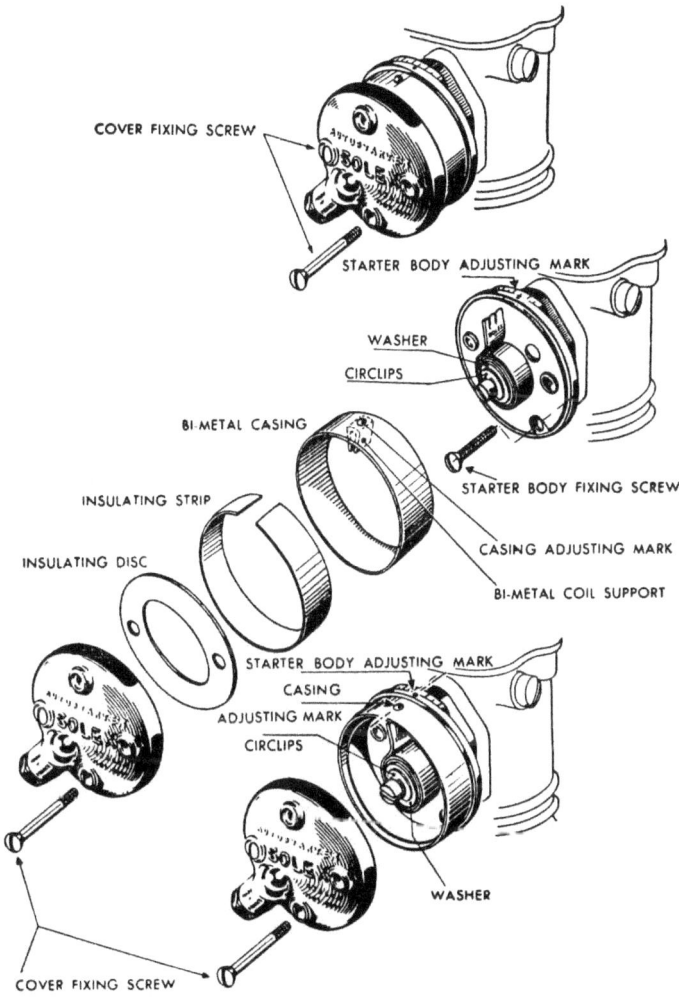

Figure 45

### b) IBT Model (Fig. 46)

(1) Unscrew the biconical joint of the warm air intake tube.
(2) Unscrew the 3 ring fixing screws.
(3) Take off the adjusting ring.
(4) Take off the casing.
(5) Unscrew the 4 body screws of the Autostarter.
(6) Take off the Autostarter body.

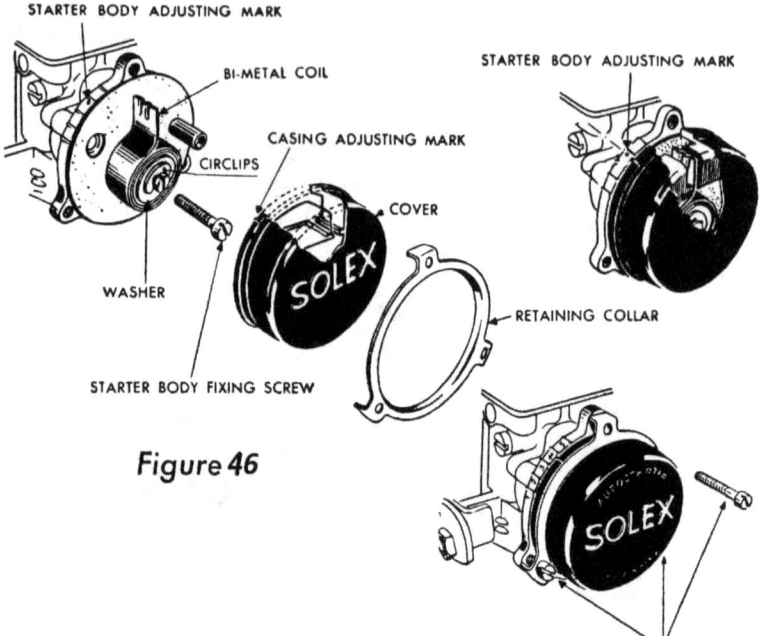

*Figure 46*

### c) BICT Model (Fig. 47)

(1) Unscrew the two cover fixing screws.
(2) Remove cover, disengaging it from the upper end of the hot air pipe.
(3) Take off cover insulating washer.
(4) Remove casing.
(5) Remove insulation inside casing.
(6) Unscrew the 4 body fixing screws.
(7) Remove the Autostarter body.

**IMPORTANT: Never remove the pin or the locking device of the bi-metal coil on the starter disc valve spindle.**

### 5. RE-FITTING OF AN AUTOSTARTER

When re-fitting an Autostarter onto a carburetor, the following precautions should be taken:

Firstly, check that the word Solex stamped on the straight

end of the bi-metal coil is well to the right on the inner face, looking at the starter from the plan view (see **Fig. 45**).

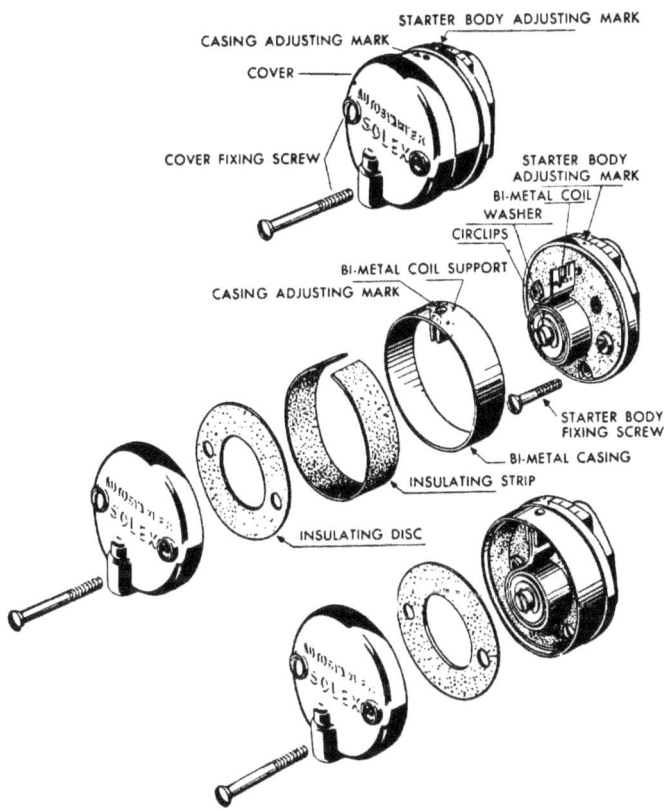

*Figure 47*

Secondly, ensure that the free end of the bi-metal coil is securely affixed in the bracket forming part of the casing, or in the slot provided in the starter cover (depending on the type of starter).

Thirdly, that the mark situated (according to the type of starter) either on the casing or on the Autostarter cover, is correctly located in relation to the "pop" mark made on the starter body during setting in our Works.

The complete Autostarter should be fitted to the carburetor body with the fixing screws, of which, depending on the model, there are either four or two.

Next, connect the hot air pipe to the Autostarter with the union and olive, which must seal perfectly. Beforehand, it is suggested that compressed air be blown through the hot air pipe, to ensure that it is quite free of obstruction.

## OPERATING FAULTS

There is no need to fear a complete failure of the Solex carburetor. At the worst fitting or adjustment faults may arise.

In the following section various faults and their causes are described. They may be in the carburetor—very often however they are due to other circumstances and their effect is erronenously connected with the carburetor.

### 1. LEAKAGES
**a) Fuel pipes**

Fuel pipes broken or badly soldered—Fuel tap leaking—Fuel filter washers loose or damaged.

**b) Fuel level too high**

Needle valve damaged or too large—dirt preventing the needle valve from closing—float leaking or too heavy—float jamming or sticking—fuel pump pressure too high.

**c) Washers and gaskets in the carburetor**

Insufficiently tightened (i.e. main jet carrier).

### 2. COLD STARTING DIFFICULT OR IMPOSSIBLE
**a) Carburetor**

No fuel—fuel pump not working—air leaks (throttle spindle, flange washer)—quality of the fuel (Octane rating too low or alcohol content too high) — incorrect starter setting — starter valve incorrectly assembled — starter cable badly fixed — fuel pipe blocked or damaged—needle valve sticking—float chamber empty due to evaporation of fuel.

**b) Ignition**

Ignition as a whole—battery flat—magneto or distributor in bad condition—incorrectely adjusted—dirty or damaged spark plugs—plug gaps wrong (magneto ignition 0.4 m/m, battery ignition 0.6-0.8 m/m)—contact breaker gaps incorrectly set—condensation on the plugs (inside or outside).

**c) Engine**

Should have the highest possible vacuum. If this is not the case the cause may be:

Poor sealing: induction pipe badly fitted—badly worn valve guides—valves sticking—valve springs broken—fault in any components connected to the induction manifold.

Cranking speed too low: battery flat—starter faulty—quality and viscosity of lubricating oil (of great importance)—grease in transmission parts too stiff—new or reconditioned engine not run-in.

## 3. HOT STARTING DIFFICULT OR IMPOSSIBLE
**a) Carburetor**
Fuel pump supply faulty (vaporization)—percolation of fuel from float chamber—pilot jet too small or blocked—idling set too slow or too weak—induction pipe flooded (with downdraft carburetors start with throttle butterfly fully open).

**b) Ignition**
Fault in the ignition system.

**c) Engine**
Valves burnt—valve springs broken.

## 4. BAD IDLING
**a) Carburetor**
Incorrect adjustment of the idling—air leaks (see 2 Cold Starting).

**b) Ignition**
Ignition faulty—plugs oiled up—wrong type of plugs (too cold)—plug gaps different.

**c) Engine**
Mostly fuel shortage—carburetor setting incorrect (choke tube too large, or pump jet too small)—air leaks (see 2 Cold Starting)—insufficient or too much heating of induction pipe - too much cooling—carburetor controls badly assembled (jamming)—over richness in induction pipe due to percolation from the float chamber.

**b) Ignition**
Ignition incorrectly adjusted—automatic advance and retard mechanism erratic—coil too hot—damaged plugs.

**c) Engine**
Engine not running freely (new or reconditioned)—poor compression.

## 6. INSUFFICIENT TOP SPEED
**a) Carburetor**
Carburetor too small—carburetor setting incorrect (choke tube too small, main jet too small, air correction jet too large)—dirt in fuel—throttle butterfly not opening fully—insufficient fuel due to vaporization in fuel pipe—insufficient pump pressure—needle valve too small—too much heat (in summer).

**b) Ignition**
Ignition insufficiently advanced—automatic advance and retard mechanism sticking—wrong type or damaged plugs.

c) **Engine**

Bearings "dragging" or some other operating fault — poor compression—engine not running freely (new or reconditioned) — cooling insufficient — lubricating oil too thick — silencer choked—brakes binding—wheel alignment not correct.

## 7. INSUFFICIENT POWER WHEN CLIMBING
a) **Carburetor**

Carburetor setting incorrect (choke tube too large or too small, main jet too small)—carburetor setting not suitable for fuel in use.

b) **Ignition**
Ignition incorrectly adjusted.

c) **Engine**
Engine not yet warm.

## 8. OVERHEATING
a) **Carburetor**
Carburetor setting incorrect (too weak)—fuel starvation.

b) **Ignition**
Ignition incorrectly adjusted.

c) **Engine**

Engine not running freely (new or reconditioned)—shortage of water—insufficient cooling—choked radiator—unsuitable lubricating oil—insufficient lubrication—silencer choked.

## 9. PINKING
a) **Carburetor**
Carburetor setting too weak—octane value of fuel too low.

b) **Ignition**

Ignition too far advanced—advance and retard mechanism unsuitable or out of adjustment.

c) **Engine**
Too much carbon deposited (very important).

## 10. MIXTURE TOO RICH
a) **Causes**

Carburetor setting incorrect (main jet too large, air correction jet too small)—main jet opened out or deformed—not genuine Solex jets—jets loose—starter in operation or not completely out of action—fuel level to high (see 1. b)—air filter not correctly fitted or clogged—pump pressure too high.

b) **Indications**

Color of plug points black—black smoke—smell of fuel—engine "hunting"—bad performance.

## 11. MIXTURE TOO WEAK
**a) Causes**

Carburetor setting incorrect (main jet too small, air correction jet too large)—main jet damaged (reduced in size)—no genuine Solex jets—air leaks (see 2a)—fuel pipes blocked.

**b) Indications**

Color of plug points white—fused deposits on plug insulators—backfiring in carburetor—pinking—engine overheating—lack of performance—burnt valves.

## 12. BACKFIRING IN THE CARBURETOR
**a) Carburetor**

Carburetor setting too weak (main jet too small, air correction jet too large).

**b) Ignition**

Pre-ignition (plugs too hot, carbon deposits)—fault in ignition system—plug insulator broken.

**c) Engine**

Valves sticking—valve springs broken.

## 13. DETONATION IN THE EXHAUST
**a) Carburetor**

Idling too weak.

**b) Ignition**

Ignition faulty.

**c) Engine**

Tappet clearance too small—valves sticking—air leaking exhaust (silencer leaking)—wrong type of plugs.

## 14. HEAVY FUEL CONSUMPTION

Consumption depends upon the following factors: weight of the vehicle, engine speed and average speed, condition and quality of all parts connected with the mechanical transfer of power, carburetion, the way in which the vehicle is driven, road conditions (hills, bends), climate conditions and the fuel in use.

Before the fuel consumption of a vehicle can be judged it is necessary to make an accurate fuel consumption test. This must be done very carefully as errors can easily be made when filling up and taking readings. The following directions should be followed:

1. Fit a small auxiliary fuel tank which should be connected by a flexible pipe to the fuel pump, or alternatively, direct to the carburetor and placed high enough to supply the carburetor by gravity feed.

2. The auxiliary fuel tank should be filled with a glass measure so that the quantity of fuel which is put in can be accurately measured.

3. The vehicle should then be driven over a distance, the length of which is accurately known. The distance should be at least 25 km (15 miles) long and should be similar to the conditions under which the vehicle is normally used.

4. After completing the distance the unused fuel should be measured with the same glass measure.

If the use of an auxiliary fuel tank is not possible the vehicle should be placed in a perfectly level position and the fuel tank filled to the brim. The vehicle should then be driven for about 100 km (60 miles) and, after placing the vehicle in a level position again, the fuel tank should be refilled using a measure.

In both cases the fuel consumption can be easily calculated, on the amount of fuel used.

If the results indicate that the fuel consumption is heavy the following points should be methodically checked, one by one:

a) **Carburetor**

Fuel leakage through washers—float sticking or leaking or too heavy (i.e. after changing to another fuel)—needle valve dirty, worn or too large (when a fuel pump is in use)—air leakage—throttle spindle worn—bad fitting—carburetor setting incorrect (too rich or too weak)—use of enlarged or deformed jets —not genuine Solex jets—main jet carrier or main jet cap loose—starter not completely out of action when starter control pushed fully home—induction pipe heating insufficient (especially if fuels of low volatility or containing alcohol are used)— air filter badly fitted, unsuitable or choked.

b) **Ignition**

Ignition incorrectly adjusted (too early or too late)—vacuum operated ignition advance mechanism of the distributor damaged—plugs damaged, too old or not suitable for the engine (too hot or too cold)—everything affecting the quality of the spark (plug gaps, contact breaker point setting etc.)

c) **Engine**

Engine not running freely (new or reconditioned)—lack of compression — valve timing incorrect — burnt valves or valve springs too weak — exhaust pipe choked — slipping clutch — everything which reduces the performance and can cause overheating of the engine.

d) **Chassis**

Everything which can increase the rolling resistance of the

vehicle.

e) **Radiator**

In winter it is sometimes advantageous to limit the cooling (thermostat, radiator blinds).

Finally, it should not be forgotten that there are many other factors which can influence fuel consumption appreciably, bad weather, headwinds, frequent stopping, erratic driving (rapid acceleration, heavy braking) and so on.

# NOTES

# ALFA ROMEO

## SOLEX 32 PAIA 4 CARBURETORS

### CLEANING AND CHECKING JETS
1. Remove jets **1, 2, 8** and **9** and blow through with compressed air. Do not use a metal probe as this could alter the jet diameter.

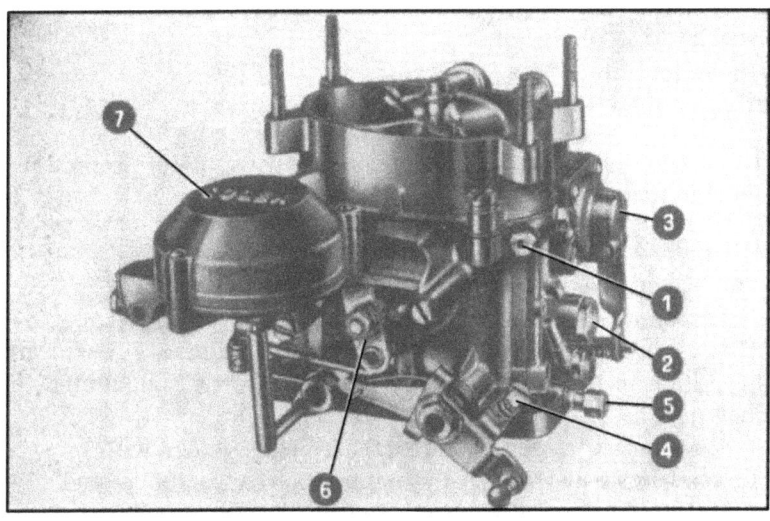

1. Idling jet, no. 1 barrel.
2. Main jet, no. 1 barrel.
3. Accelerating pump.
4. Adjusting screw for minimum opening of 1st throttle.
5. Idling mixture adjusting screw.
6. Choke control lever.
7. Vacuum capsule.
8. Main jet, no. 2 barrel.
9. Idling jet, no. 2 barrel.
10. Filter.
11. Adjusting screw for minimum opening of 2nd throttle.

2. Check that the numbers stamped on the jets are the same as those prescribed (see table).

| Jet specifications | 1st Barrel | 2nd Barrel |
| --- | --- | --- |
| Venturi | 20 | 23 |
| Main jet | 105 | 110 |
| Idling jet | 45 | 70 |
| Main air metering jet | 220 | 200 |
| Idling air metering jet | 100 | 60 |
| Accelerating pump jet | 40 | — |
| Choke jet | 120 | — |
| Mixture tube | 17 T | 17 T |

To prevent enlarging jet diameter never use a metal probe when checking jets.

## IDLING ADJUSTMENT (warm engine)
Numbers in bold type refer to images on previous page
1. Disconnect the control linkage from carburetor lever.
2. Give the screw **11** one quarter turn, in order to prevent any hesitation in the opening of the second throttle and tighten the lock nut.
3. Lightly tighten screw **4** to increase engine speed.
4. Slacken screw **5** until the engine starts to "hunt" and then tighten gradually until the engine runs evenly.
5. Slacken screw **4** very slowly until engine speed is about 500/600 rpm.
6. If the engine again starts to "hunt," slightly tighten screw **5**. **Under no circumstances must this screw be tightened to its maximum extent.**
7. Connect the throttle control linkage and, if necessary, adjust the length of push-pull rods so as to allow for a proper free travel of about 1/8" before opening throttles.

## REMOVAL FROM CAR
1. Remove covers and take out the filter elements.
2. Slacken the nuts securing filter body to carburetors and take out filter body.
3. Remove:
A. Accelerator control.
B. Suction pipe for distributor vacuum advance regulator.
C. Fuel feed pipe.
D. The four nuts of studs securing the carburetor to the intake manifold (tool No. A.5.0108).
E. Choke control from carburetors.

## DISMANTLING - See Fig. 1 & Fig. 2

1. Remove:
A. The acceleration pump valve **1**.
B. The four screws **2** securing the bowl cover to the carburetor.
C. The float from bowl.
2. Unscrew the fuel filter retaining plug **3** and clean filter of impurities.

Fig. 1

3. Check that the mating flange of the float chamber cover is perfectly flat; if not, smooth it on emery cloth placed on a surface plate.

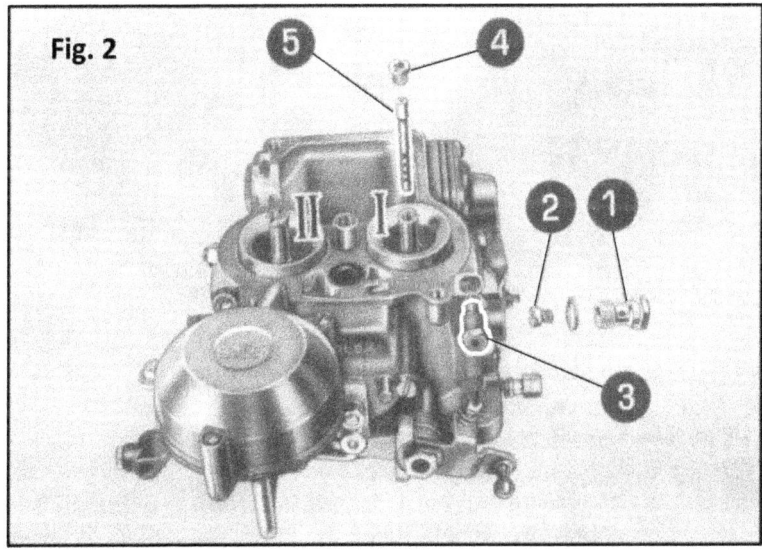
Fig. 2

4. Remove the carriers **1** and main jets **2**, the idling jets **3**, the air metering jets **4** and mixture tubes **5**.
5. Check that the numbers stamped on the jets are as shown in the following list:

|                  | 1st Barrel | 2nd Barrel |
|------------------|------------|------------|
| Main jet         | 105        | 110        |
| Air metering jet | 220        | 200        |
| Idling jet       | 45         | 70         |
| Mixture tube     | 17 T       | 17 T       |

**To prevent enlarging jet diameter never use a metal probe when checking jets.**

### ACCELERATION PUMP - See Fig. 3, Fig. 4 & Fig. 5
1. Disconnect the pump jet **1** from bottom of bowl.
2. Turn over carefully the carburetor body for removing the ball of the inlet valve:
   **Pump discharge nozzle = 40.**
3. Slacken the six screws **2** securing pump to carburetor body.
A. Remove split pin **3** securing the pump lever to control linkage.
B. Check that pump diaphragm is sound.

Fig. 3

Fig. 4

4. Refit pump securing split pin **3** in first hole.
5. Check pump delivery:
   **The flow should be: 4 - 6 cc per 20 strokes.**
   If the quantity of fuel discharged is not within the prescribed limits it is possible to correct it by working on the pump stroke. Small alterations can be obtained by inserting shims between

the split pin **3** and the pump lever. Shifting the pin by one hole in the adjuster rod causes a 100% increment in pump flow.

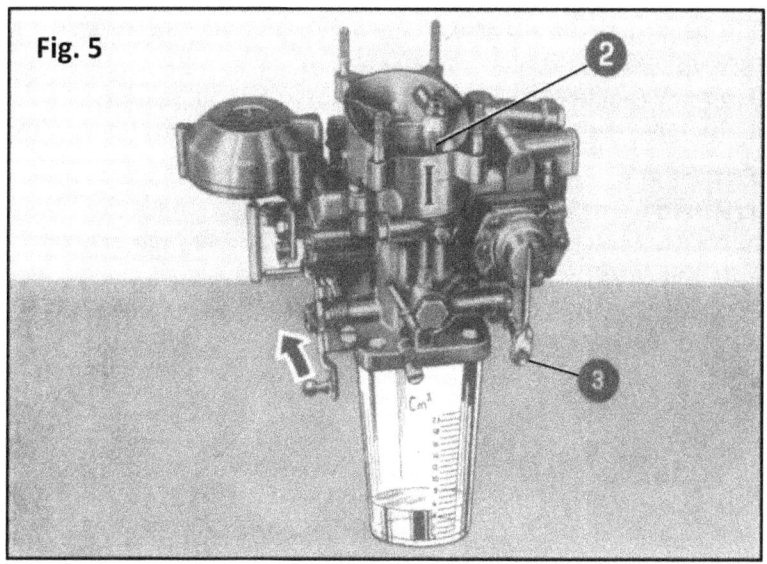

Fig. 5

**NOTE:**

The pump nozzle **2** (above) works also as a calibrated jet, is not turnable, but fixed in the position for giving the best result. It is **absolutely forbidden to use metal tools or gauge rods to avoid enlarging jet diameter.**

Fig. 6

Fig. 7

## CHOKE - See Fig. 6 & Fig. 7

1. Slacken the two screws **1** securing the choke assembly to carburetor body.
2. Check that the surface of the valve disc and the mating surface on carburetor body are flat and smooth.
3. Check that choke plunger **2** slides freely in its seating.
4. Remove choke jet **3** from bottom of bowl **choke jet = 120**.

## THROTTLE - See Fig. 8

It is not advisable to remove the throttles unless it is absolutely necessary. For removing the throttles slacken screws **1**.

If the throttle spindles show sign of damage or seizing it is necessary to replace them. (Bore and bush the seatings in the body of carburetor, if necessary.)

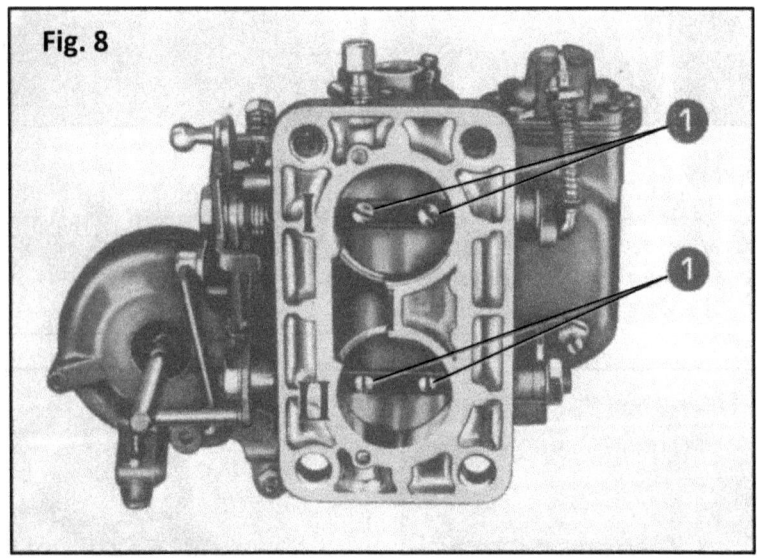

Fig. 8

## VENTURIS - See Fig. 9

1. Slacken the set screws **1**.
2. Take out venturis from carburetor body.

When refitting them take care of alignment of suction holes for second throttle vacuum control capsule.

When screwing in the setscrew take care that it is well centered in mating hole which is in the venturi; if this is not the case the venturi obstructs the suction duct compromising the carburetion.

Fig. 9

## SECOND THROTTLE VACUUM CONTROL CAPSULE - Fig. 10

The vacuum control for the opening of the second throttle, enters into action when the engine needs power.

Usually, if the engine is accelerated with no load, the vacuum capsule should not operate. If the vehicle, when road tested, continues to run below its maximum speed limit it is necessary to check the vacuum chamber proceeding as follows:

A. Check that the throttle is not jammed in its duct owing to wrong adjustment of the throttle opening screws.

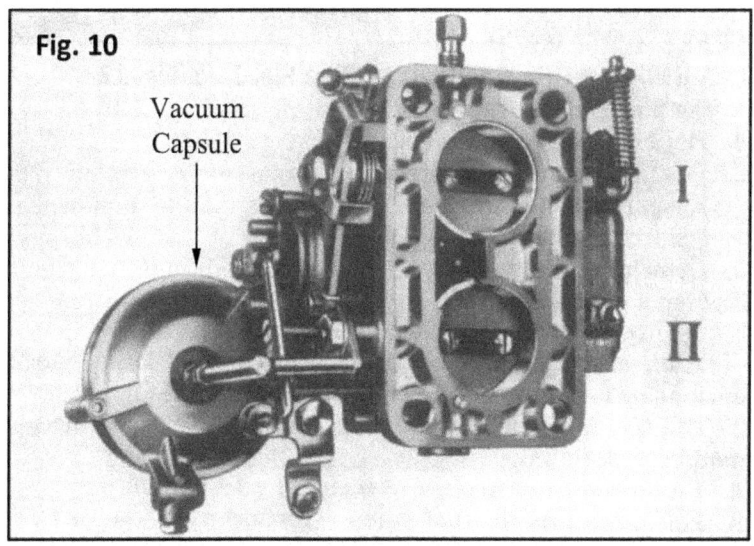

Fig. 10

Vacuum Capsule

B. Check that the small levers connecting the chamber to the throttle work freely without binding.
C. Check that there are no obstructions along the suction duct from 1st venturi port up to the vacuum chamber.
D. Check that the rubber diaphragm is fitted perfectly and is not squeezed between the two walls of the vacuum capsule, so to obstruct the duct section.

Unless it is absolutely necessary, it is advisable not to dismantle the vacuum capsule to avoid damaging the rubber diaphragm during reassembly.

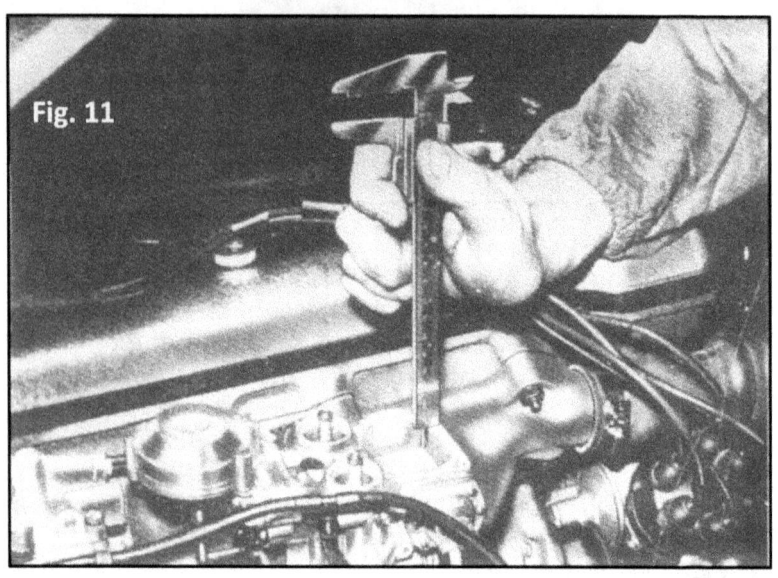

Fig. 11

## LEVEL OF FUEL IN BOWL - See Fig. 11 & Fig. 12

1. For checking the fuel level in bowl proceed as follows:
A. Refit carburetor to vehicle.
B. Position vehicle on a horizontal surface.
C. Run the engine for approximately one minute at slow speed then stop the engine.
D. Detach the fuel feed pipe from carburetor and discharge the fuel from pipe completely.
E. Remove cover and float from bowl.
F. With gauge measure the distance of the fuel level from the bowl flange surface it must be 18-19 mm (.71 .75 in.)
2. The fuel level can also be measured with the more accurate method as follows:
A. Fit the indicator in place of main jet ( See Fig. 30).
B. Put into action the fuel pump and check that level is 13 mm

Fig. 12

(.51 in.) below the flange mating surface.
  If the rating is not as prescribed check the needle valve and the float:
   Needle valve = 175
   Copper shim under valve seat = 1 mm (.039 in.)
   Weight of float = 7.2 grs (.25 oz.).
  Do not touch at all the float arm; eventually insert shims under the valve seat as required.
  If the trouble persists check the delivery of fuel pump.
**NOTE:**
  After refitting the carburetor to engine adjust idling.

## SOLEX C 32 PAIA-7 CARBURETOR
**CLEANING AND INSPECTION OF JETS - See Fig. 15 & 16**
1. Remove jets **1, 2, 8** and **9** and blow through with compressed air. Do not use a metal probe as this could alter the jet diameter.
2. Check that the numbers stamped on the jets are the same as those given in the table.

**IDLING ADJUSTMENT** (with engine hot) **- See Fig. 15 & 16**
1. Tighten the screw **11** for a quarter turn (to prevent binding of the 2nd throttle) and lock in the jam nut.
2. Screw slowly in the screw **4** to make the engine run faster.
3. Loosen the screw **5** unti the engine begins begins to hunt, then gradually screw it in until the engine runs smoothly.
4. Unscrew the screw **4** very slowly until the engine speed is approximately 500-600 rpm.

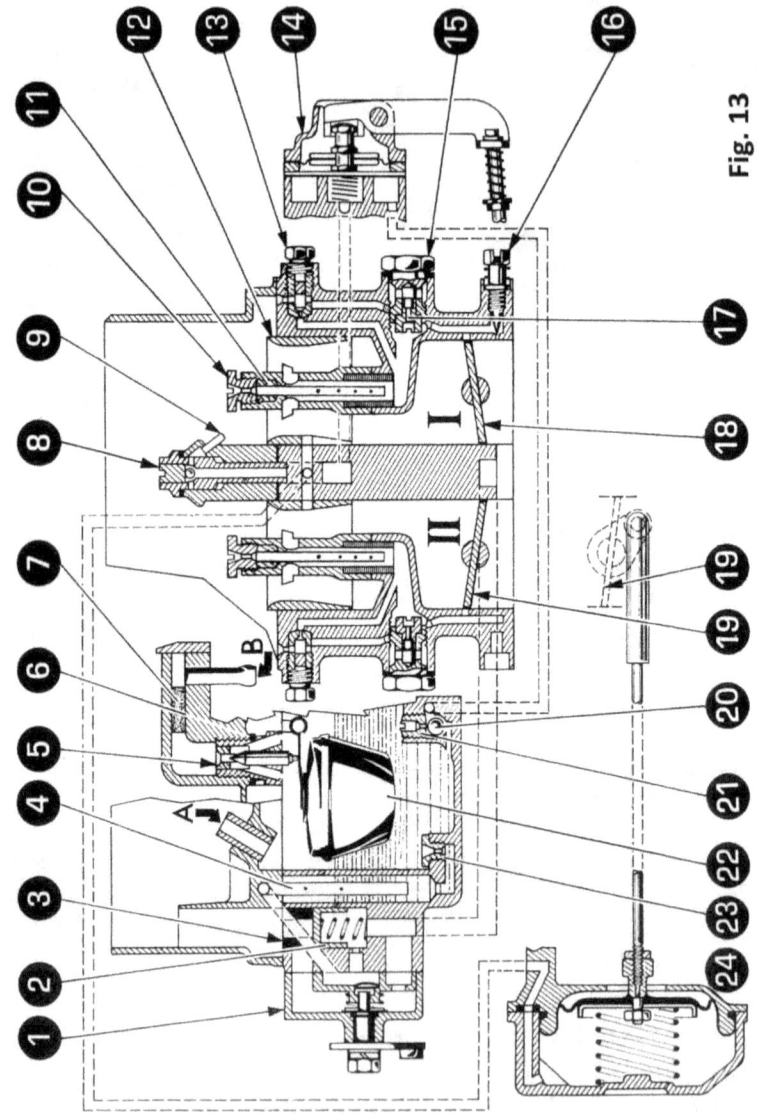

Fig. 13

## Key to Fig.13 & Fig. 14

- A  Air inlet
- B  Fuel inlet
- 1  Choke assembly
- 2  Choke plunger
- 3  Choke plunger limit stop
- 4  Choke air metering
- 5  Needle valve seat
- 6  Copper gasket for needle valve seat
- 7  Filter gauze
- 8  Accelerating pump outlet valve
- 9  Accelerating pump nozzle
- 10 Main air metering
- 11 Mixture tube
- 12 Venturi
- 13 Idling jet
- 14 Accelerating pump
- 15 Main jet carrier
- 16 Idling mixture adjusting screw
- 17 Main jet
- 18 1st barrel throttle
- 19 2nd barrel throttle
- 20 Accelerating pump inlet valve
- 21 Accelerating pump bypass jet
- 22 Float
- 23 Choke jet
- 24 Vacuum capsule
- 25 Setscrew and locknut for securing venturi
- 26 Accelerating pump stroke adjuster
- 27 2nd barrel throttle adjusting screw
- 28 Suction port for distributor vacuum advance regulator
- 29 1st throttle idle adjusting screw
- 30 Choke control lever

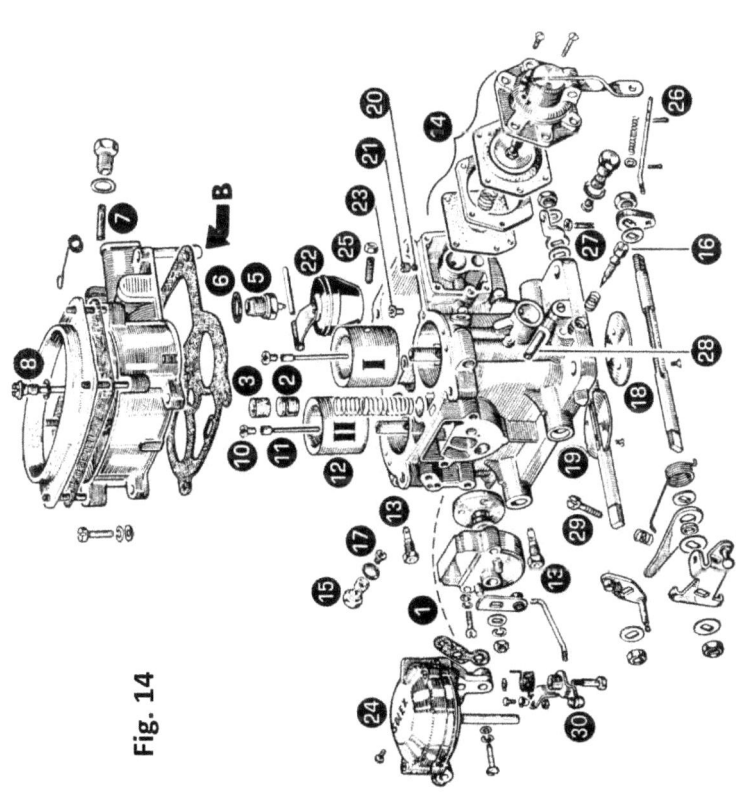

Fig. 14

Fig. 15

1 Idling jet, no. 1 barrel.
2 Main jet, no. 1 barrel.
3 Accelerating pump.
4 Adjusting screw for minimum opening of 1st throttle.
5 Idling mixture adjusting screw.
6 Choke control lever.
7 Vacuum capsule.
8 Main jet, no. 2 barrel.
9 Idling jet, no. 2 barrel.
10 Filter.
11 Adjusting screw for minimum opening of 2nd throttle.

Fig. 16

5. If the engine again begins to hunt, slightly tighten screw **5**; **in no case must this screw be tightened to its maximum extent.**

| Jet specifications | 1st Barrel | 2nd Barrel |
|---|---|---|
| **Venturi** | 23 | 23 |
| **Main** | 125 | 130 |
| **Idling** | 45 | 70 |
| **Main air metering** | 190 | 190 |
| **Idling air metering** | 100 | 60 |
| **Accelerating pump** | 45 | — |
| **Choke** | 120 | — |

## REMOVAL FROM CAR - See Fig. 17 & Fig. 18
Remove:
A. The cover from air cleaner housing; to do this unscrew the wing nut and the clamp on carburetor.
B. The choke control **1** from carburetor.
C. The accelerator control **2** from carburetor.
D. The suction pipe **3** for distributor vacuum advance regulator.
E. The fuel feed pipe **4**.
F. The nuts **5** from the studs securing the carburetor body to intake manifold (special tool A.5.0108).

## DISASSEMBLY - See Fig. 19 & Fig. 20
1. Remove:
A. The accelerating pump outlet valve **1**.
B. The four screws securing the cover to the carburetor body.
C. The float from its chamber.
2. Unscrew the gauze element seat **3** and clean the element from foreign matter that may have ben collected on it.
3. Check the cover flange for warping and the joining surface for smoothness; if not, smooth it on emery cloth laid on a surface plate.
4. Take out from both barrels the jet carriers **1** with the main jets **2**, the idling jets **3**, the main air meterings **4** and the mixture tubes **5**.

Check that the figures stamped on the jets are as shown in the table below.

**Do not alter the jet diameter with the use of sharp tools or metal probes.**

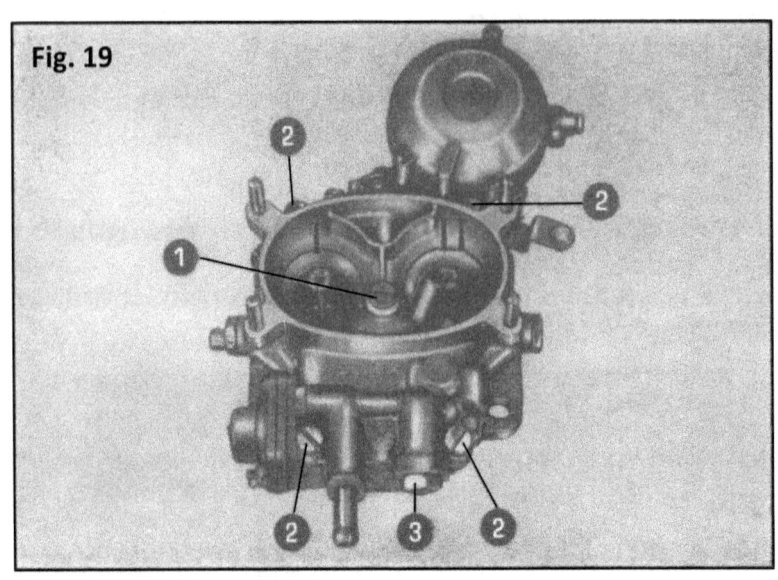

Fig. 19

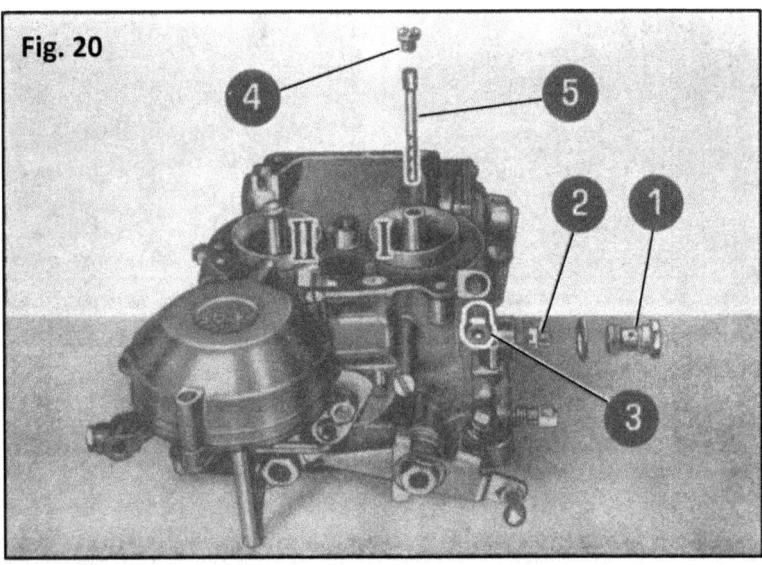

Fig. 20

|  | 1st Barrel | 2nd Barrel |
|---|---|---|
| Main jet | 125 | 130 |
| Main air metering | 190 | 190 |
| Idling jet | 45 | 70 |
| Mixture tube | 17 T | 17 T |

**ACCELERATING PUMP - See Fig. 21, Fig. 22 & Fig. 23**
1. Unscrew the accelerating pump bypass jet **1** from the bottom

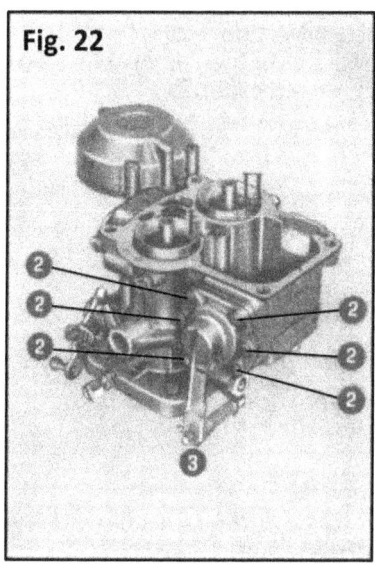

of float chamber.

2. Upset the carburetor with care in order to take the ball out of the valve seat.

**Pump bypass jet: 40.**

3. Loosen the six screws 2 securing the pump to carburetor body.

A. Withdraw the split pin which locks the control lever 3 to the linkage.

B. Check the diaphragm for good operating condition.

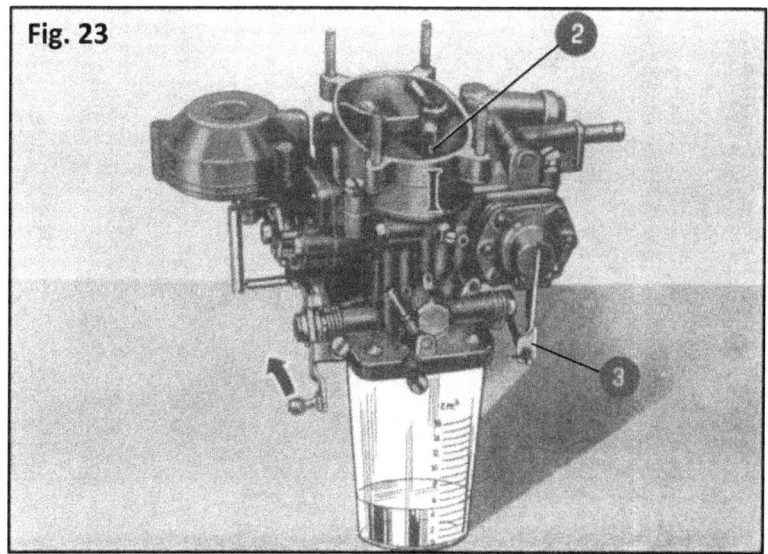

4. Reassemble the pump and temporarily insert the split pin into the first hole of stroke adjuster rod.
5. Check pump delivery:
The flow should be: **4-6 cc. per 20 strokes.**
If the flow is not within the specified limits correct it by adjusting the pump stroke. Small increments can be obtained by inserting shims between the split pin and the control lever 3.
Shifting the pin by one hole in the adjuster rod causes a 100% increment in pump flow.

**NOTE:**
The pump nozzle **2**, a calibrated jet, is not turnable but fixed in the position giving the best results. **It is strictly prohibited to alter the nozzle calibrated hole.**

## CHOKE - See Fig. 24 & Fig. 25

1. Loosen the two screws **1** securing the choke assembly to carburetor body.
2. Check that the surface of the valve disc and the mating surface on carburetor body are flat and smooth.
3. Withdraw the limit stop **2** and check that the plunger **3** slides freely without binding.
4. Check the spring **4** for proper operation.
5. Take the choke jet **5** out of float chamber bottom.
    **Choke jet: 120.**

Fig. 24

Fig. 25

## THROTTLE VALVES - See Fig. 26

It is not advisable to remove the throttles unless absolutely

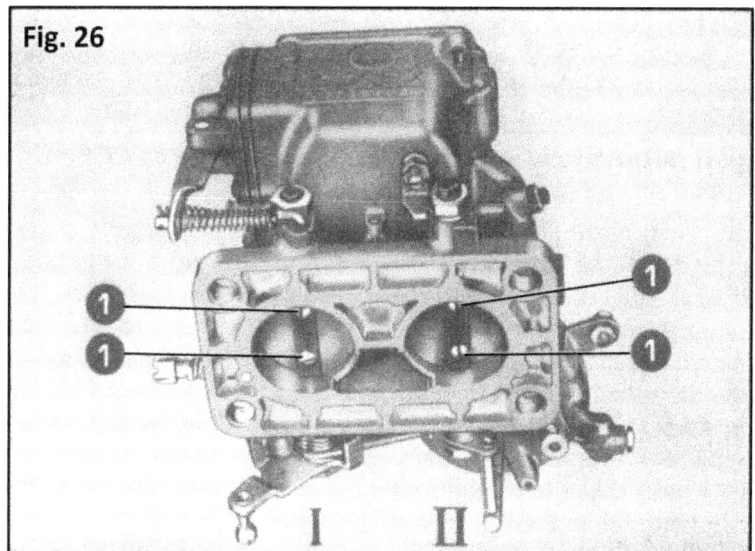

necessary.

To remove the throttles loosen the screws **1**. If the throttle spindles show signs of scoring or seizing, replace them (bore and rebush the seats in the carburetor body, if necessary).

## VENTURIS - See Fig. 27
1. Loosen the setscrews **1**.
2. Take the venturi tube out of carburetor body.

**NOTE:**
A built-in dowel properly position the venturi tubes with respect to carburetor body so that any misfit on reassembly is avoided.

## 2ND THROTTLE ACTUATING VACUUM CAPSULE - Fig. 28

The second throttle actuating vacuum capsule starts to operate when more power is needed. Usually, if the engine is accelerated with no load, the vacuum capsule should not operate. If the car, during a road test, should not attain the maximum speed range, check the vacuum capsule for proper operation as follows:

A. Check that the throttle is not seized in its barrel owing to wrong adjustment of throttle opening screws.
B. Check the linkage connecting the throttle to the vacuum capsule works freely without any binding.
C. Check that the vacuum pipe is not obstructed throughout its run from 1st venturi to vacuum chamber.
D. Check that the rubber diaphragm is properly fitted but not squeezed between the capsule halves in such a way as to obstruct the suction port.

**Unless strictly necessary, it is recommended not to disassemble the vacuum capsule to avoid damaging the rubber diaphragm on reassembly.**

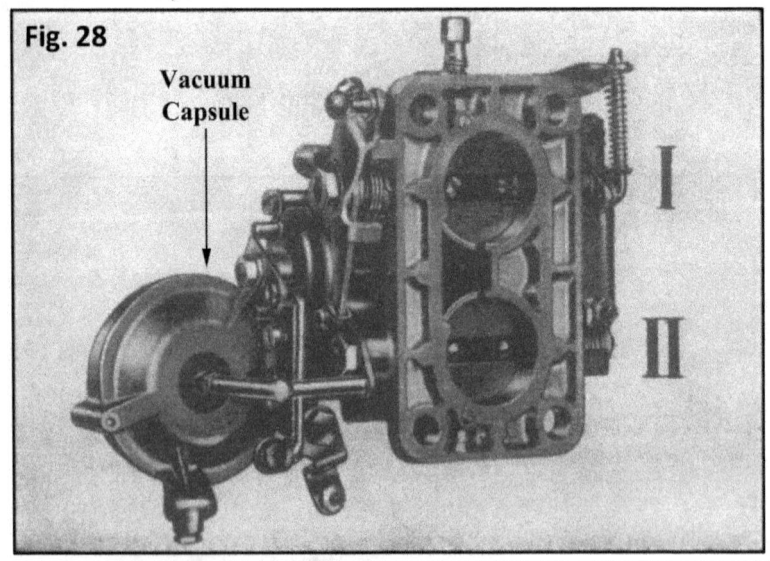

Fig. 28 — Vacuum Capsule

## LEVEL OF FUEL IN FLOAT CHAMBER - See Fig. 29 & 30

To check the level of fuel in float chamber proceed as follows:
1. Reinstall the carburetor onto car.
2. Place the car on level ground.

Fig. 29

3. Run the engine at slow speed for about one minute then stop the engine.
4. Detach the feed pipe from carburetor and discharge the fuel from pipe completely.
5. Remove cover and float from chamber.
6. Take measurement with a gauge as shown.
7. The distance from fuel level to float chamber flange should be 18-19 mm (.71 .75 in.).

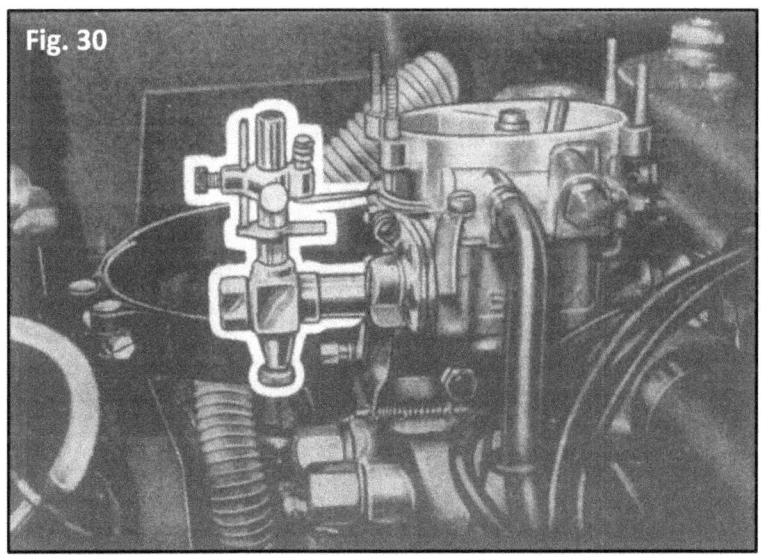

Fig. 30

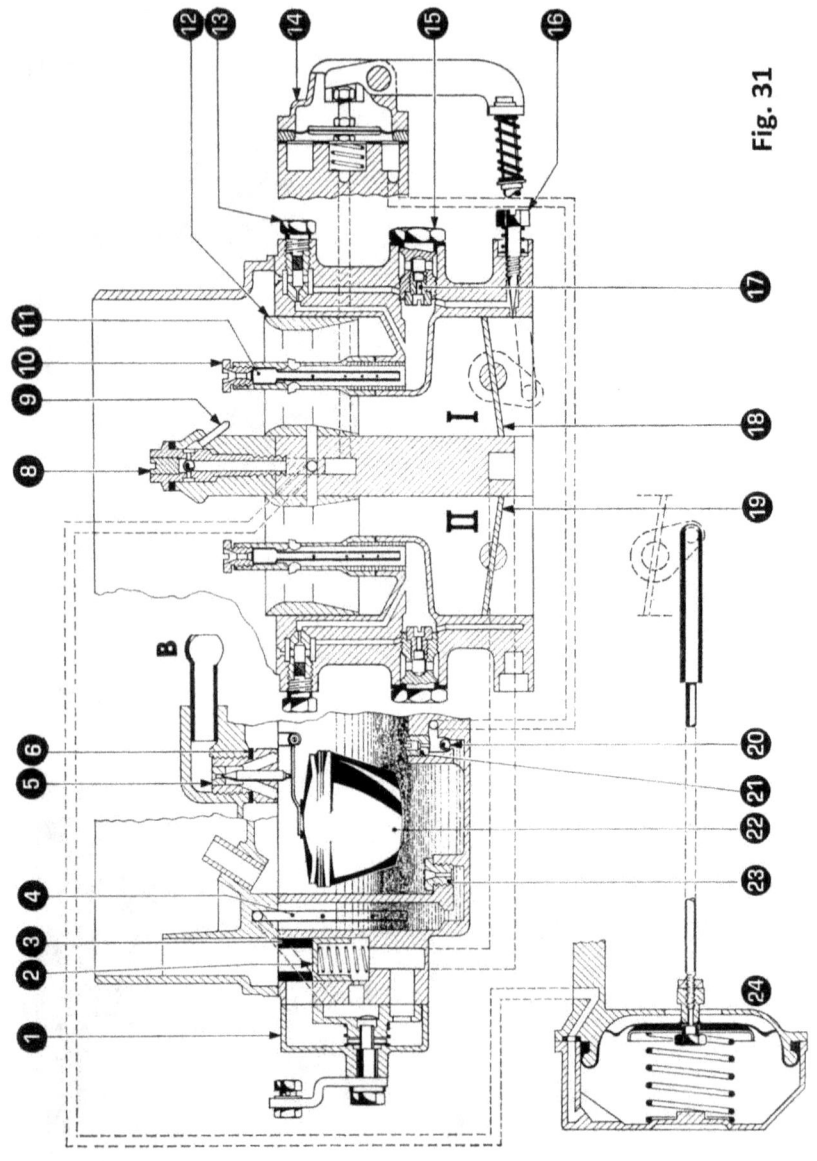

Fig. 31

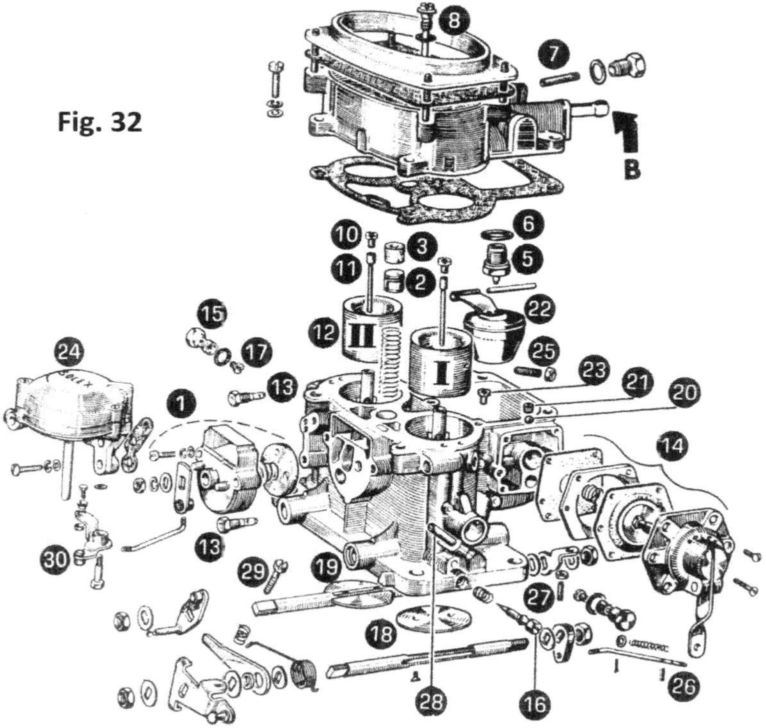

## Key to Fig. 31 & Fig. 32

- B. Fuel inlet
- 1. Choke assembly
- 2. Choke plunger
- 3. Choke plunger limit stop
- 4. Choke air metering
- 5. Needle valve seat
- 6. Copper gasket for needle valve seat
- 7. Filter gauze
- 8. Accelerating pump outlet valve
- 9. Accelerating pump nozzle
- 10. Main air metering
- 11. Mixture tube
- 12. Venturi
- 13. Idling jet
- 14. Accelerating pump
- 15. Main jet carrier
- 16. Idling mixture adjusting screw
- 17. Main jet
- 19. 1st barrel throttle
- 19. 2nd barrel throttle
- 20. Accelerating pump inlet valve
- 21. Accelerating pump bypass jet
- 22. Float
- 23. Choke jet
- 24. Vacuum capsule
- 25. Setscrew and locknut for securing venturi
- 26. Accelerating pump stroke adjuster
- 27. 2nd barrel throttle adjusting screw
- 28. Suction port for distributor vacuum advance regulator
- 29. 1st throttle idle adjusting screw
- 30. Choke control lever

Fig. 32

The fuel level can also be measured with the more accurate and quicker method as follows:
1. Fit the indicator in place of main jet ( See Fig. 30).
2. Actuate the fuel pump and check that the level is 13 mm (.51 in.) below the flange mating surface.

If the level is not as above specified, check the needle valve and the float:
**Needle valve seat = 175.**
**Copper gasket under valve seat: 1 mm (.039 in.) thick.**
**Float weignt: 7.2 gr (.25 oz.).**
Do not touch at all the float arm; insert shims as required under the valve seat.

**NOTE:**
After refitting the carburetor to engine adjust idle.

## SOLEX 44 PHH CARBURETORS

The engine is fitted with three carburetors, in line to a manifold suitably shaped to balance the proportion of mixture to each pair of cylinders.

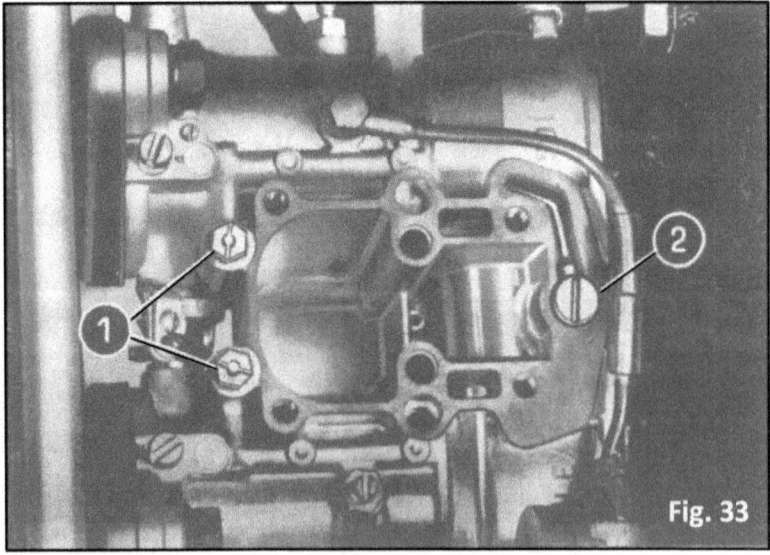

Fig. 33

| Jet specifications | 1st Barrel | 2nd Barrel |
|---|---|---|
| Venturi | 24 | 32 |
| Main jet | 120 | 145 |
| Main air metering jet | 160 | 160 |
| Idling jet | 45 | 65 |
| Acceleration pump jet | 50 | — |
| Spring-loaded needle valve | 200 | — |

## CLEANING AND CHECKING JETS - See Fig. 33 & Fig 34

1. Remove idling jets **1**, pump jet **2** and main jets **3** and blow through with compressed air.

**Never use** a metal probe which could alter metering diameter.

2. Check that jets are stamped with the prescribed figures.

Fig. 34

## IDLING ADJUSTMENT (warm engine) - See Fig. 35 & Fig. 36

1. Disconnect the throttle linkage from carburetor lever.

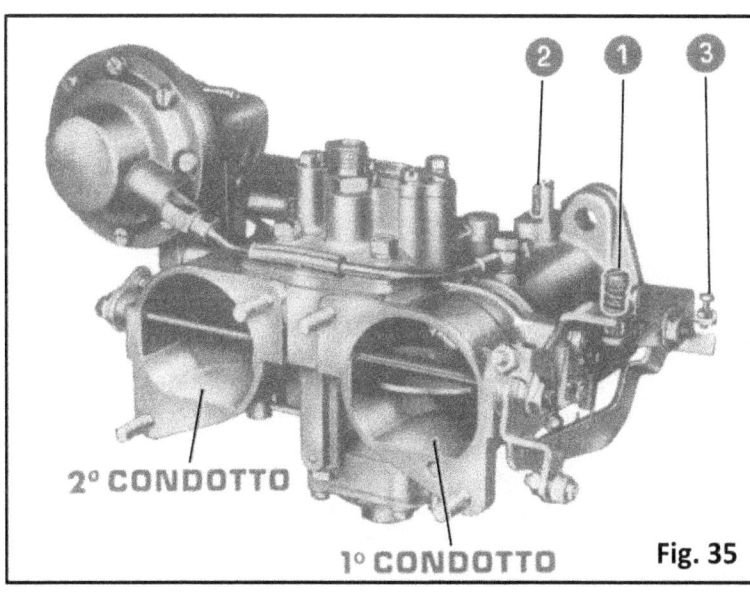

Fig. 35

1 Adjusting screw of main barrel minimum throttle opening.
2 Adjusting screw for main barrel idling mixture.
3 Choke control lever adjuster.
4 Secondary barrel throttle control adjuster.

**Fig. 36**

1° condotto = 1st barrel

2° condotto = 2nd barrel

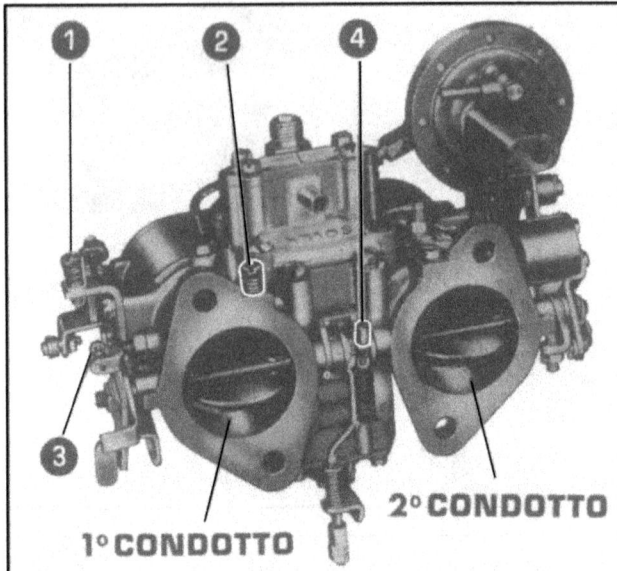

1° CONDOTTO    2° CONDOTTO

| Jet specifications | 1st barrel | 2nd barrel |
|---|---|---|
| Venturi . . . . . . . . . . | 24 | 32 |
| Main jet . . . . . . . . . . | 120 | 145 |
| Main air metering jet . . . . . . . | 160 | 160 |
| Idling jet . . . . . . . . . | 45 | 65 |
| Acceleration pump jet . . . . . . | 50 | — |
| Spring-loaded needle valve . . . . | 200 | — |

2. Slacken off almost completely: screw **1**, adjuster **3** and adjuster **4** (1-1½ turns approximately) after slackening lock nuts.
3. Set adjuster **3** so that the gap between lever and screw tip is .7-.8 mm (.028-.031 in.) (corresponding to about 1½ turn of adjuster) when the main barrel throttle is completely closed.
Then adjust to the following approximate settings:
Screw **1**: tighten one turn from the point at which it just makes contact.
Screw **2**: slacken one turn from the fully closed position.

4. Start the engine and, if necessary, slightly readjust screws **2** until the engine runs evenly and screws **1** until the idling speed is about 700/750 rpm.
5. Check that, during adjustment, the secondary barrel throttle is kept completely closed by the counterweight.
6. Tighten adjusters **4** so that there is no play on the main throttle spindle when the throttles are in the minimum open position.
7. Connect carburetors to accelerator linkage adjusting the length of the tie rods so as to have a free movement of about ⅛" before actuating carburetors.
8. Check that the accelerator control stop is effected, when throttles are fully open, by the adjustable stop on the pedal and not by the adjusting screws on the throttle spindle. This is to prevent strain on the throttle control levers.
9. Check that the accelerator control return is stopped by the adjustable stop on the pedal and not by the adjusting screws **1**. This is to prevent strain on the throttle valve control levers.
10. Check that the whole accelerator assembly is working properly and that the throttle valves return freely to the idling position when accelerator is released.

## REMOVAL FROM VEHICLE - See Fig. 37
1. Disconnect:
A. Fuel Feed pipe **2**.
B. Air filter rubber hose **1**.
C. carburetor tie rods **4**.

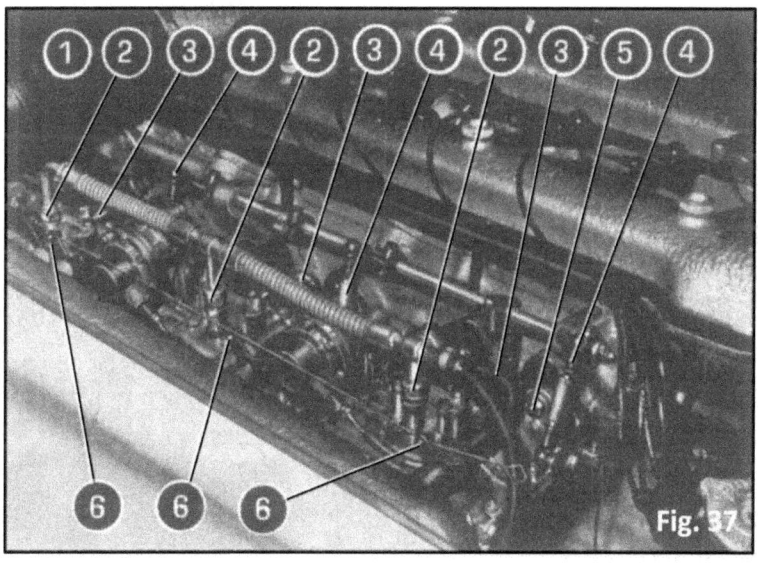

Fig. 37

D. Mixture tube air pipes **3**.
E. Fuel vapor vent pipes.
F. Choke operating flexible cable **6**.
2. Unscrew nuts **5** securing carburetors to rubber blocks and remove the whole assemly.
3. Disconnect air intake from carburetors.

**DISMANTLING AND CHECKING - See Figs. 38 Through 48**
1. Disconnect the vacuum capsule suction tubes **1**.

The main carburetor vacuum capsule has the selector valve **2** connected with the vacuum chambers of the other two carburetors.

Fig. 38

Fig. 39

2. Disconnect the vacuum capsule **3** from carburetor body by removing lever **4** and unscrewing the screws **5**.
3. Open the capsule chamber and check that the diaphragm is not damaged.
4. Check spring efficiency.
5. Disconnect acceleration pump **6** from carburetor.
6. Check that the diaphragm, the spring and the gasket are in sound condition.

The selector valve does not need any checking or replacement. Its function is to cancel at slow speeds the difference in pressure existing between the two chambers of the vacuum capsule: in this way the atmospheric pressure in the chamber at the control rod side is displaced by the vacuum originated from engine (balance of pressure) which, at idling speeds, keeps the throttles completely closed.

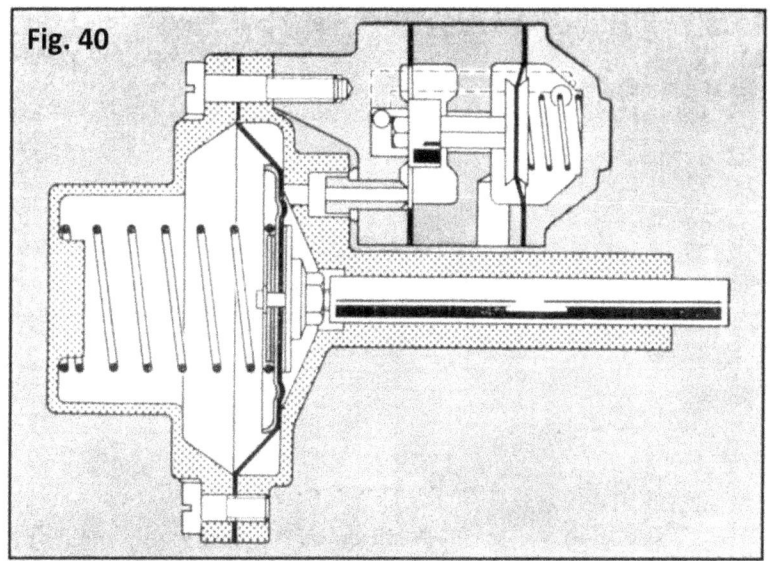

**Fig. 40**

7. Remove the two covers **1** and **2** from bowl and check that the float **5** and its arm are perfectly sound.
   **Weight of float = 10 grs. (.35 oz.).**
8. Check that there is no leak past the needle and that the needle is working properly. If the needle is worn, change both needle and seat.
   3 Copper shim = 1 mm (.039 in.).
   4 Spring-loaded needle valve = 200.

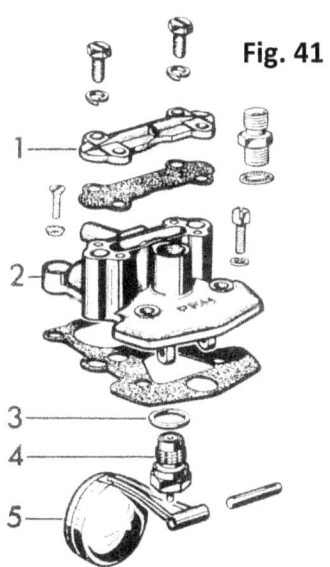

**Fig. 41**

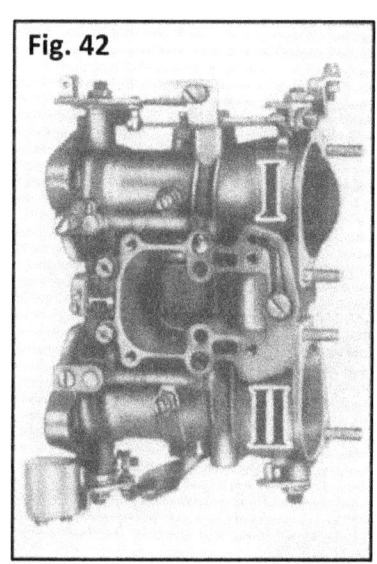

**Fig. 42**

9. Remove jets, jet carriers and air meterings.
10. Check that the numbers stamped on the jet carriers are as listed below:

1  1st barrel main jet . . . . . . . . . . . . . . . . . . . . . . . . . . . . . .  120
2  Secondary barrel main jet . . . . . . . . . . . . . . . . . . . . . . .  145
3  1st barrel idling jet . . . . . . . . . . . . . . . . . . . . . . . . . . . . .  45
4  Secondary barrel idling jet . . . . . . . . . . . . . . . . . . . . . . .  65
5  **Main and secondary barrel air metering** . . . . . . . . . . . .  160
6  **Acceleration pump jet** . . . . . . . . . . . . . . . . . . . . . . . . . .  50

11. Check that the ball valve **7**, the acceleration pump are working properly and clean pump strainer.

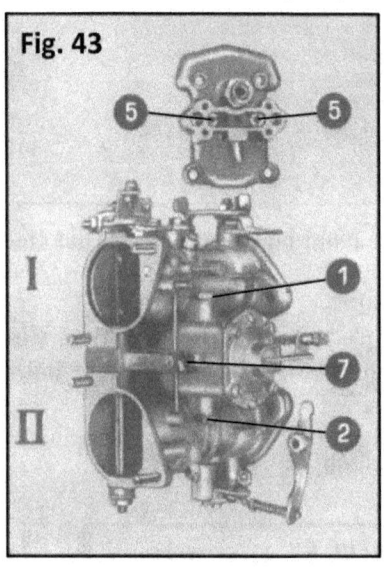

Fig. 43

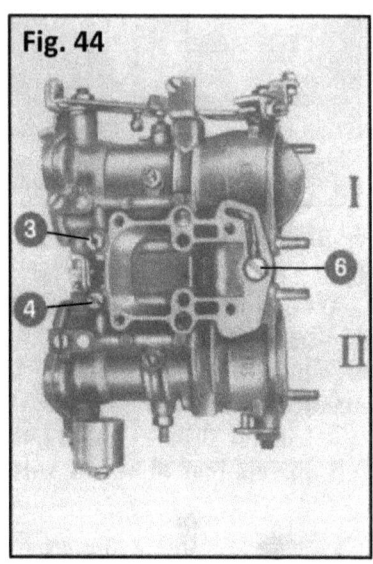

Fig. 44

12. Check that the throttles are not excessively worn.
13. Dismantle the choke and main barrel throttle control linkages.

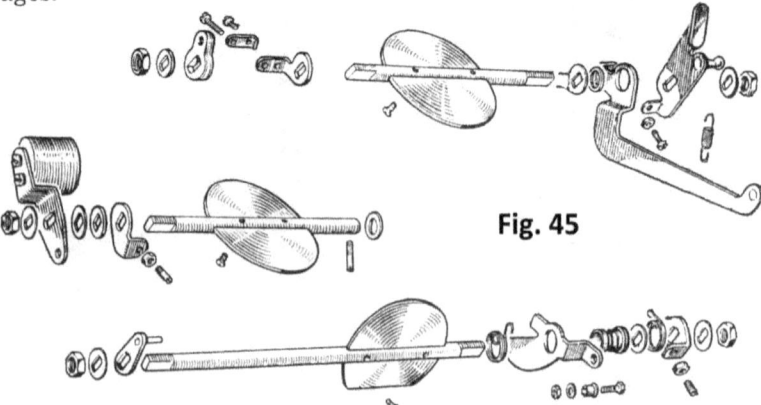

Fig. 45

14. Remove the nuts and screws securing throttle spindles and take out the spindles.
15. Check play of spindles in their seatings. If play is excessive change the spindles and bore and rebush the seatings, if necessary.
16. Take the mixer and the venturi out of 1st barrel by removing the securing screws 1 and 2.
   I. 1st barrel venturi = 24
17. Take the mixer and the venturi out of second barrel by removing the securing screws 3 and 4.
   II. 2nd barrel venturi = 32.

Fig. 45

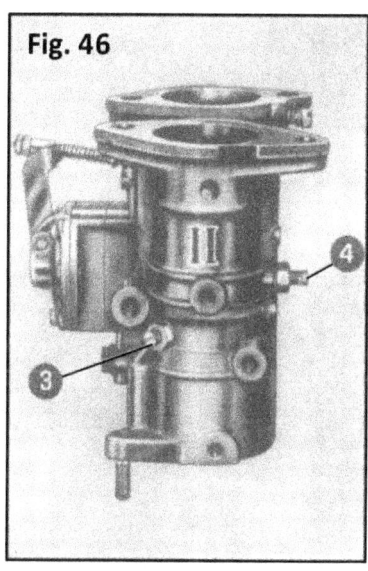

Fig. 46

18. Wash the whole unit thoroughly with gasoline, blow through with compressed air and reassemble the carburetor.

See next page for illustrations relating to the following text.

19. Acceleration pump delivery is adjusted using nut **A**.
The pump should deliver 6-8 cc per 20 strokes.
20. Check fuel level in the float chamber as follows:
A. Refit carburetor to vehicle.
B. Run the engine for a short time to restore the fuel level in bowl.
C. Remove the bowl cover and the float and check that fuel level is 28-30 mm (1.10-1.18 in.) below the cover mating surface.

If the fuel level is higher or lower, check the needle valve and float for proper operation. Do not touch at all the float arm; add shims as required under the needle valve seat.

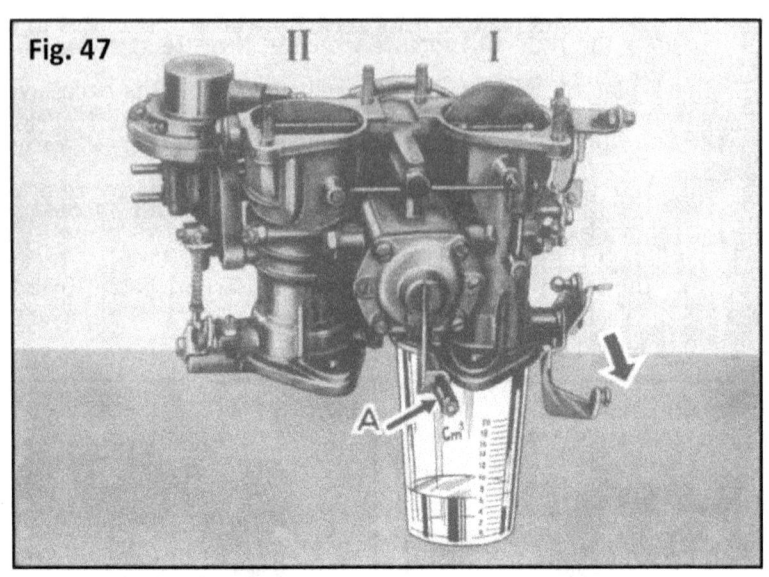

Fig. 47

Fig. 48

# JAGUAR 2.4

## SPECIFICATIONS

| | |
|---|---|
| Make and type | Solex B32, PBI-5 (twin) |
| Choke (venturi) | 7 to 1 CR: 23 mm |
| | 8 to 1 CR: 24 mm |
| Main jet | 110 |
| Air correction jet | 7 to 1 CR: 200 |
| | 8 to 1 CR: 180 |
| Emulsion tube | 14 |
| Pump jet | 55 |
| Pilot jet | 50 |
| Pilot air bleed | 1.2 mm |
| Needle valve | 1.5 mm |
| Needle valve washer | 1 mm |
| Starter fuel jet | GS 105 |
| Starter air jet | GA 4.5 |

Early Mk I model carburetors may be fitted with different jets and choke tubes to those listed above. These early carburetors can be brought up to the later specifications if desired, but a type 72 accelerator pump must also be fitted.

If the car operates at an altitude of between 5,000 and 10,000 feet, it is recommended that the main jets be reduced by one size, ie, from 110 to 105. Above 10,000 feet, reduce the main jets to 100.

## SOLEX B32 PBI-5

This type of carburetor is fully dust-proofed and has a progressive starting device with fast idle; it also incorporates an anti-percolation device and accelerator pump.

**DUST-PROOFING**

The carburetors are made dust-proof by causing all air to the engine (ventilating float chambers, starting, slow-running and the main spraying circuits) to be drawn through the air cleaner. This ensures maintenance of a balanced mixture and complete filtration of all inducted air, even if the air cleaner gradually becomes clogged in service.

**THE STARTING DEVICE**

The starting device, operated by a control on the instrument panel, ensures immediate starting from cold and quick drive-away. The control in the full rich position supplies a very rich mixture, to enable starting at low temperatures.

## Fig. 1
## Exploded View of the Solex Carburetor

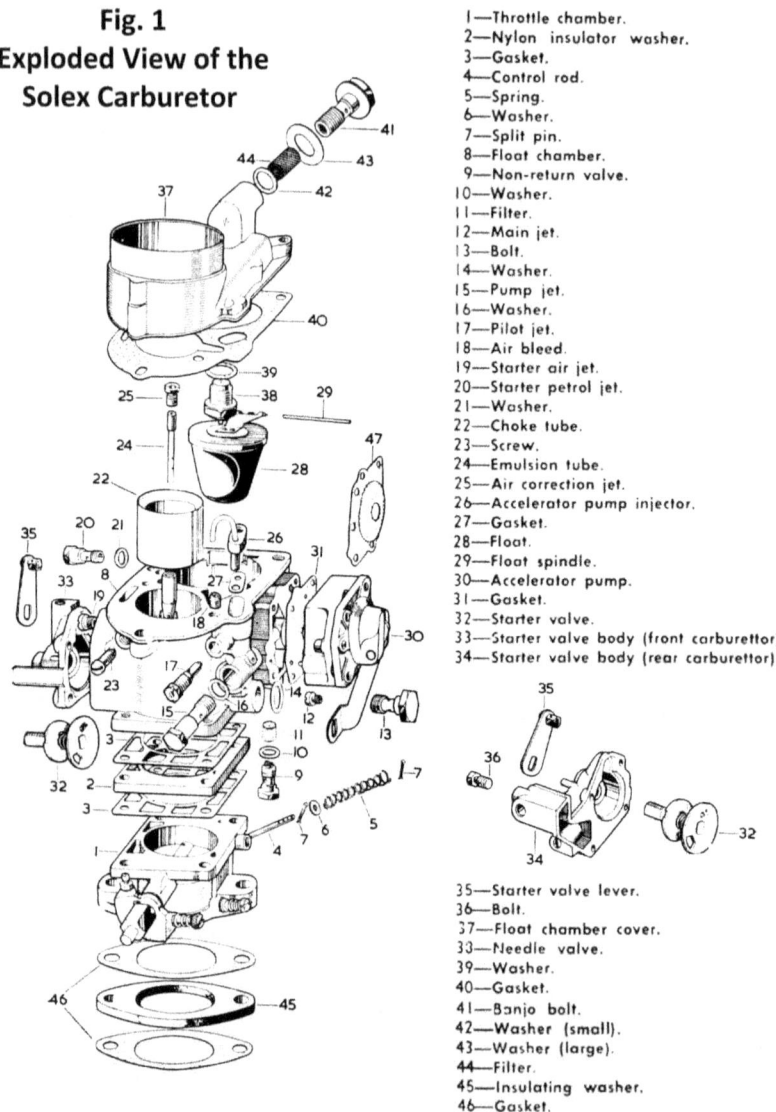

1—Throttle chamber.
2—Nylon insulator washer.
3—Gasket.
4—Control rod.
5—Spring.
6—Washer.
7—Split pin.
8—Float chamber.
9—Non-return valve.
10—Washer.
11—Filter.
12—Main jet.
13—Bolt.
14—Washer.
15—Pump jet.
16—Washer.
17—Pilot jet.
18—Air bleed.
19—Starter air jet.
20—Starter petrol jet.
21—Washer.
22—Choke tube.
23—Screw.
24—Emulsion tube.
25—Air correction jet.
26—Accelerator pump injector.
27—Gasket.
28—Float.
29—Float spindle.
30—Accelerator pump.
31—Gasket.
32—Starter valve.
33—Starter valve body (front carburettor).
34—Starter valve body (rear carburettor).
35—Starter valve lever.
36—Bolt.
37—Float chamber cover.
38—Needle valve.
39—Washer.
40—Gasket.
41—Banjo bolt.
42—Washer (small).
43—Washer (large).
44—Filter.
45—Insulating washer.
46—Gasket.

After starting, the mixture control should be placed in the intermediate position (half-way). This supplies a weaker mixture of greater volume, and enables the car to be driven away immediately. This position can also be used when the engine is not stone cold.

During the warming up period of the engine the control should be moved gradually towards the off position, thus progressively reducing richness until the starting device is out of action.

## IDLING

For idling, the mixture is supplied to the engine past the butterfly and from the pilot jet and the pilot jet air bleed. Engine speed can be varied by the slow-running adjustment screw which opens or closes the throttle as required, while adjustment of the volume control screw varies the mixture strength and volume from the pilot jet and the pilot air bleed.

## THE MAIN CIRCUIT

For normal running, fuel is supplied from the float chamber through the main jet; it is mixed in the main well with air metered through the air correction jet and carried into the well via the emulsion tube. The mixture is then discharged from the main spraying well into the air stream passing through the choke tube.

## ACCELERATING AND ECONOMY PUMP

The pump unit attached to the float chamber is operated by interconnected throttle linkage. The main components are a membrane and spindle, a return spring, an inlet valve and a spring controlled outlet valve. When the accelerator is released, the membrane is pushed back by the spring, thereby drawing in fuel via the inlet valve. When the accelerator is depressed, the membrane is pushed forward and this causes the fuel in the pump to close the inlet valve, and calibrated through the pump jet, to be discharged into the main air stream via the injector tube.

The pump has the additional function of supplementing the output of the main jet for full power, the size of the latter being chosen for most economical cruising. When the throttle is held fully open the pump lever holds the membrane forward, which in turn keeps the outlet valve open, thus creating an open circuit through which fuel is drawn by engine vacuum via the injector tube. Easing the accelerator to return to cruising speed closes the outlet valve and stops the supplementary supply.

## STARTING FROM COLD

For starting from cold the mixture control (marked Start) should be moved up to the fully rich (Cold) position.

Switch on the ignition and press the starter switch button but do not touch the accelerator. Release the starter button as soon as the engine fires — this is important. If for any reason the engine does not start, do not operate the starter switch again until both the engine and the starter motor have come to rest.

As the engine speed increases, progressively move the mixture control to the off (Run) position until the knob is at the bottom of the slide and the red warning light is extinguished.

### STARTING IN MODERATE TEMPERATURE

In warm weather, or if the engine is not absolutely cold, it is usually possible to start the engine with the mixture control in the intermediate (Hot) position by adopting the procedure given above.

### STARTING WHEN HOT

Do not use the mixture control. If the engine does not start immediately, slightly depress the accelerator pedal when making the next attempt.

Do NOT pump the accelerator pedal. The action of an accelerating pump in the carburetor will admit an excessively rich mixture into the engine.

### DIFFICULT STARTING (ENGINE HOT)

On extremely hot days, or when the engine is stopped after a fast climb, occasionally difficult may be experienced in starting immediately.

This may be due to a temporary richness of mixture. On no account pump the accelerator, but slowly depress it to about one-third of its travel, maintaining this position until the engine fires.

### USE OF THE MIXTURE CONTROL — IMPORTANT

Use of the mixture control (marked Start) brings into operation a starting device which provides the richer mixture necessary for starting. Do NOT permit the starting device to remain in operation longer than is necessary but return the control to the (Run) position as soon as the engine will allow. Unnecessary use of the mixture control will result in increased cylinder bore wear.

A reminder that the starting device is in operation is provided by a red warning light immediately below the mixture control slide. When the control is returned to the (Run) position the starting device is taken out of action and the warning light is extinguished.

## TO REMOVE CARBURETORS

Bend the rubber seal joining the air intake pipe to the air cleaner back on to the air cleaner flange. The air intake pipe can now be removed by applying a steady pressure under the center, care being taken not to lose the two connecting sleeves from the top of the carburetors.

Disconnect the distributor vacuum feed pipe from the front carburetor by unscrewing the union. Disconnect the fuel feed pipe by removing the banjo bolts. Disconnect the accelerator linkage from the carburetor. By removing the two retaining setscrews from the mixture control levers and also the outer cable retaining setscrews, the control cable can be withdrawn from the carburetors. Remove the four carburetor flange securing nuts and washers and lift off the carburetors.

## TO REFIT

Refitting is the reverse of the removal procedure. Always fit two new gaskets to each side of the carburetor insulating distance piece. When refitting the mixture control, ensure that the mixture lever inside the car is in the Run position and that the levers on the carburetor are as far forward as possible. Thread the control wire into position, remembering to replace the distance tube between the two choke levers.

## TO DISMANTLE - See Fig. 2

Remove the air cleaner. Unscrew the banjo bolts **Bb** (**Fig. 2**) and remove the filter gauzes.

Unscrew the float chamber cover fixing screws and gently remove each cover **Fc**. The needle valves **Nv** are now exposed for removal.

Lift and remove the float toggles **Ft**, spindles **Fs** and floats **F**. Remove the pilot **g**, pump **Gp** and starter jets, the latter being situated at the bottom lefthand side of the starter box, then the pump non-return valve and wire mesh, situated at the base of the pump chamber, plug **Gu** and main jets located in the holders **T**. The emulsion tubes may be lifted out with a matchstick after removing the air correction jets **a**. (Before doing so, make sure that the throttles are closed in case parts are accidentally dropped.)

## TO CLEAN AND INSPECT

Cleanliness during servicing is of the utmost importance and on no account should a rag be used for cleaning or drying the interior of the carburetor. A clean tray filled with gasoline or solvent, a small stiff paint brush (no loose hairs) and compressed air for the dismantled instruments and parts, are desirable.

Sediment can be quickly removed by gently brushing, followed by swilling out with fuel.

The interior of the carburetors and exposed passages should be blown out, to ensure that all loose particles of foreign matter are cleared.

For cleaning jets use compressed air only; never use wire as a probe as this can easily result in increased fuel consumption and a possible reduction in engine performance.

**THE FLOATS**

Inspect the floats for leakage and dents. Leaking or dented floats should be renewed; never repair (except in cases of dire emergency) as the volume and weight of the floats are important.

**THE NEEDLE VALVES**

Thoroughly clean with fuel, blow out and check the needles for quick drop and seal. Any tendency for a needle to stick can usually be cured by a short immersion in a degreasing tank, otherwise the unit should be renewed.

Should the occasion arise where the pump and starter units have to be dismantled, careful note should be made of the position of the various parts, as incorrect assembly will result in complete failure of either component.

It is stressed that the accelerating pump is specially set at the factory, therefore the unit should not needlessly be dismantled. However, should the membrane require replacing, it is not supplied separately it is only available as part of a replacement accelerating pump assembly.

**TO REASSEMBLE**

Before reassembling, check all carburetor assembly screws and flange nuts for tightness; do not use undue force.

When replacing jets and needle valves, fit new fiber washers, using genuine parts only; failure to do so may upset the calibration of the carburetor.

The nose of the pilot jet makes seating contact in the casting, therefore it should be screwed in tightly, but not with undue force or the seating will be damaged.

Refit the toggles and spindles, taking care that the toggles are fitted with the letters TOP uppermost and move freely on their spindles. Refit the needle valves to the float chamber covers, using the correct washers, as their thickness partly determine the fuel level; make a final check on the needle stems for free movement.

**Fig. 2**

View of the Solex carburetors with float chamber covers removed.

Bb—Banjo bolt.
Fc—Float chamber cover.
Nv—Needle valve.
F—Float.
Fs—Float spindle.
Ft—Float toggle.
g—Pilot jet.
Gp—Pump jet.
Gu—Plug.
T—Main jet holder.
a—Air correction jet.
B—Clamping bolt.
Z—Slow running adjusting screw.
W—Volume control screw.

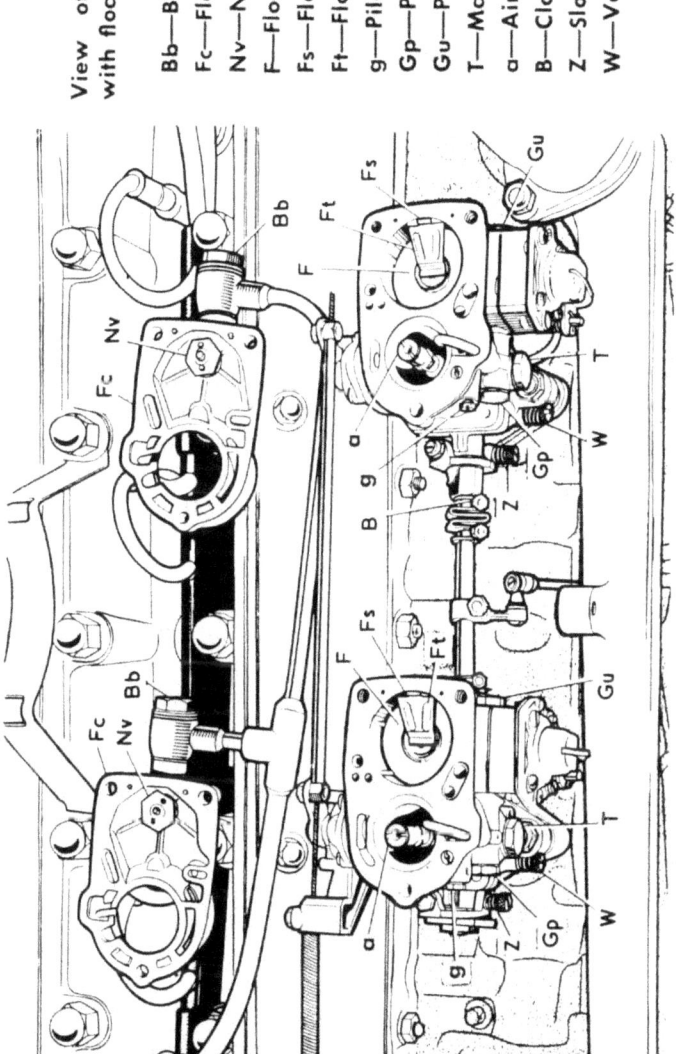

Fit new gaskets to the float chambers before replacing the covers — the carburetors, being dustproof, require a seal at this joint. Refit the fuel pipe and air cleaner.

If the carburetors have been removed from the manifold, new flange gaskets must be used on reassembly. At the same time it is advisable to check the flatness of the face of the carburetor flanges before refitting them to the manifold, to eliminate any possibility of air leaks at this point.

### SLOW RUNNING ADJUSTMENT - See Fig. 2

Adjustment and synchronization of the carburetors is quite simple, but is dependent on cylinder compressions, valve clearances, the ignition setting, spark plug gaps and contact breaker gap being set as laid down in the specifications.

The idling must be set with a fully warmed up engine.

Each carburetor has two external adjustments, the slow-running adjustment screw **Z** (**Fig. 2**) and the mixture volume control screw **W**.

Switch off the engine and loosen the clamping bolt **B** on the flexible link between the carburetors. Each instrument should now be separately adjusted. Starting with the front carburetor:

Unscrew the screw **Z** and ensure the throttle is closed by manual pressure on the slow-running screw. Insert a .002 feeler (or strip of paper) between screw **Z** and the casting stop, screw in **Z** one further complete turn from this point.

Gently screw the volume control screw **W** clockwise until light contact is made with the casting seat, then unscrew three-quarters of a turn.

Repeat the above adjustments to the rear carburetor.

Start the engine and, watching the Rev counter; adjust each slow-running screw **Z** equally until the engine is turning at 650 rpm. Then screw out each volume control screw **W** a quarter of a turn at a time until a drop in rpm is registered, indicating richness.

Carefully screw in each volume control screw **W** by quarter turns until the engine reaches the highest and steadiest idling speed, taking care not to go beyond this point where erratic running will be evident.

Should the engine speed now be other than 650 rpm, adjust the slow-running adjustments in order to obtain the required idling speed and synchronization.

The throttle connecting linkage between the carburetors should now be securely tightened, care being taken that both throttles are against their stops during the process.

FAULT FINDING
### Sudden Loss of Performance
This may be due to tiny particles of foreign matter or water escaping the filters in the carburetors and fuel pump and blocking one or more of the metering jets.

### Poor Slow Running
Sudden failure to idle smoothly may be due to one or both pilot jets becoming obstructed and failing to meter the quantity of fuel required by the engine.

Pilot jets should then be removed and the metering orifices cleared by blowing through.

When replacing jets, screw in securely but do not use undue force.

### Failure to Respond to Throttle Opening (Engine Hot)
If the engine will idle but suddenly fails to respond to throttle opening, the main jets should be removed for cleaning. Main jets are assembled in holders, the heads of which are clearly marked "Main Jet Holder." The latter are easily removed with an adjustable wrench, the jets then being exposed. Gripping the holder between the jaws of the wrench, the jets can be removed with a screwdriver and blown out. During this operation the float chamber will have drained, thereby carrying away impurities.

Important: Do not probe the jet metering orifices with wire.

### Flat Spot (Engine Hot)
Should the engine become reluctant to acelerate from slow to normal speeds the pump jets may be partly or completely obstructed and should be removed for cleaning. After replacing jets and priming the carburetors, pump action may be checked in the following manner: Remove the air cleaner and open the throttles. A discharge should then occur from each pump injector, visible in the choke tubes of the carburetors.

### Difficult Starting (Engine Cold)
Provided the carburetors contain fuel and the ignition spark is good, the engine should start immediately.

If it does not and there is no smell of fuel after considerable cranking, the starter jets may need blowing out to clear obstructions.

# NOTES

# PORSCHE 356

For many years the 32 PBI and 40PBIC (or PICB) were standard equipment on Normal and Super types respectively (except the 1954-55 1300 S which mounted the 32 with a strange assortment of jets). The carburetor types are identical in design but the 40 is somewhat larger as befits a more powerful higher revving engine. An accompanying table lists the normal factory-installed venturis and jets commonly found in these carburetors. Not always, mind you, but generally.

The Solex is a fine carburetor, easy to understand, capable of being adjusted to a fine degree and relatively trouble-free. The home workshop tuner need ordinarily concern himself with two elements: Idling speed and idling mixture, should his car come to him correctly jetted for his locality and the type of driving he prefers. If the second condition is not met, there are many happy hours in store (if he is the experimenting type) or possible avenues of frustration.

The first step in tuning is the simple one of adjusting the idling speed and mixture—balancing the two carburetors. We will begin with this, and for those who have passed this stage, it can be skipped over until the level you are currently operating on has been reached.

With the engine warm and idling:
1. Loosen the linkage between the two carburetors (a few turns on each nut will suffice)
2. Tighten **idling adjusting** screw on each carb slightly to bring engine up to fast idle (1,000 rpm) **See Fig. 1**

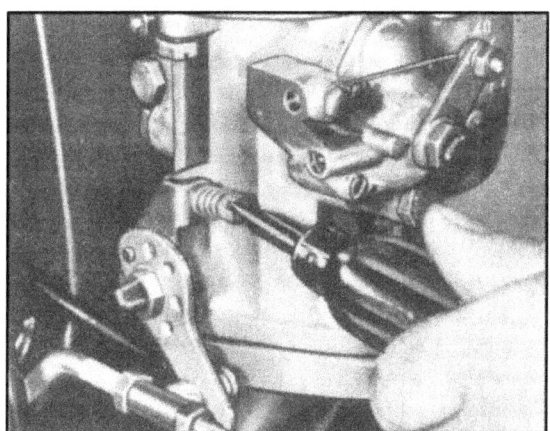

**Fig. 1** - Idling Adjusting screw regulates idle speed

**Fig. 2** - Volume control screw regulates idle mixture

3. Close **volume control** screw fully on one carburetor, then back it out 1½ turns **See Fig. 2**
4. Repeat on second carb.
5. With this idling mixture as a starting place turn the volume control screw on one carb back and forth until the engine attains its best speed. If you don't trust your ear have someone watch the tachometer.
6. Repeat on second carburetor.
7. Back off each idling adjusting screw until both carburetors are "sucking" the same amount. (With air cleaners removed place the ear close to each carburetor in turn, the sound each makes is a guide) and engine is idling at 600-800 rpm.
7a. Use a Unisyn or vacuum gage to determine airflow through each carburetor. The instructions in the Unisyn box cover the use of this simple but valuable instrument.
8. Tighten adjusting nuts on carburetor linkage.

The idling mixture on the Solex (determined by the size of the idling jet and the volume control screw) carries well up the rpm range—to 3,000 rpm or so. Therefore it is an important function of performance. After you have set the idling mixture in the above manner run the engine up, either in free revs or by driving around the block, to clean it out. Then rev it up to 3,000 and release the throttle suddenly. The engine should drop to idling speed smoothly and not sputter or die. If it hesitates or runs poorly, run the volume control screws in (clockwise) ½ turn to lean the mixture slightly. If it is necessary to run the volume control screws closed or within a half-turn of being closed to attain best speed the idling jet is too rich. With the proper setting and pump stroke correct, the engine will not falter on sudden application of throttle.

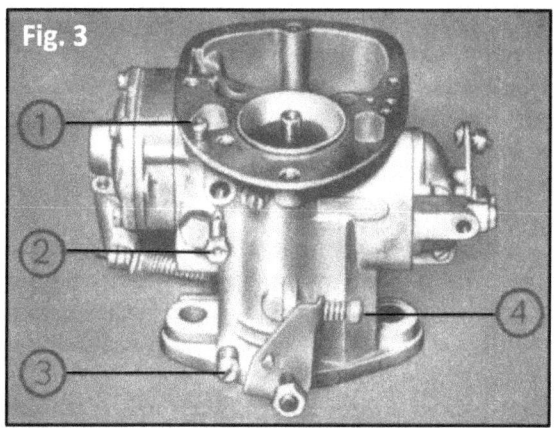

**These components influence idle and performance to 3,000 rpm: (1) Idling air jet, (2) Idling Jet, (3) Volume control screw, (4) Idling adjusting screw**

The carburetor serves two purposes: it is a metering device to provide the right amount of fuel and it is an emusifier which breaks the liquid into a fine mist for better mixing. The carburetor must also be versatile. At low rpm, where residual exhaust gases dilute the mixture, a richer than normal condition must prevail and at high rpm additional fuel is needed to provide extra cooling. (Actually; to absorb more heat and prevent detonation.) This versatility is provided by jets or other mixture controls within the carburetor body.

Before beginning a discussion of jets, let us review the principle of carburetion: The internal combustion gasoline engine operates on 80-90 octane gas—most efficiently on an air/fuel ratio of a little more than 12 (air) to 1 (fuel) by **weight.** Since the **weight** of atmospheric air varies with temperature, humidity and altitude but the engine requires a fixed **volume,** because of fixed bore/stroke, we can only vary the weight (or volume) of the fuel by varying the jets that admit the fuel.

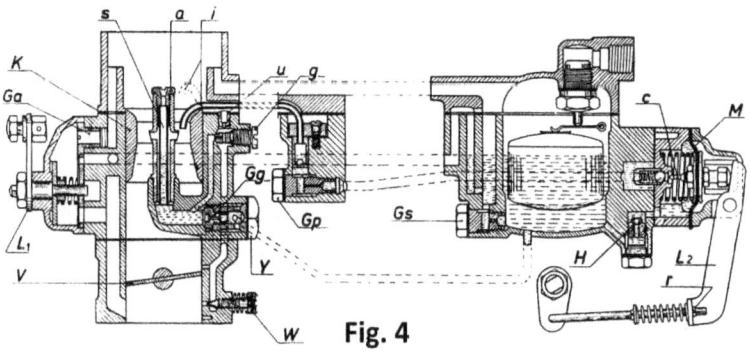

Fig. 4

The Solex embodies the following jets to control fuel volume through different ranges. (See Fig. 4 & Specification Charts)
1. Main jet (Gg)
2. Air correction jet (a)
3. Idling jet (g)
4. Idling air jet (u)
5. Pump jet (Gp)

Two other adjustable units, not properly classified as jets, enter into the picture: The volume control screw (W) and the pump operating rod with its adjustable nuts. The choke (called "starter" on the diagrams) and its jets need not concern us since it is seldom used and then only for a brief period.

The **Main** jet controls the fuel air mixture over the entire range, the **Air Correction** jet combined with the **Mixture** (or **emulsion) tube** (s) makes the mixture leaner with increasing vacuum in the venturi. The **Idling** jet and its volume control screw companion take over when the throttle is only partly open and negative pressure in the venturi is not sufficient to draw a good mixture from the main jet. The **Pump** jet richens the mixture on acceleration and also corrects for high speed leanness. The high vacuum opens it at about ¾ throttle.

As can be seen from the diagram and explanation, two variations are possible at each jet except the pump . . . air and fuel . . . this means a most precise adjustment of the ratio can be made.

Without going into myriad combinations which can be covered under "tuning" let us familiarize ourselves with the components and specifications. The jet **numbers** have no meaning other than to show a size relationship . . . they do not represent millimeters, inches or ells, but they do increase and decrease arithmetically: The higher the number the larger the cross section. A grand selection of jets is available from Porsche dealers or parts houses that handle Solex carburetors. The two you will probably be most concerned with are the Main Jet and the Air Correction jet. Their designations run from around 100 to 130 (Main) and 150 to 260 (Air). The Main jet is reached by removing the Jet Holder in the side of the carburetor body adjacent to the pump. The Air Correction jet can be reached by removing the air cleaner. It is positioned in the center of the venturi.

The Idling jet is directly above the volume control screw, it has no cover. The slot in the head is at right angles to the orfice in its tip. When replacing it, be sure that this slot is horizontal. The Idling air jet is reached by removing the cover from the carburetor. It will be found above the Idling jet.

All jets are marked on the heads.

## Solex Carburetor Specifications

| Engine | 1100 | 1300N | 1300S | | 1500N |
|---|---|---|---|---|---|
| Year* | '50-54 | '51-54 | '55-57 | '53 | '54-57 | '52-55 |
| Carb. | 32PBI | 32PBI | 32PBI | 40PBIC | 32PBI | 32PBI |
| Venturi | 23mm | 24mm | 23mm | 26mm | 24mm | 24mm |
| Main jet | 110 | 115 | 125 | 105 | 160 | 120 |
| Air Corr. | 230 | 240 | 220 | 150 | 160 | 260 |
| Idling jet | 60 | 60 | 50 | 50 | 55 | 55 |
| Idling Air | 1.0 | 1.0 | 1.0 | 2.0 | 1.0 | 1.0 |
| Pump jet | 50 | 55 | 60 | 50 | 80 | 55 |
| Needle | 1.5 | 1.5 | 1.5 | 2.0 | 2.0 | 2.0 |
| Mixture Tube # | 23 | 23 | 31 | 28 | 0 | 28 |
| Float Wt. | 12.5g | 12.5g | 12.5g | 21g | 12.5g | 12.5g |

*Note: Many cars with the factory designation 1954 were delivered here into 1956, '57s in '58 and so on. Generally the 1955 (as we bought it) was the last of the 1500 series.

## Solex Carburetor Specifications

| Engine      | 1952        |       | 1500S<br>1953 |         |       | 1954-55<br>40PBIC (PICB) |       |       | 1600N<br>1956-1957<br>32PBI | 1600S<br>40PBIC |
|-------------|-------------|-------|---------------|---------|-------|--------------------------|-------|-------|-----------------------------|------------------|
| Year        |             |       |               |         |       |                          |       |       |                             |                  |
| Carb.       | 40PBIC      |       | 40PBIC        |         |       |                          |       |       |                             |                  |
| Use         | City        | Comp. | City          | Comp.   |       | City                     | Comp. |       | Normal                      | Normal           |
| Venturi     | 26mm        | 29mm  | 26mm          | 29mm    |       | 26mm                     | 29mm  |       | 26mm                        | 29mm             |
| Main jet    | 117.5       | 135   | 107.5         | 117.5   |       | 085                      | *     |       | 110                         | 130              |
| Air Corr.   | 160         | 160   | 160           | 160     |       | 160                      | 160   |       | 200                         | 200              |
| Idling jet  | 55          | 55    | 50            | 50      |       | 55                       | 55    |       | 55                          | 55               |
| Idling Air  | 2.2         | 2.2   | 1.0           | 1.0     |       | 2.0                      | 2.0   |       | 1.0                         | 2.0              |
| Pump jet    | 60          | 60    | 85            | 110     |       | 80                       | 90    |       | 60                          | 80               |
| Needle      | 2.0         | 2.0   | 2.0           | 2.0     |       | 2.0                      | 2.0   |       | 2.0                         | 2.0              |
| Mixture Tube # | 23       | 23    | 28            | 28      |       | 28                       | 28    |       | 28                          | 28               |
| Float Wt.   | 21g         | 21g   | 21g           | 21g     |       | 21g                      | 21g   |       | 21.5g                       | 21g              |

*Factory admonition. "Try jets #97.5 to 102.5, find out correct jet by testing."

## FLOAT LEVEL - See Fig. 5

Proper level of fuel in the float bowl is important and the condition of the float needle valve often determines whether performance is good or ragged. Checking the fuel level with the carburetors on the car is not the easiest task in the world because of their position in the engine compartment, but the alternate method of removing them from the car and filling the bowl by running fuel in from a tank held above the carburetors is cumbersome, to say the least. However it can be done either way.

Remove the carburetor air cleaners and the bowl covers after having shut off the engine at the idle. With a depth gage or a narrow pocket rule of the sort that has a spring clip, gage the height of the fuel in the bowl at the **meniscus:** the point where the fluid creeps up the side of the bowl. The distance from the top of the bowl to this point should be .63" in the 32 PBI and .79" in the 40PBIC. Tolerance is .06" and .04" in the 32 and 40 respectively. (Some factory workshop manuals list this as plus or minus 0.6 and 0.4 which is a misprint.)

To change the float level, bend the float toggle, The toggle bears on the needle valve in an upward direction . . . the valve being in the top section.

The needle valve in its chamber unscrews in a conventional manner.

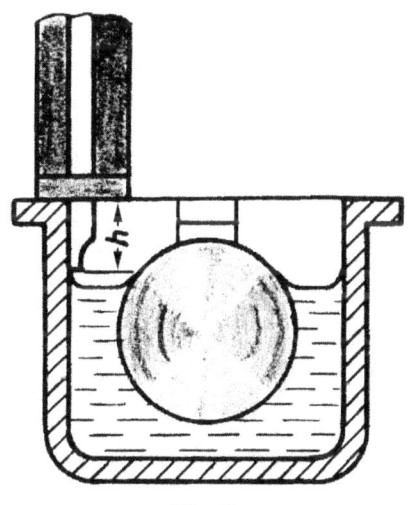

Fig. 5

'h' = .63" +/- .03" **(32 PBI)**

'h' = .79" +/- .02" **(40 PBIC)**

## ACCELERATION PUMP DELIVERY - See Fig. 6 & Fig. 7

Performance in the Zero to 30 mph range is much affected by the volume of the charge delivered by the acceleration pump. The amount discharged at each stroke should be .5 to .7cc in the 32 PBI and .7 to .9cc in the 40 PBIC and both carburetors should deliver an identical amount as closely as can be determined.

In the absence of "liquid measure P25" used by the factory, seal the small end of an eyedropper of the glass variety by holding in a gas stove flame for a few minutes. Then take another dropper and put 10 drops of ethyl gas (it's red and easy to see) into the first dropper. With the edge of a file, scribe a line at this level. This is .7cc. (Add 3 drops and you have .9cc.) The average dropper is too long for our purposes, so cut it off with a glass cutter or hot wire to about ½" above your mark, loop a piece of wire around it for a handle and you have your own "liquid measure P25".

With the engine idling and air cleaners removed, work the throttle a couple of times to clean out the jets then make a full stroke of the pump with the throttle rod holding the "liquid measure" under the delivery tube that curves above the venturi. Do this several times until consistent results are obtained. If the amount in the dropper does not come up to the .7 or .9 level (depending on the carburetor) unscrew the adjusting nuts with an 8mm wrench and set the stroke until this ideal is attained. Clockwise lengthens the stroke, counter clockwise shortens it.

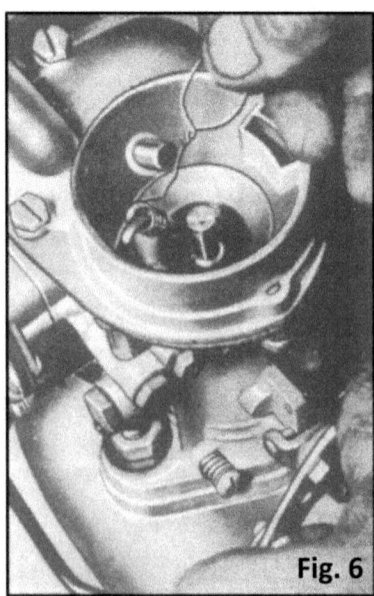

Fig. 6

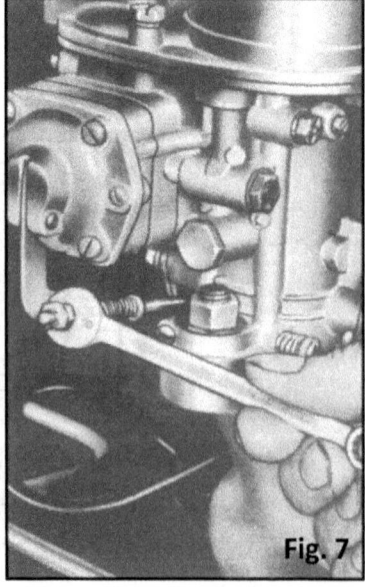

Fig. 7

## DISASSEMBLY AND CLEANING

After using our domestic highly leaded and dyed gasolines for a while, the carburetors become unsightly and are suspected of having the same sort of internal appearance. To clean them they should be disassembled and washed thoroughly in cleaning solvent, unleaded gas or carburetor cleaner. This is the sequence:

1. Remove carburetors from manifold.
2. Unscrew hex screws that hold cover, remove carefully, watching for sticking gasket. **(Fig. 9)**
3. Screw float needle valve out of cover. **(Fig. 8)**
4. Take out float toggle pin and float. **(Fig. 10 & 11)**
5. Remove air correction jet and mixture tube. ⎫
6. Remove main jet cover, main jet. ⎬ **(See Fig. 4 and text on page 98)**
7. Take out idling jet and idling air jet. ⎭
8. Release venturi retaining screw and take out venturi. **(Fig. 12)**
9. Unscrew adjusting nut on pump lever. **(Fig. 7)**
10. Remove pump chamber cover, take out diaphragm **(Fig. 13)** and spring.
11. Screw out discharge nozzle plug (alongside discharge tube) and remove tube.

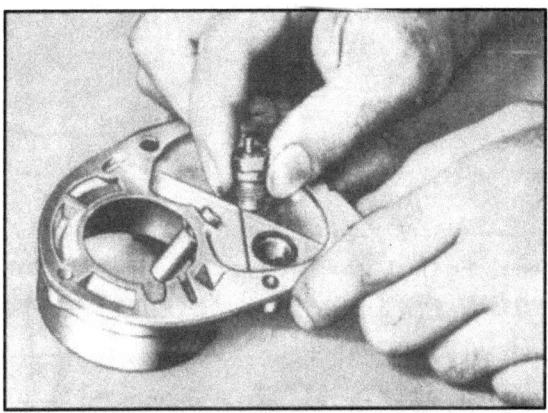

**Fig. 8 -** Remove float needle valve after top is off

After cleaning, blow compressed air through all orfices. Do not use wire to unplug a jet because you may roughen the bore. Check the following items before re assembly: **Float.** Hold it near your ear and shake it, if there is fluid inside it must be replaced. As a double check immerse it in hot water, air bubbles rising to the surface are a giveaway. Do not solder a leak, this will change the weight which is critical.

Fig. 9 - Solex 32 PBI with cover removed

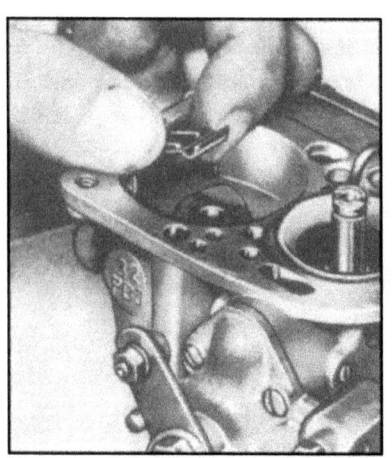

Fig. 10 - Removing float, step 1

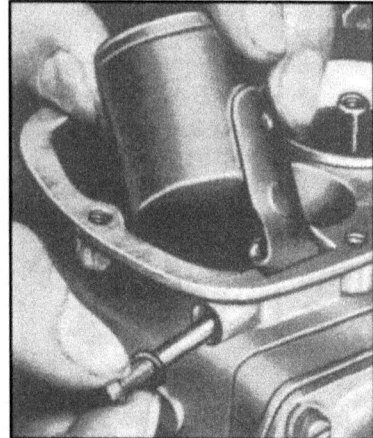

Fig. 11 - Removing float, step 2

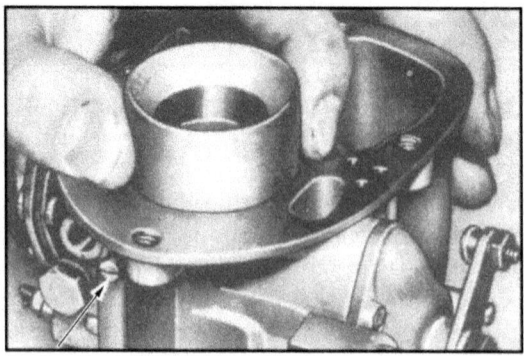

Fig. 12 - Release venturi retaining screw, lift venturi

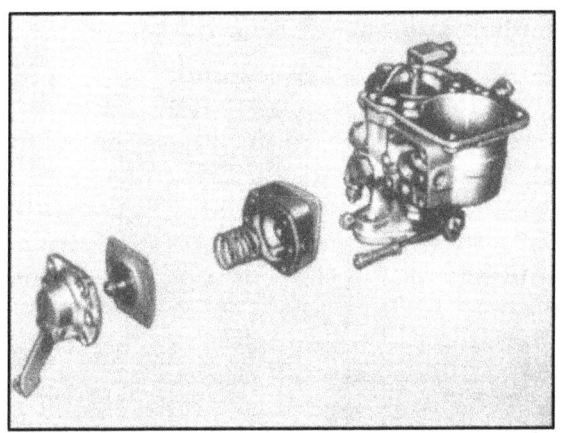

**Fig. 13** - Exploded view of accelerator pump assembly

**Pump diaphragm:** Should be firm, flexible and whole.
**Pump spring:** Check these against each other, they should be equal in resistance.
**Volume control screw:** Be sure tip is tapered, not blunted.

To re-assemble, follow the above pattern in reverse, of course, paying attention to these points: **Venturi;** Be sure that the venturi is in the bore right side up. The restricted "waist" of the venturi is offset toward the top. **Throttle valve (butterfly) shaft:** The clearance between shaft and carburetor body should be minimal. If this is a loose fit, outside air can be drawn in to ruin the mixture. **Toggle lever:** The word "OBEN" is stamped on the upper side of the toggle in the 32PBI; replace it this way.

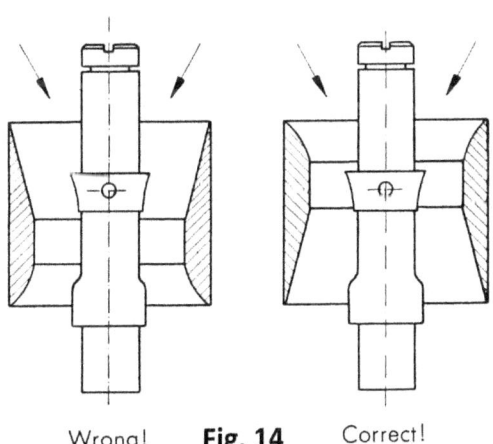

Wrong!    **Fig. 14**    Correct!

## Carbureter Specifications For Engine Type 1600 S-90

| Title | Specifications | Remarks |
|---|---|---|
| Carbureter | Solex 40 PII-4 | 2 per engine |
| Main venturi (K) | 32 | 2 per carbureter |
| Main jet (Gg) | 0115 | 2 per carbureter |
| Air correction jet (a) | 180 | 2 per carbureter |
| Idle metering jet (g) | 57.5 | 2 per carbureter |
| Idle air bleed (u) | 1.8 | 2 per carbureter |
| Accelerating pump | No. 72 | 1 per carbureter |
| Pump jet (Gp) | 50 | 2 per carbureter |
| Accelerating pump nozzle | high-type, with 0.4 restrictor | 2 per carbureter |
| Float needle valve (spring-loaded) | 175 | 1 per carbureter |
| Float | 7.4 g | 1 per carbureter |
| Emulsion tube | No. 25 | 2 per carbureter |
| Main jet carrier | 6 | 2 per carbureter |
| By-pass ports | 1.7; 1.4; 1.0 | |
| Injection quantity (warm season) | 0.45 cc (.122 fl. dram.) from 2 strokes, each nozzle | 2 nozzles per carbureter |
| Injection quantity (cold season) | 0.65 cc (.176 fl. dram.) from 2 strokes, each nozzle | |

Main jet metering is of great importance when operating at considerably varying altitudes for which the following rule-of-thumb may be applied: Change main jet calibration +/- 6% for each 1,000 m (3,280') altitude variation. For example: normal main jet calibration at an altitude of 400 m (1,312') is 0115; proper jet size for an altitude of 1,400 m (4,592') is 0110.

# NOTES

# PORSCHE 911

With the 911 six cylinder model Porsche specified a three-barrel solex carburetor, the 40 PI, which has a unique fuel supply system.

## CARBURETOR DESCRIPTION (Fig. 1 & Fig. 2)

Contrary to common carburetors with float-contolled fuel level, the Solex 40 PI downdraft carburetor employs a so-called overflow system incorporating a spill tube in close proximity of the metering jets for maintaining the desired fuel level in the metering system.

The actual float chamber has been detached from the carburetor and relocated to a point below it to serve as a supply or overflow reservoir for a desired number of carburetors.

A primary pump delivers the fuel from the fuel tank to the supply reservoir. A secondary pump, functioning as a recirculating twin pump, delivers the fuel to the carburetors; there are 2 triple-throat carburetor assemblies in the opposed-cylinder arrangement of the Type 911 engine. Fuel pumped into the carburetors in excess of demand flows from the spill tubes and returns into the overflow bowl.

This carburetor design makes it possible to maintain a constant fuel level in the metering system, being completely immune to conditions brought about through acceleration, deceleration, changed vehicle attitude, and especially considerable centrifugal and inertia forces exerted upon the fuel mass, as encountered in vigorous negotiations of curves.

The layout of this carburetor differs from the usual designs in that all jets are clustered in one assembly which is located in its own compartment within the carburetor body, extending through the cover; the jet cluster is easily accessible and can be removed for servicing.

The accelerating pump is of the diaphragm type and is actuated through the throttle arm at the carburetor, a pump rod and spring, and the pump lever. The pump circuit has a system of check valves permitting an added flow of fuel into the induction throat at higher power settings, i.e., increased velocities of induction air. The purpose of this enrichment system is to further enrich the fuel/air mixture at higher engine loads and rpm when maximum engine power is required.

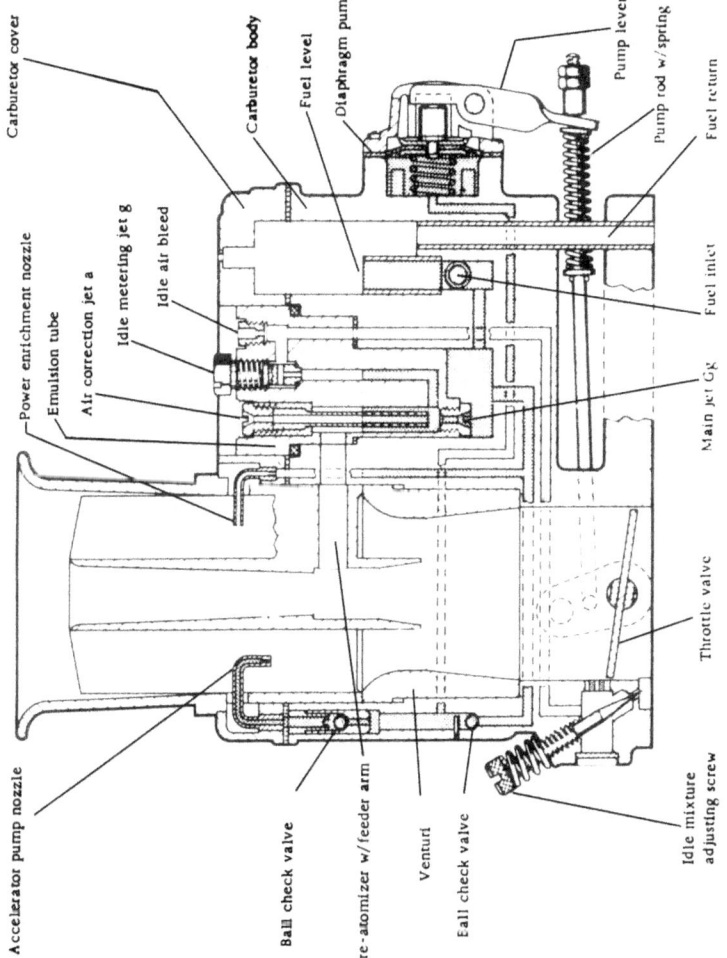

Fig. 1 Schematic view of Type 40 PI carburetor

### Schematic View of Carbureter

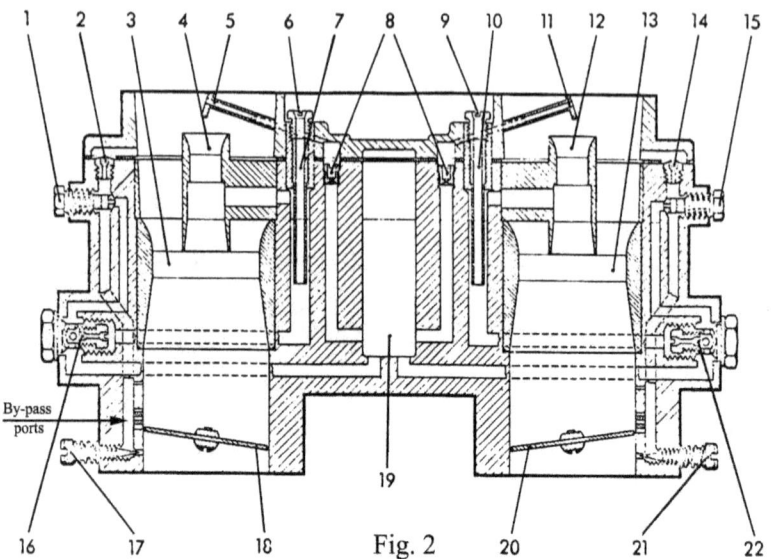

Fig. 2

For reasons of schematic clarity the throttle shaft is purposely shown in an untrue, transverse arrangement.

① Idle metering jet
② Idle air bleed
③ Main venturi
④ Primary venturi
⑤ Power enrichment nozzle
⑥ Air correction jet
⑦ Emulsion tube
⑧ Power enrichment jets
⑨ Air correction jet
⑩ Emulsion tube
⑪ Power enrichment nozzle

⑫ Primary venturi
⑬ Main venturi
⑭ Idle air bleed
⑮ Idle metering jet
⑯ Main jet carrier
⑰ Idle mixture adjustment
⑱ Throttle valve
⑲ Float chamber
⑳ Throttle valve
㉑ Idle mixture adjustment
㉒ Main jet carrier

## POWER ENRICHMENT (Fig. 3)

The carburetor is equipped with an enrichment nozzle which is connected to the fuel inlet point by way of a port. The enrichment nozzle outlet is situated in a low-vacuum area; the vacuum here is not strong enough to draw fuel from the enrichment nozzle at low engine rpm or light throttle settings. At full power settings, when the vacuum has considerably increased, the enrichment nozzle begins to discharge additional fuel.

In addition, a separate port connects the accelerating pump nozzle with the fuel supply to further enrich the fuel/air mixture.

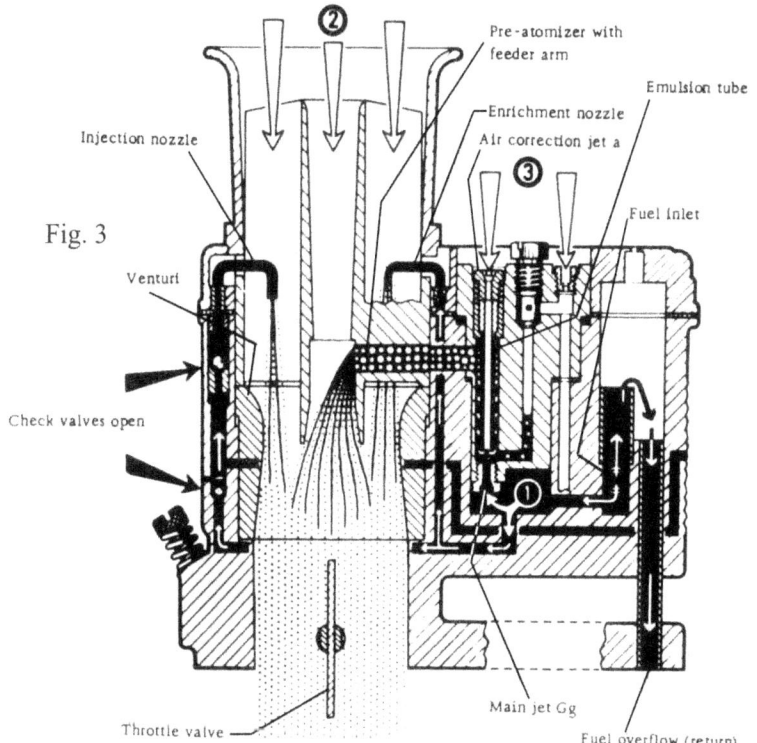

Fig. 3

The fuel enrichment takes place progressively, that is, the enrichment continues to increase until the engine has been brought to its full operating load. This system has been devised to provide economical cruising power and low specific fuel consumption in the lower power range without affecting the engine's maximum power performance.

## ACCELERATION (Fig. 4 & Fig. 5)

The accelerating pump system is filled with fuel entering from the inlet point. When the pump is at rest, a spring presses the pump diaphragm outward (Fig. 4). When the throttle valve is opened, this motion is transmitted to the pump lever over the throttle arm, and the pump rod and spring causing the diaphragm to be pushed inward. This results in delivery of fuel into the carburetor throat by way of the pump nozzle, thus enriching the fuel air mixture and providing quick acceleration (Fig. 5). A check valve located at the pump inlet prevents the fuel from "backing up" on the pump pressure stroke.

The injection volume is controlled by the pump stroke; duration of injection is determined by appropriately calibrating the size of the injection nozzle.

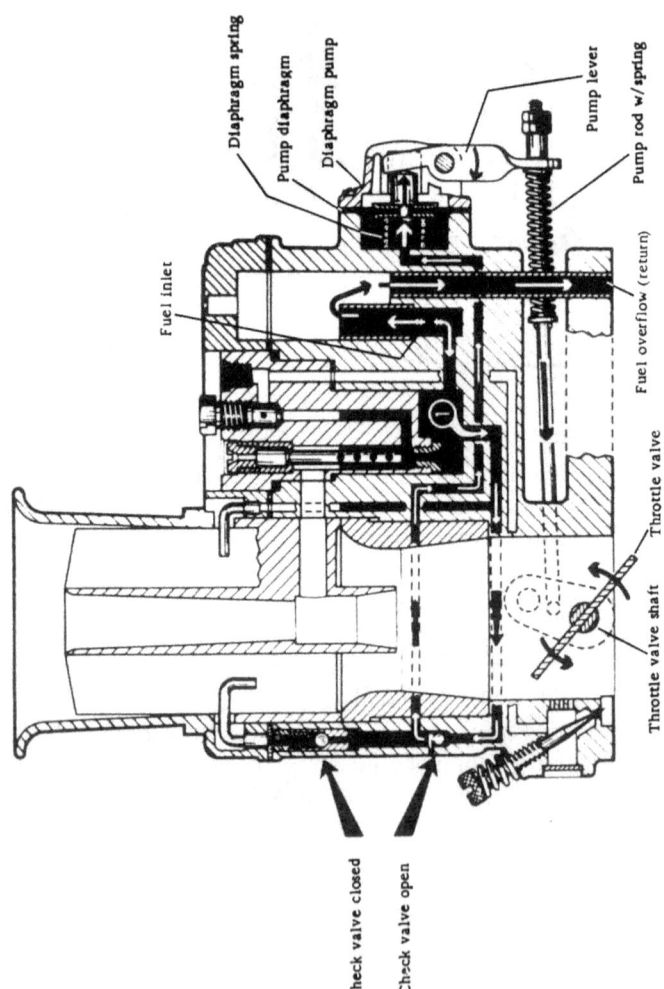

Fig. 4  40 PI accelerator pump - Intake stroke

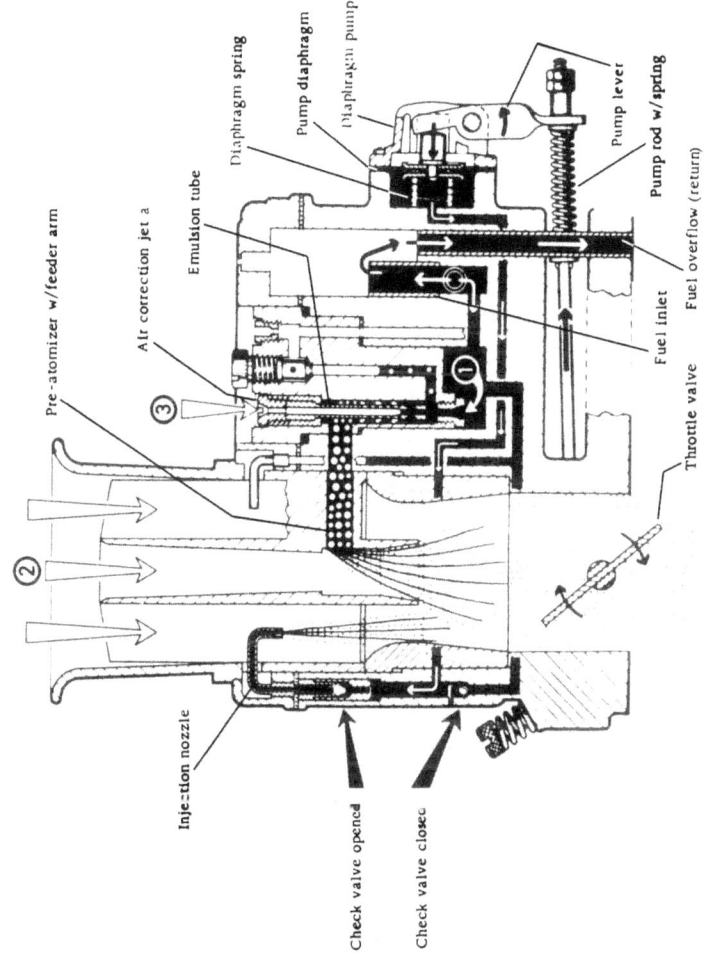

Fig. 5 40 PI accelerator pump - Pressure stroke

## IDLE METERING (Fig. 6 & Fig. 7)

The fuel passes through the idle metering jet (g) where it mixes with air entering through the idle air bleed (4), and changes into a fuel/air emulsion. This emulsion is channeled to four small discharge ports located adjacent to the throttle valve. The emulsion flow through the lowest port is controlled by the idle mixture adjusting screw. Idle mixture required for idling is drawn from this port when the throttle valve is set for idling. The upper three orifices are known as by-pass ports (Fig. 6 & Fig. 7) and have mixed functions. The port located at the level of the throttle valve disc serves as an idle mixture booster. The two topmost ports, located just above the throttle valve disc, become active as the throttle valve opens, and supply additional fuel emulsion to provide a smooth response from idling to power (Fig. 7). The emulsified fuel mixture leaving these ports mixes with induction air which is entering past the throttle valve (2), and is then atomized into the actual idle mixture.

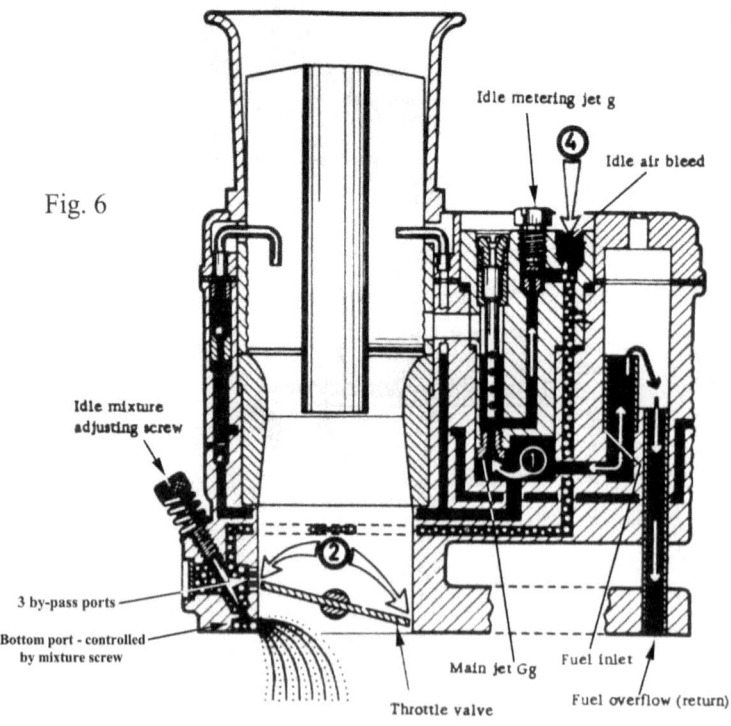

Fig. 6

Fig. 7

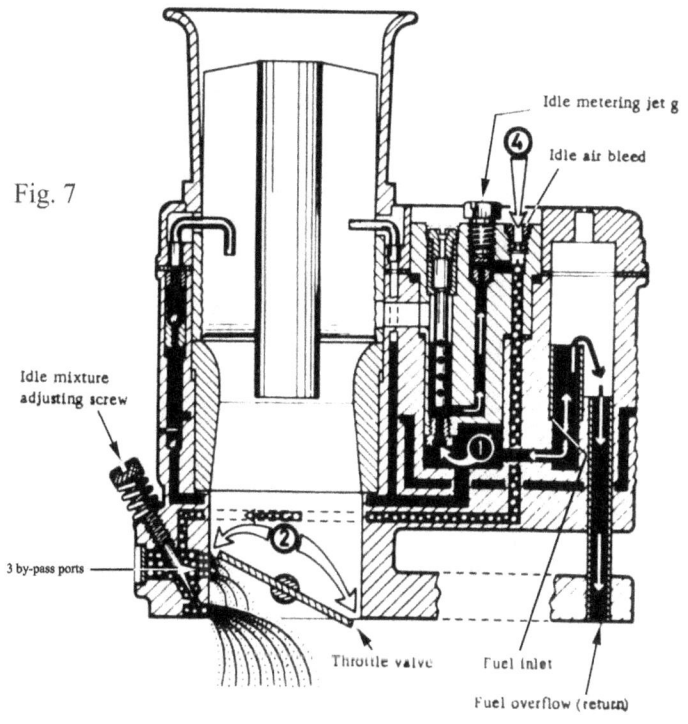

## CRUISING POWER METERING (Fig. 8)

The fuel flows, in part, from the fuel inlet through the main jet and into a cavity containing the emulsion tube which protrudes from above. Located above the emulsion tube is the air correction jet a. When the fuel is sucked out of the feeder arm due to negative pressures prevailing in the carburetor throat, the fuel level in the emulsion tube drops to a greater or lesser degree, depending upon the intensity of the negative pressures. As a result, air can enter through the air correction jet and flow further through the small orifices in the emulsion tube to mix with the outflowing fuel to convert into an emulsion so that a mixture in the right proportions is created throughout a wide range of engine rpm.

Fig. 8

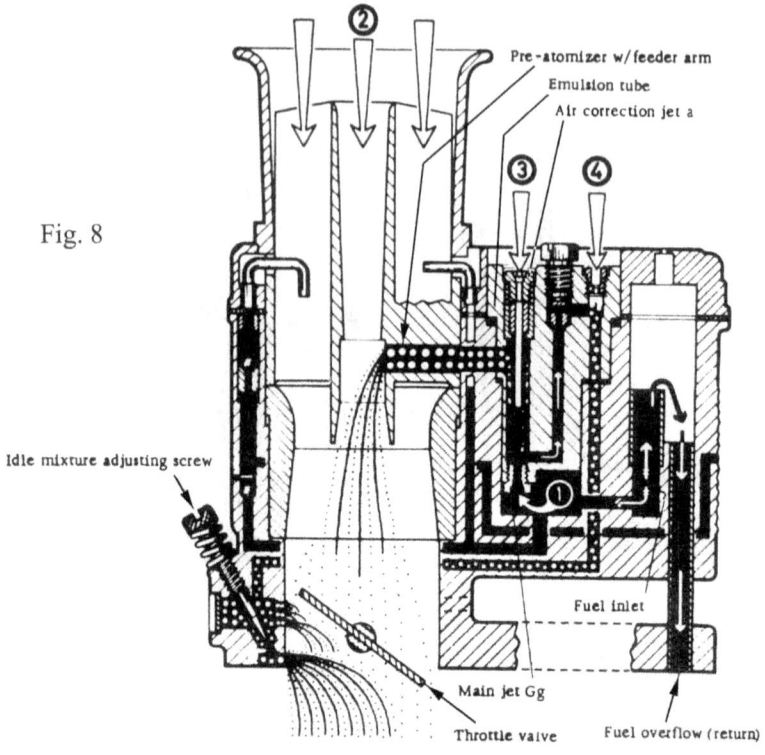

## SYNCHRONIZATION

Tuning these carburetors and balancing them seems to be highly complex to the new owner or mechanic who sees them for the first time. However, the same principles of synchronization, idling speed, pump injection and jetting which apply to the other Porsche Solexes can be transferred to the 40 PI. Reference to previous material on the carburetors in this book is advised before beginning with the 40 PI type.

The most important factor in synchronization of throttles is to disconnect **all** linkage — from the accelerator rod to the individual throttle rods — to be sure that all butterflies are closed. This should be done after the engine is warmed up and running. Adjustment of the idling mixture control screws can be made to keep the engine idling while this is being done. Then, connect the individual throttle rods, with adjustment backed off, and tighten the adjustment up equally, using the Unisyn to make sure that none of the butterflies is other than closed. Select the weakest cylinder (lowest Unisyn reading) to synchronize to. With all throttle links connected on each side, but still not connected to the cross rod, set idling speed up (with curb idle screw) to approximately 1,000 rpm and adjust for best idling speed (maximum revs for throttle setting) with the volume control screws. Then set idling speed to manufacturer's recommendation, (or to idling speed owner prefers) with curb idle speed screw. Check individual carburetor throats at idling and approx. 1300 rpm with unisyn and adjust accordingly. Re-connect cross rod and accelerator rod being sure to maintain curb idle speed as set.

## PUMP DELIVERY AND JETS

Acceleration pump delivery should be checked in the usual fashion with a graduated tube. Factory recommendation for delivery amount is .4 to .6 cc and for use with domestic U.S.A. fuels, settings toward the high side are advised. Approximately .55 cc seems to be best.

If the car was picked up in Germany it may also be necessary to change main and air correction jets to compensate for differences in fuel. The 130 main jet can be replaced by 125 and the 160 air correction jet by a 180.

The 1600 Super 90 engine and the 912 engine are equipped with Solex 40 PII twin-throat downdraft carburetors. The low manifold makes it possible to dispense with choke or cold-starting enrichment devices. So the circuits are: idle, intermediate, power and acceleration. The systems are controlled by fuel and air correction jets common to Solex practice. (See previous Solex and Porsche carburetor application material.) One item of difference between the 40 PII-4 and earlier Solexes is the use of a ball check valve with a return orifice to prevent excessive enrichment due to variations in the pump plunger velocity.

Tuning, syncronization and disassembly of this type is closely related to earlier models and reference to procedures previously described is advised.

# RENAULT

The Renault 4CV was equipped with a single throat Solex 22 ICBT model carburetor. The Dauphine utilizes a Solex 28 IBT carburetor with automatic choke while the Caravelle and Caravelle Speciale are carburated with either a Solex 32 PIBT or a Solex 32 PDIST and some with a Zenith 32 IGT. The new Renault R8 models are equipped with a wet-base Solex 32 DISTA carburetor unit after first using a dry base Zenith and then a dry base Solex of basically the same configuration as the DISTA.

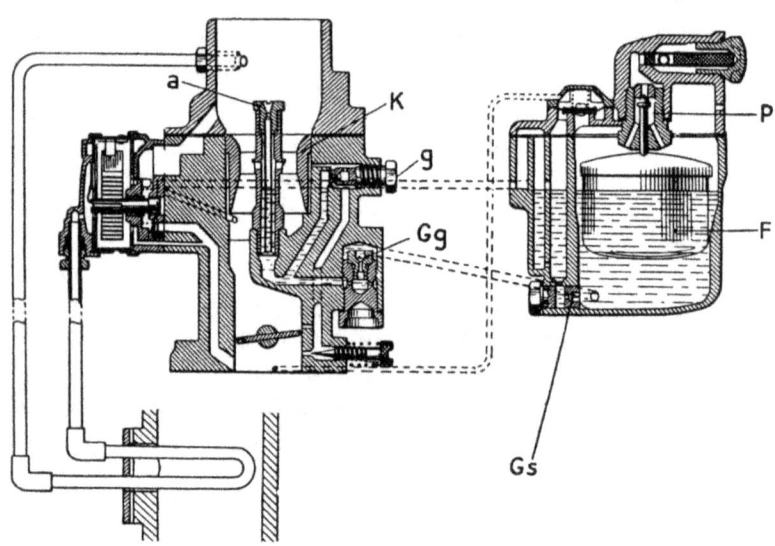

**THE SOLEX 22 ICBT CARBURETOR**

| Reference on Cutaway Drawing | Description | SOLEX 22 ICBT CARBURETOR SPECIFICATIONS | | | |
|---|---|---|---|---|---|
| | | Reference 245 | Reference 245/1 | Reference 245/2 | Reference 245/3 |
| | Type of vehicle... | R. 1 062 and R. 1 062 U.S.A. | R.1 062 Tropics | R. 1 062 High altitude | R. 1 062 Tropics High altitudes |
| | **Normal operation:** | | | | |
| Gg | Main jet........ | 100 | 95 | 100 | 95 |
| | Air correction jet.. | 165 K | 160 K | 165 K | 160 K |
| | **Slow running:** | | | | |
| g | Slow running jet.. | 40 | 40 | 40 | 40 |
| | **Choke:** | | | | |
| Gs | Choke fuel jet.... | 95 | 95 | 95 | 95 |
| K | Spray chamber... | 18 | 18 | 18 | 18 |
| P | Needle valve..... | 1.5 | 1.5 | 1.5 | 1.5 |
| F | Float.......... | 12.5 gr (.43 oz) | 12.5 gr (.43 oz) | 12.5 gr (.43 oz) | 12.5 gr (.43 oz) |
| | Altitude corrector. | none | none | with | with |

# DISMANTLING AND REASSEMBLING THE SOLEX 22 ICBT CARBURETOR

**DISMANTLING** — The numerical order of the reference numbers shown on the illustration corresponds to the dismantling sequence of the parts. Follow this order.

**NOTE: The components of assembly (24) should under no circumstances be separated.**

**REASSEMBLING** — Reassemble the parts in reverse sequence of numbers on the illustration, noting the characteristics concerning the following parts: (29) Check throttle plate for correct assembly, making sure the lips fit on the inside contours of the body when at the fully closed position. (22) Insert end of thermostatic spring into slot of casing (22). (18) Before tightening screws (18), align the marking on the casing (22) with the punchmark on the assembly body (24). This position is determined by the manufacturer and corresponds with correct automatic choke operation; therefore, strictly adhere to this specification. (15) Fully tighten the assembly (15) and next back off by 3 turns (approximate position of adjustment of idle mixture screw). (13) Assemble spray chamber with markings and figures upwards.

THE SOLEX 22 ICBT CARBURETOR

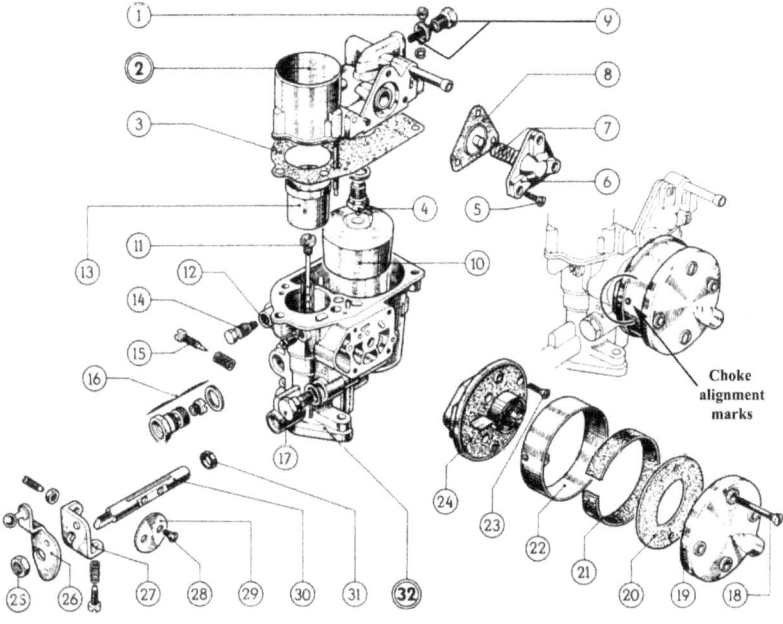

# SOLEX 28 IBT CARBURETOR

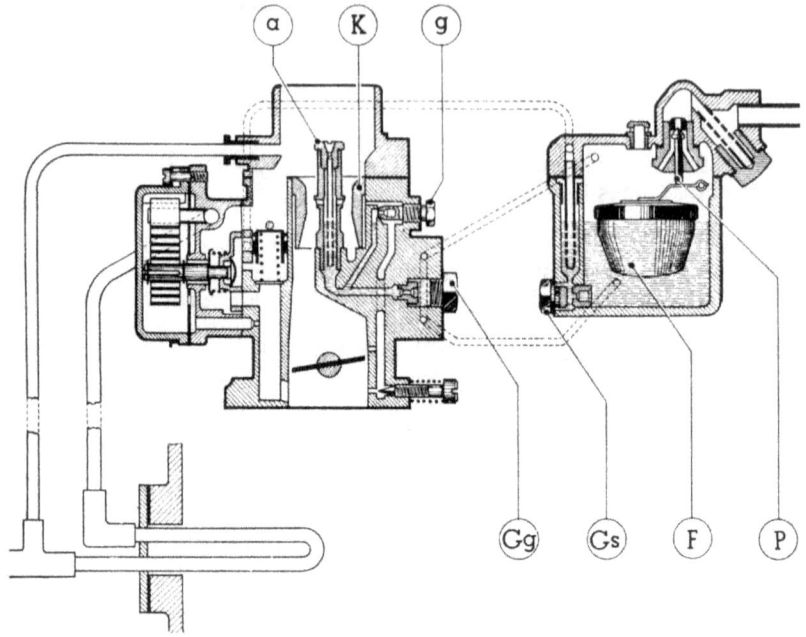

Schematic view of Solex 28 IBT

Main jet (Gg)   Venturi (K)   Idling jet (g)   Float (F)
Air correction jet (a)   Needle valve (P)   Choke jet (Gs)

| | |
|---|---|
| Main jet (Gg) | 100 |
| Air correction jet (a) | 155 K |
| Idling jet (g) | 45 |
| Choke jet (Gs) | 100 |
| Venturi (K) | 19 |
| Needle valve (P) | 1.5 |
| Float (F) | 5.79 |

**ADJUSTING IDLING SPEED**—Before attempting to adjust idling speed, make sure that the ignition system is in perfect order and that spark timing is right (clean spark plugs, check breaker and spark plug gaps).

As a preliminary adjustment, screw in idling mixture adjustment screw until it bottoms, then back off 3 turns. Start up engine and let it run at a fast idle until it is thoroughly warmed up (set up idling speed with adjustment screw 7). Adjust idling mixture (9) until engine runs smoothly. Slow down engine to approximately 600 rpm by turning idling adjustment screw. Now again adjust mixture screw to find the exact position for best mixture. If because of this adjustment idling speed increases too much, bring speed down with idling adjustment screw.

After adjustment, run up engine speed and let throttle snap shut. Engine should not stall.

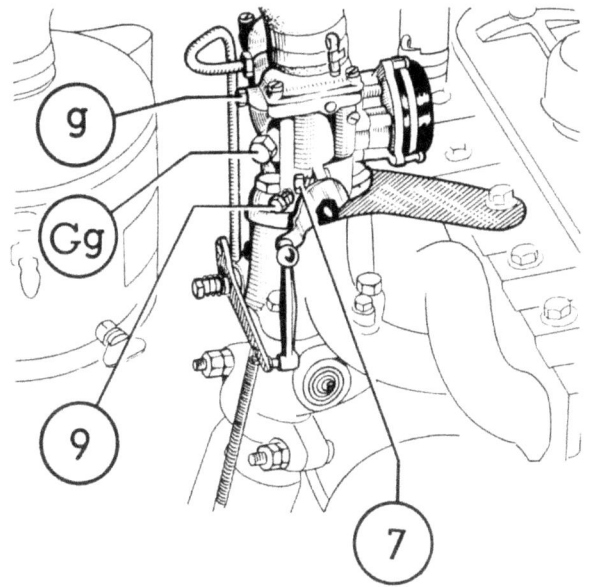

— Adjusting idling mixture and idling speed

g-Idling jet
Gg-Main jet
7-Idling speed adjustment
9-Mixture adjustment

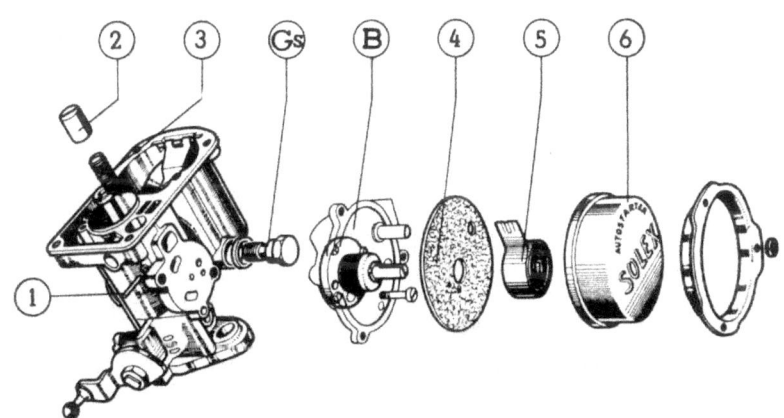

— Exploded view of choke assembly

**DISMANTLING AND REASSEMBLING AUTOMATIC CHOKE**—Remove choke cover, thermostatic spring, cover gasket, choke body assembly. With bowl cover off, remove mixture corrector stop, mixture corrector and spring.

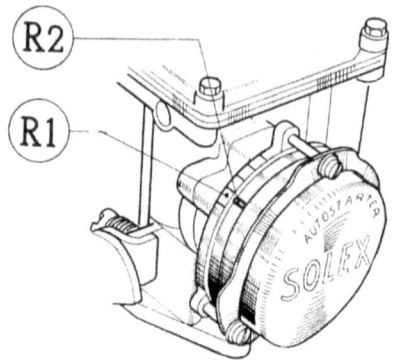

— Automatic choke assembly

To reassemble, install spring, mixture corrector. Make sure piston slides easily in bore. Install upper stop. If thermostat spring or plate is damaged, replace whole assembly. The slot for anchoring the thermostatic spring should be positioned vertically. The calibrated hole in the body should be facing the throttle control. Fit assembly to carburetor body. Position gasket (4), thermostatic spring (wind clockwise). Install cover (6) so that thermostatic spring is correctly anchored in cover. Install ring and screws but do not yet tighten screws. Line up marks as shown (R1 & R2) and tighten screws (this is the correct choke setting as determined at the works).

## SOLEX 32 PIBT CARBURETOR
(with automatic choke controlled by thermostatic spring)

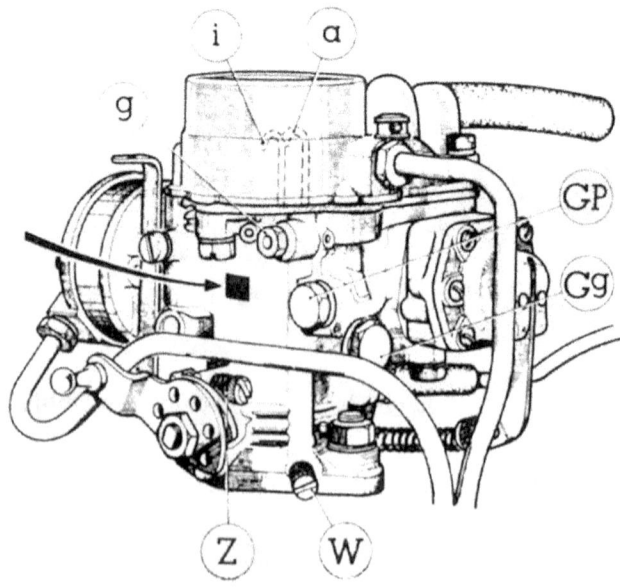

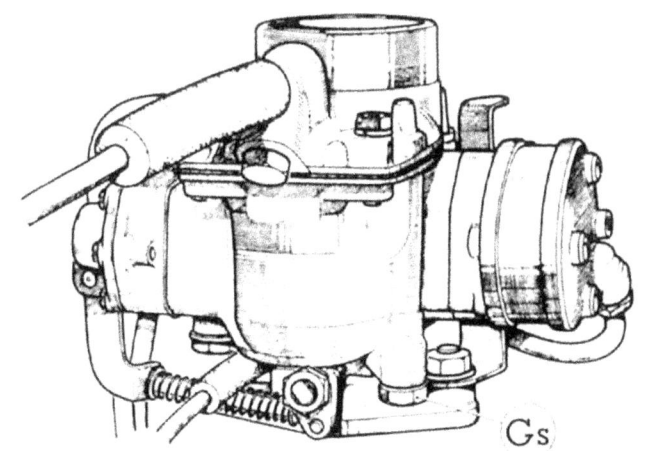

**NORMAL OPERATION :**

| | | |
|---|---|---|
| Gg = | Main jet | 117 |
| | Air correction jet | 190 |
| | Emulsion tube | 19 |
| K = | Spray chamber. | |
| | Needle valve | 1.2 mm |
| | Float | 5.7 g |

**SLOW RUNNING :**

g = Idler jet.

**CHOKE :**

Gs = Choke fuel jet.

**PUMP, mark 72 (Standard) :**

| | | |
|---|---|---|
| Gp = | Pump jet | 40 |
| i = | Pump injector high calibrated to | 50 |
| a = | Pick-up enriching device, calibrated to | 50 |
| Z = | Idler stop screw. | |
| W = | Idling mixture screw. | |

# SUNBEAM ALPINE & RAPIER

This section covers the carburetors used on the Sunbeam Alpine Series III and IV and Sunbeam Rapier Series IV.

## SOLEX B. 32 P.A.I.A.

The Solex B. 32 P.A.I.A. Carburetor is a twin choke downdraft carburetor. Its twin choke and twin throttle barrel arrangement overcome certain disadvantages met with on single choke carburetors when engine outputs are increased beyond moderate ratings.

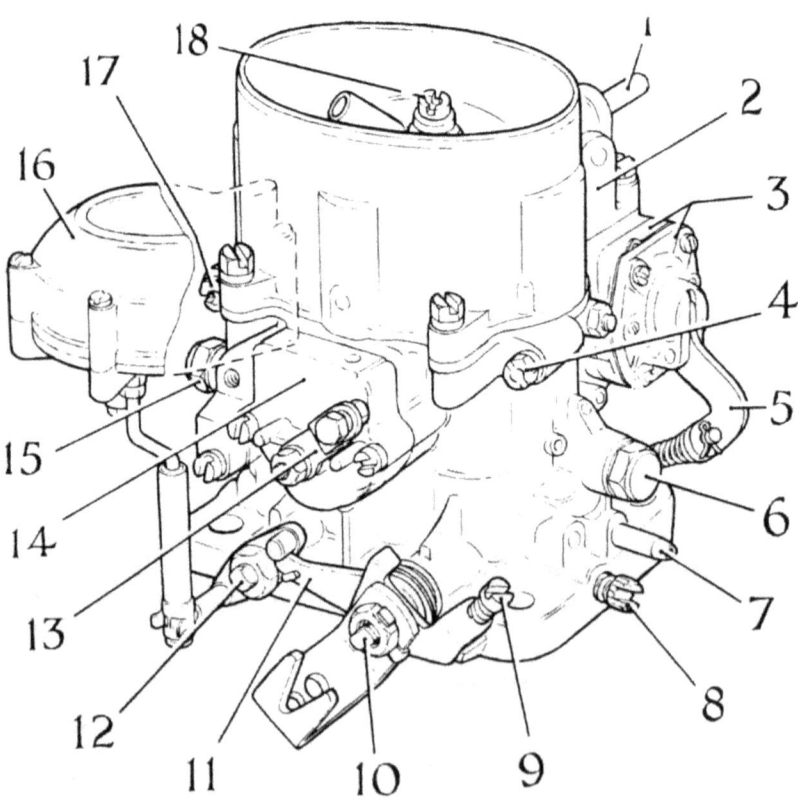

Fig. 1 - Solex B. 32 P.A.I.A. Carburetor

## CARBURETTOR

### Alpine (Later Series III models) and Rapier IV

Make ... ... ... ... ... Solex compound (twin choke)
Type ... ... ... ... ... 32 PAIA

### Settings

|  | Primary throttle | | Secondary throttle | |
|---|---|---|---|---|
|  | STD. | GT. & Rap. | STD. | GT. & Rap. |
| Choke | 24mm | 24mm | 26mm | 26mm |
| Main jet | 120 | 117·5 | 155 | 130 |
| Air correction | 210 | 190 | 210 | 190 |
| Pilot jet | 60 | 60 | 60 | 60 |
| Pilot air bleed | Nil | 1·0 | Nil | ·8 |
| Pump jet | 70 | 70 | Nil | Nil |

Pump back bleed—50 ...  } in float chamber
Needle valve—2·5 x 1·0mm

### Key to Fig. 1

1. FUEL INLET.
2. FLOAT CHAMBER COVER AND CARBURETTOR TOP BODY.
3. ACCELERATOR PUMP.
4. PRIMARY THROTTLE BARREL PILOT JET (SLOW RUNNING JET)
5. ACCELERATOR PUMP OPERATING LEVER.
6. PRIMARY THROTTLE BARREL MAIN JET HOLDER.
7. VACUUM ADVANCE CONNECTION.
8. SLOW RUNNING VOLUME CONTROL SCREW.
9. SLOW RUNNING SPEED ADJUSTMENT.
10. PRIMARY THROTTLE.
11. OVERRIDING LEVER.
12. SECONDARY THROTTLE.
13. STARTER ASSEMBLY OPERATING LEVER.
14. STARTER ASSEMBLY.
15. SECONDARY THROTTLE BARREL MAIN JET HOLDER.
16. SECONDARY THROTTLE OPERATING UNIT.
17. SECONDARY THROTTLE BARREL PILOT JET (NOT SLOW RUNNING).
18. CARBURETTOR TOP BODY CENTRE FIXING SCREW.

(Refer to Fig. 1 for numbers in the following description)

With a single fixed choke carburetor the power output of an engine can be increased by using a larger choke tube with suitable jet settings, provided the engine valves, valve ports and manifolds do not obstruct the extra air that can pass through the larger choke tube. At the higher possible engine outputs, however, the choke tube size needed to obtain the required power is often too large to allow satisfactory tuning of the carburetor for proper part throttle performance.

This difficulty suggests that two carburetors are needed, one tuned to give economy and good part throttle performance when operating alone, and the other tuned so that when operating with the first primary carburetor, the maximum performance is obtained. The Solex B. 32 P.A.I.A. does this by combining the advantages of two carburetors in one unit by having two throttle barrels.

This carburetor is known as the Solex Automatic Twin. It has a single float chamber, single cold starting assembly, single accelerator pump and single slow running system, together with twin choke tubes, twin by-pass (progression) circuits and twin main spraying circuits. The slow running circuit operates in the primary throttle barrel and is adjusted in a similar manner to that employed on a single barrel carburetor.

The primary throttle (10) of this carburetor is operated over its whole range of movement by the accelerator pedal. Its secondary throttle is operated automatically.

**SOLEX B. 32 P.A.I.A. CARBURETTOR—PARTS IN OPERATION**

| ENGINE REQUIREMENT | Float Chamber | Starting device | PRIMARY THROTTLE BARREL | | | | SECONDARY THROTTLE BARREL | |
|---|---|---|---|---|---|---|---|---|
| | | | Slow running jet | Progression holes | Main jet | Accelerator pump | Progression holes | Main jet |
| Starting from cold | ● | ● | ● | | | | | |
| Slow running | ● | | ● | | | | | |
| Light Throttle | ● | | | * | * | ● | | |
| Acceleration | ● | | | | | ● | ● | |
| Two thirds throttle Secondary throttle opening | ● | | | | | ● | ● | |
| Two thirds throttle onwards | ● | | | | | ● | | ● |
| Acceleration | ● | | | | | ● | ● | ● |
| Deceleration on closed throttle | ● | | | ● | | | | |

● In operation.   * Depending on how much throttle opening.

The above shows the more simple operation. It does not cover all carburation requirements of the engine. For example:—Driving away from cold with the choke control partly out.

As noted in the index, certain of the carburetor models discussed here are also fitted to other automobile makes. Some minor differences in mounting and linkage prevail, but all maintenance and adjustment data given here can be applied.

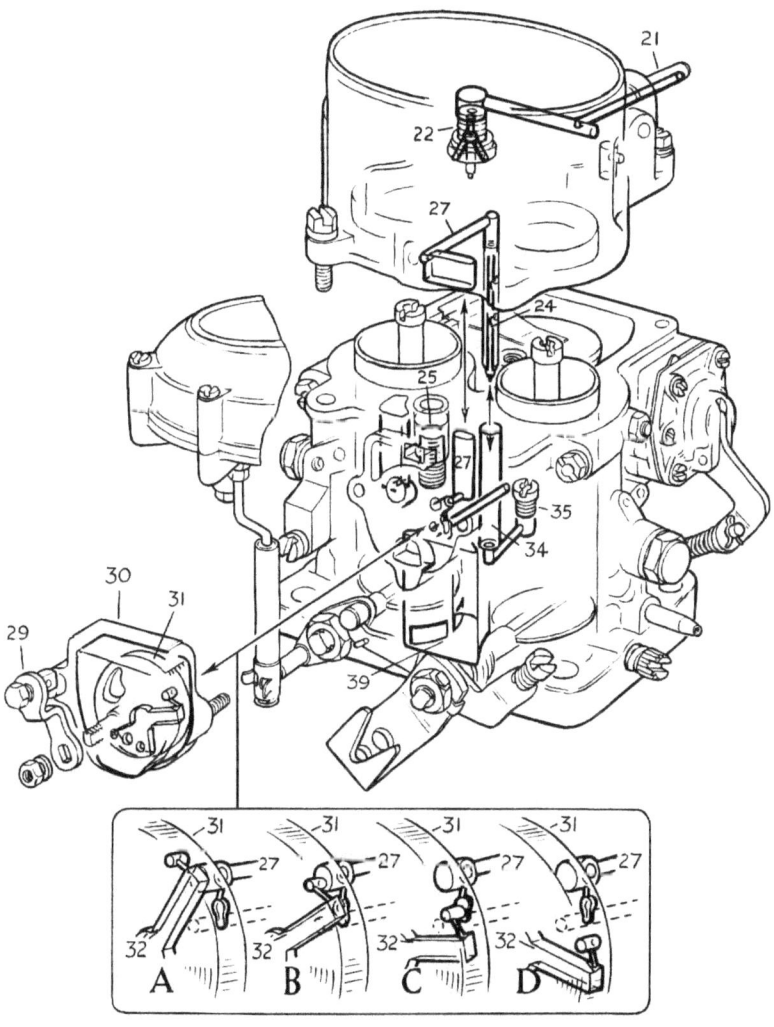

Fig. 2

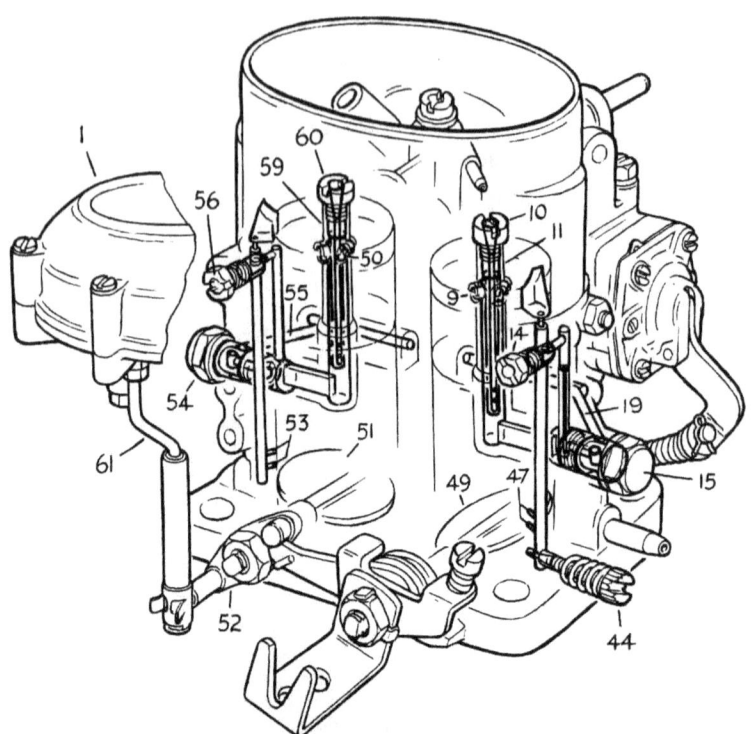

Fig. 3 - Solex B. 32 P.A.I.A. Carburetor—Slow Running and Main Spraying Passage-ways

(Refer to Fig. 1 for numbers in the following description)

The secondary throttle operating unit (16) consists of a diaphragm, diaphragm return spring, diaphragm cover, and a rod and ball joint connecting the diaphragm to the secondary throttle spindle lever (12). An internal passage connects the vacuum side of the diaphragm to the cross drillings in the choke tubes.

The secondary throttle is prevented from opening during the first two thirds of the primary throttle opening by the lever (11). After this amount of primary throttle movement, the lever (11) moves clear of the secondary throttle spindle lever, and allows the secondary throttle operating unit (16) to open the secondary throttle if the air speed through the primary throttle choke tube is high enough to create the necessary suction for atmospheric pressure to lift the diaphragm in the operating unit. The amount of the secondary throttle opening is dependent on the position of the lever (11).

When the primary throttle (10) is closed from fully open to its two thirds position, the lever (11) overrides the action of the secondary throttle operating unit and closes the secondary throttle (12).

The automatic opening and closing of the secondary throttle ensures that it only operates when its action is required.

**Note:** The secondary throttle is NOT operated by inlet manifold vacuum.

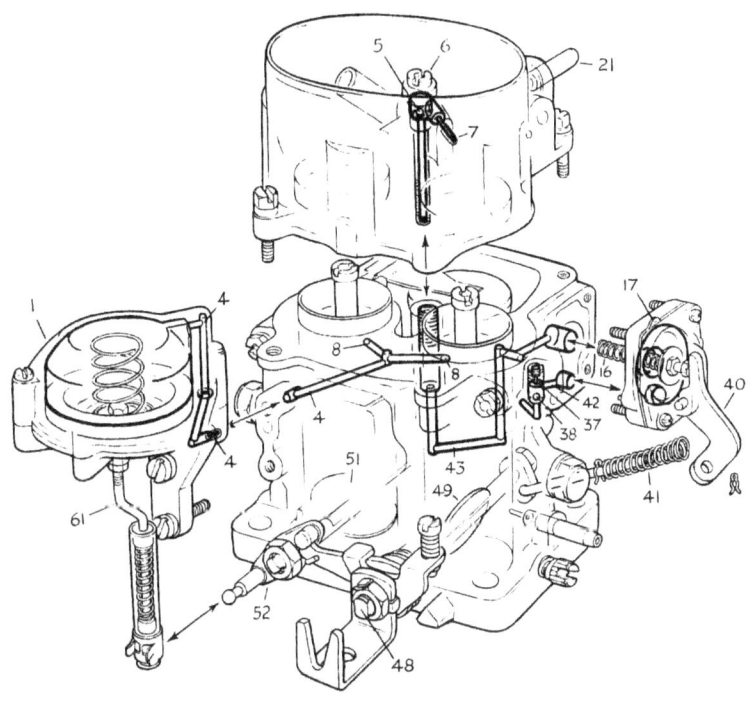

Fig. 4 - Solex B. 32 P.A.I.A. Carburetor—Accelerator Pump and Secondary Throttle Operating Unit Passage-ways

## Carburetor Operation

### Float Chamber - See Fig. 5

Fuel enters the float chamber through the connection (21) in the float chamber cover and passes through the float needle valve (22) into the float chamber. The float needle is operated by the lever attached to the plastic float (36) which rises and closes the float needle valve when the fuel level is correct. This action is entirely automatic and maintains the correct fuel level under all conditions of engine speed and load. The float chamber is vented internally by the short pipe (23) into the carburetor air intake and by an external hole in the top of the float chamber not shown in the illustrations.

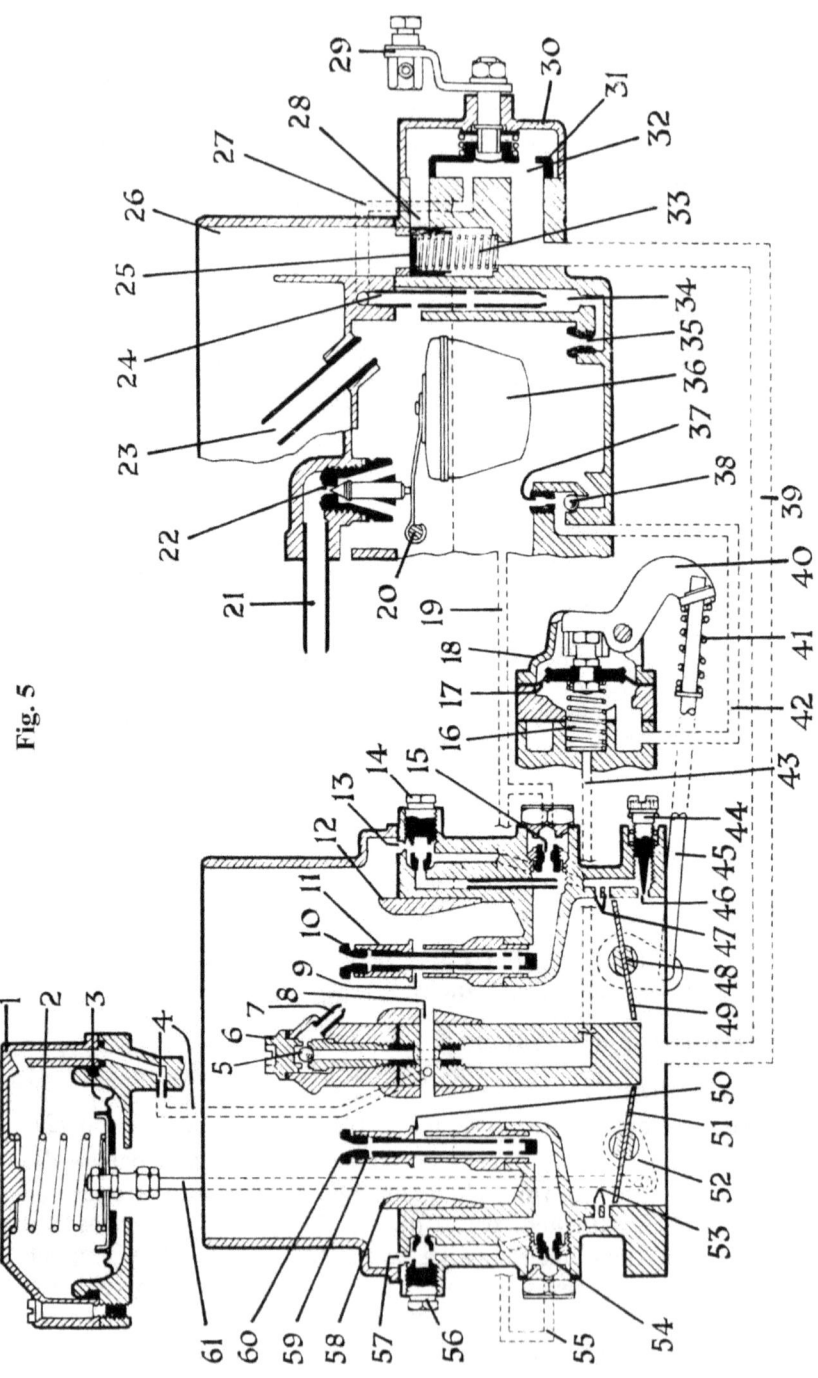

Fig. 5

1. SECONDARY THROTTLE OPERATING UNIT HOUSING.
2. DIAPHRAGM RETURN SPRING.
3. SECONDARY THROTTLE OPERATING UNIT DIAPHRAGM.
4. DEPRESSION FEED PASSAGE AND PASSAGE RESTRICTOR.
5. ACCELERATOR PUMP DELIVERY BALL VALVE.
6. ACCELERATOR PUMP DELIVERY ASSEMBLY.
7. ACCELERATOR PUMP DELIVERY NOZZLE.
8. DRILLING IN CHOKE TUBES CONNECTED TO PASSAGE 4.
9. PRIMARY THROTTLE BARREL MAIN SPRAYING ORIFICES.
10. PRIMARY THROTTLE BARREL AIR CORRECTION JET.
11. PRIMARY THROTTLE BARREL EMSULSION TUBE.
12. PRIMARY THROTTLE BARREL CHOKE TUBE.
13. PRIMARY THROTTLE BARREL PILOT JET AIR BLEED.
14. PRIMARY THROTTLE BARREL PILOT (SLOW RUNNING) JET
15. PRIMARY THROTTLE BARREL MAIN JET.
16. ACCELERATOR PUMP DIAPHRAGM RETURN SPRING.
17. ACCELERATOR PUMP DIAPHRAGM.
18. ACCELERATOR PUMP END COVER.
19. FEED PASSAGE TO PRIMARY BARREL MAIN JET.
20. FLOAT LEVER PIVOT PIN.
21. FUEL INTAKE CONNECTION TO FLOAT CHAMBER.
22. FLOAT NEEDLE VALVE AND SEAT.
23. INTERNAL AIR VENT TO FLOAT CHAMBER.
24. STARTER FUEL FEED DIP TUBE.
25. STARTER ASSEMBLY AIR CONTROL PISTON.
26. CARBURETTOR TOP BODY.
27. FUEL PASSAGE TO STARTER DISC VALVE.
28. AIR PASSAGE.
29. STARTER ASSEMBLY OPERATING LEVER.
30. STARTER ASSEMBLY COVER HOUSING.
31. STARTER ASSEMBLY DISC VALVE.
32. PASSAGE IN STARTER DISC VALVE.
33. STARTER DEVICE PISTON RETURN SPRING.
34. STARTER WELL.
35. STARTER JET.
36. FLOAT.
37. JET CONTROLLING ACCELERATOR PUMP OUTPUT (BY BLEED BACK TO FLOAT CHAMBER).
38. ACCELERATOR PUMP INTAKE NON RETURN VALVE.
39. STARTING MIXTURE FEED PASSAGE.
40. ACCELERATOR PUMP OPERATING LEVER.
41. ACCELERATOR PUMP OPERATING SPRING.
42. FEED PASSAGE TO ACCELERATOR PUMP.
43. DELIVERY PASSAGE FROM ACCELERATOR PUMP.
44. SLOW RUNNING VOLUME CONTROL SCREW.
45. ACCELERATOR PUMP OPERATING LINK ROD.
46. SLOW RUNNING OUTLET IN PRIMARY THROTTLE BARREL.
47. BY-PASS (PROGRESSION) HOLES IN PRIMARY THROTTLE BARREL.
48. PRIMARY THROTTLE LEVER.
49. PRIMARY THROTTLE.
50. SECONDARY BARREL MAIN SPRAYING ORIFICES.
51. SECONDARY THROTTLE.
51. SECONDARY THROTTLE.
52. SECONDARY THROTTLE OPERATING LEVER.
53. SECONDARY THROTTLE BARREL BY-PASS (PROGRESSION) HOLES.
54. SECONDARY BARREL MAIN JET.
55. FEED PASSAGE TO SECONDARY BARREL MAIN JET.
56. SECONDARY THROTTLE BARREL PILOT (PROGRESSION) JET.
57. AIR BLEED TO PILOT JET IN SECONDARY BARREL.
58. SECONDARY BARREL CHOKE TUBE.
59. SECONDARY THROTTLE BARREL EMULSION TUBE.
60. SECONDARY THROTTLE BARREL AIR CORRECTION JET.
61. SECONDARY THROTTLE OPERATING ROD

Fig. 5 - Solex B 32 PAIA, Sectional Views

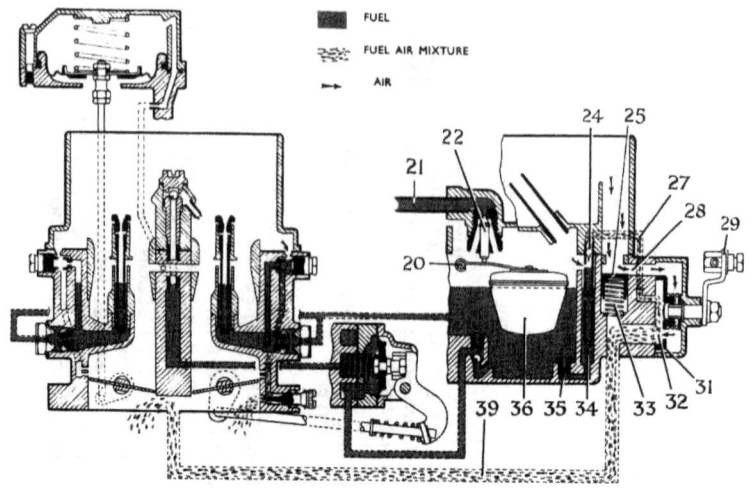

Fig. 6 - Cold Starting Operation

## Starter Assembly Operation - See Fig. 6

Cold starting conditions require a very rich fuel/air mixture and a progressively weaker mixture until the engine is warm enough to run on the normal settings of the main carburetor.

These requirements are provided by the manually controlled cold starting assembly which is a small auxiliary carburetor fed from the float chamber and situated on the outside of the carburetor.

The lever (29) is operated by the choke control inner cable and when moved fully overturns the disc (31) which rotates to open up the passage-way (32) in the disc (31) for the starting fuel/air mixture to enter the inlet manifold.

Fuel from the starter jet (35) feeds the starter well (34) where it rises to the fuel level as shown. Suction created by engine rotation draws fuel from the starter well (34) through the starter feed tube (24) and the passage (27). This emulsified fuel is drawn through the disc (31) and through the passage way (39) to provide the very rich mixture needed for cold starting.

Directly the engine starts the considerably increased depression in the starting passage-way (39), causes the piston (25) to move down against its return spring (33) due to the action of air pressure on its top face. This allows more air to mix with the emulsified mixture controlled by the disc (31), and prevents the supply of excess fuel after the engine starts.

When the engine starts, the fuel in the starter well (34) is used up quickly and the engine continues to run on fuel supplied to the starter well by the starter jet (35).

As the choke lever is pushed inwards the lever arm (29) turns the disc which progressively weakens the mixture but increases its volume, thus giving a fast idle, after the full rich start position. Further movement of the lever reduces the volume progressively and decreases the fast idling speed.

When the choke control is pushed fully in, the lever arm (29) moves against its back stop and the disc (31) closes off the passage (39) from the starting device fuel and air supply system.

Fig. 2, Inset A. —Shows the fuel delivery from the starting well (34) through the passage (27) which is used for starting from cold when the choke control is pulled out as far as possible.

Inset B.—Shows the two small metering drillings, in the disc (31) in "parallel" with the passage (27). These provide a volume of air and fuel suitable for fast idle when the choke control is pushed partly inwards.

Inset C.—Shows the two metering holes in "series" which allows a reduction of mixture supply as the choke control is pushed further in reducing the fast idle speed.

Inset D.—Shows how the disc valve (31) cuts off the passage (39) when the choke control is pushed fully inwards.

## Slow Running - See Fig. 7

When primary throttle (49) is in the slow running position fuel is metered by the slow running jet (14) which is fed from the float chamber by fuel that passes through the main jet (15) in the primary throttle barrel.

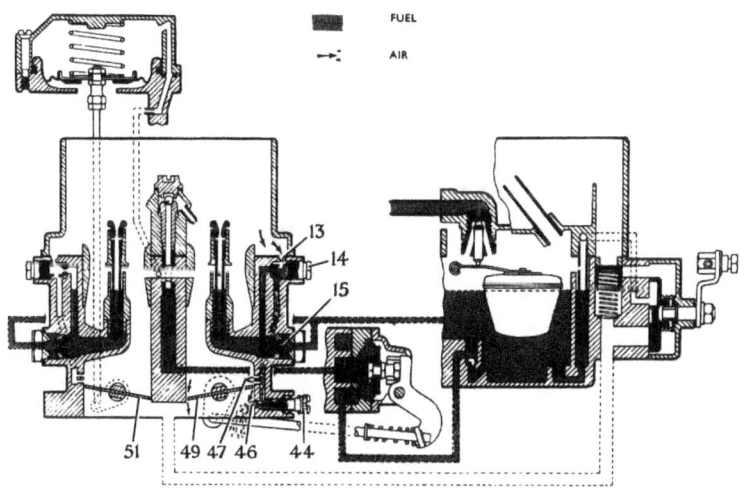

Fig. 7 - **Idling Operation**

Air to emulsify the fuel metered by the slow running jet is drawn through the calibrated air bleed (13). Air is also drawn through the nearly closed primary throttle (49) and by adjusting the slow running volume control screw (44), the amount of emulsified fuel drawn from the slow running outlet (46) can be adjusted so that when mixed with the air passing through the throttle, a suitable slow running mixture passes into the inlet manifold.

Further opening of the throttle allows more air to be drawn past the throttle and also uncovers the by-pass orifice (47), sometimes called progression holes, from which additional emulsified fuel is drawn. This maintains the correct mixture strength as the engine speed is increased from slow running to a fast idle speed.

**Note:** Whenever the engine is idling the secondary throttle (51) is always closed.

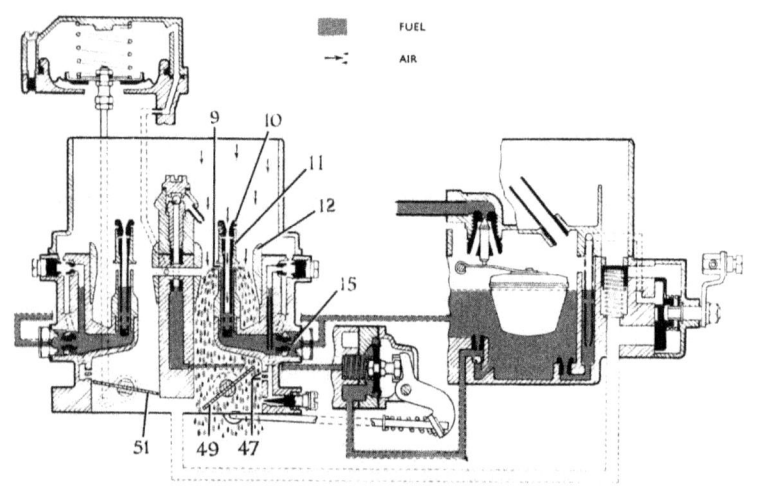

Fig. 8 - Part Throttle Driving Operation

## Normal Acceleration to Cruising Speed - See Fig. 8

As the primary throttle (49) is opened past the by-pass orifice (47), the air velocity through the primary choke tube (12) increases. This causes sufficient suction to be exerted on the spraying orifices (9) in the primary barrel, for fuel to be drawn from the emulsion tube well, below the emulsion tube (11) and the main jet (15), into the air stream. The amount of fuel, drawn from the emulsion tube well before drawing on the main jet (15), gives the temporary mixture enrichment needed for this condition of operation.

## Part Throttle Driving - See Fig. 8

This driving condition uses the main jet (15) emulsion tube (11) and air correction jet (10) for supplying the correct amount of fuel to the air stream passing through the primary throttle choke tube (12). If only the main jet were used to control the fuel flow as the throttle was opened, too rich a mixture would be given at wide throttle openings, assuming that the main jet size was correct for a small throttle opening.

As the throttle is opened and air speed through the choke tube (12) in the primary throttle barrel rises and the increased depression acting on the spraying orifice (9) brings the main spraying system into operation. Under this condition fuel flows from the float chamber and is metered by the main jet (15) before passing into the spraying well, below the emulsion tube (11), where it mixes with air metered by the air correction jet (10); the air entering the fuel stream by means of small holes in the emulsion tube (11). From the main well the mixture finally discharges from the spraying orifice (9) into the main air stream. As engine speed increases, the fuel level in the well drops and uncovers the remaining holes in the emulsion tube (11). In this way additional air enters the fuel stream and corrects the output from the main jet (15) to meet the engine requirements according to speed and load.

**Note:** During this driving condition, which occurs during the first two thirds of the primary throttle movement, the secondary throttle (51) cannot open because it is held closed by the spring loaded lever "L" (Fig. 11) on the primary throttle spindle.

---

## Wide and Full Throttle Driving - See Fig. 9 & Fig. 10

After the primary throttle (49) is two thirds open the primary choke tube (12) and main spraying system can no longer provide sufficient fuel air mixture for further increases of engine speed, and to meet the high speed driving requirements the secondary throttle (51) begins to open. This allows air to pass through the secondary throttle barrel choke tube (58) and for fuel to discharge through the by-pass orifices (progression holes) (53), and then the main spraying orifices (50) in this throttle barrel. In this way for the last third of the primary throttle movement both throttle barrels can operate together to provide the correct quantity of fuel air mixture for higher and maximum speed requirements.

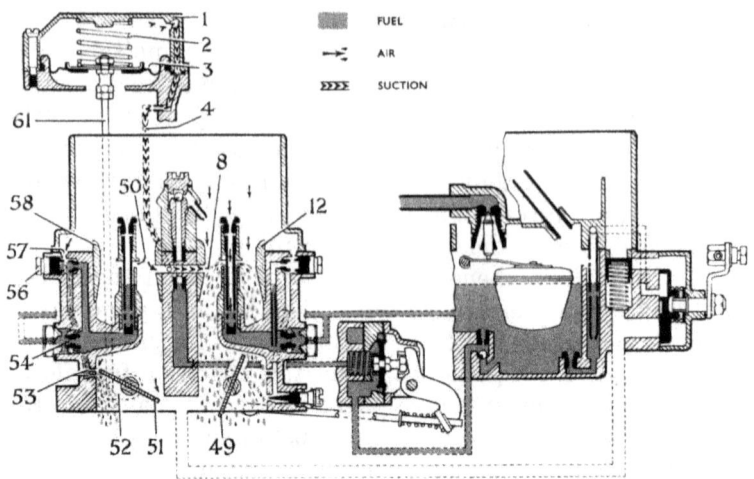

Fig. 9 - Secondary Throttle Coming Into Operation

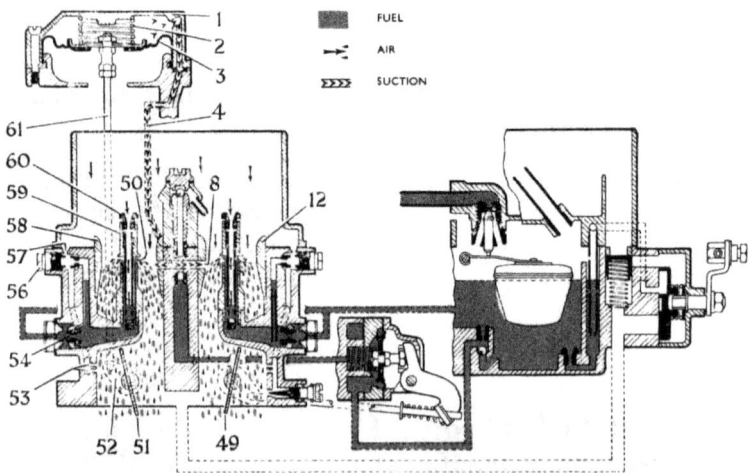

Fig. 10 - Wide Throttle Driving Conditions

## Secondary Throttle Barrel Operation - See Fig. 10

The secondary throttle is opened automatically by its operating unit which is shown in sectional form. It consists of a diaphragm housing (1), diaphragm (3), diaphragm return spring (2), and rod (61) that connects the diaphragm by a spring loaded ball joint connection to the lever (52) on the secondary throttle spindle.

The secondary throttle can only open when the following two conditions exist:
1. The primary throttle is open beyond two thirds of its travel.
2. The air speed through the primary choke tube is high enough to create enough suction to allow atmospheric pressure to move the diaphragm (3) in the secondary throttle operating unit.

At low engine speeds, with the engine under load, it is possible for the primary throttle (49) to be fully open and the secondary throttle (51) to remain closed. This is because air speed through the primary choke tube (12) is too low to provide the suction needed in the passage (4) to operate the diaphragm (3).

Movement of the diaphragm (3) in the secondary throttle operating unit, takes place when air pressure is reduced on the spring loaded side of the diaphragm. This occurs when the air flow through the primary choke tube (12) is high enough to create the necessary suction at the cross drilling (8) which connects to the passage (4). The secondary throttle (51) then opens, the amount being dependent on the position of lever "L"(**Fig. 11**).

When the secondary throttle (51) is open wide enough, air flow through the secondary throttle choke tube (58) increases the suction at the cross drilling (8). This provides the increased suction needed to move the diaphragm (3) against the force of its return spring (2) which becomes greater as the secondary throttle opens.

The secondary throttle barrel has its own choke tube (58) air correction jet (60) emulsion tube (59), pilot jet (56) and pilot jet air bleed (57) that feeds the by-pass orifice. It has no slow running outlet orifices. These parts function in similar manner to those in the primary throttle barrel. The secondary by-pass system is necessary to ensure that fuel is fed into the secondary air stream directly the secondary throttle is open, and to prevent air only passing through the secondary throttle before the secondary main spraying circuit comes into operation.

When the accelerator pedal is released from its full or above two thirds travel position, the secondary throttle, if open, is progressively closed by the heavily spring loaded lever "L" on the primary throttle spindle, and is fully closed against its adjustable stop when the primary throttle returns to less than its two-third open position.

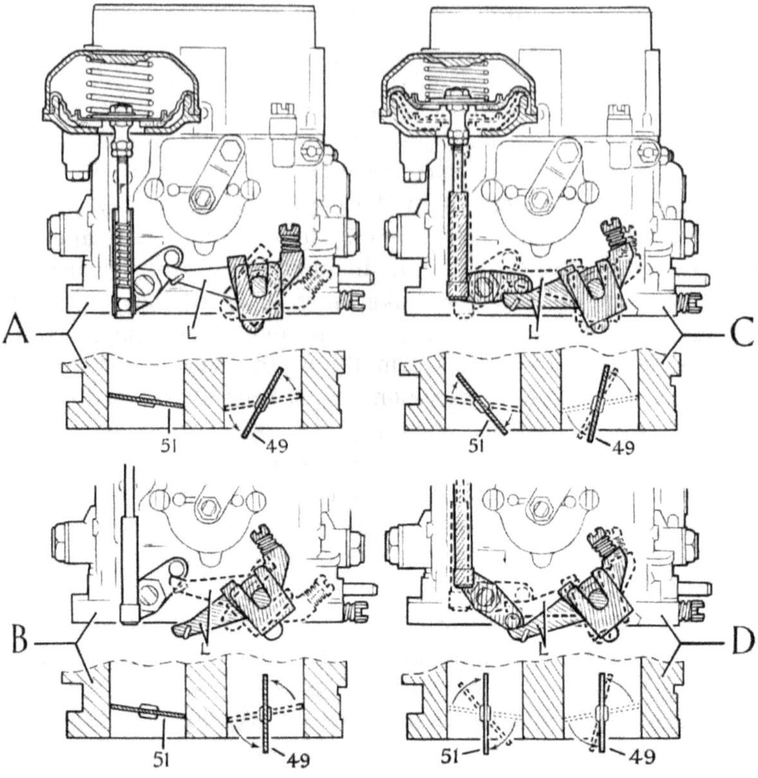

Fig. 11 - Primary and Secondary Throttle Operation

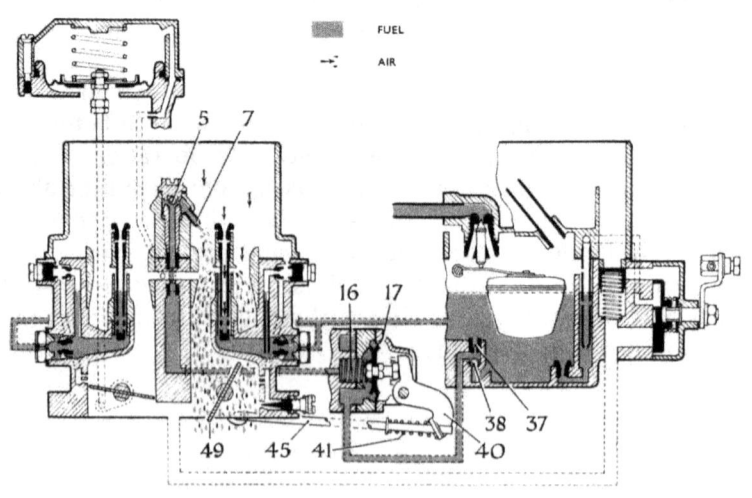

Fig. 12 - Acceleration—Accelerator Pump in Operation

## Acceleration and Accelerator Pump - See Fig. 12

To ensure immediate engine response, when the primary throttle is suddenly opened, a temporary metered supply of extra fuel is needed. This fuel is provided by a mechanically operated diaphragm type accelerator pump connected to a short lever on the primary throttle spindle.

When the accelerator pedal is released the pump diaphragm return spring (16) forces the diaphragm (17) outwards which draws fuel into the accelerator pump through its non-return valve (38).

When the accelerator pedal is depressed the primary throttle (49) opens and the spring (41) is compressed on the connecting rod (45). This pushes the pump lever (40) which compresses the diaphragm (17) and causes fuel to be discharged from the jet (7) into the primary choke tube after lifting the non-return delivery ball valve (5).

The accelerator pump non-return ball valve (38) inside the float chamber is situated below the jet (37) which controls the accelerator pump output characteristic by allowing the pump to return some fuel to the float chamber during the pumping stroke.

## Starting Engine from Cold

When starting the engine from cold, the choke control is pulled fully out, the ignition switched on and the starter operated **without moving the accelerator pedal**. When the engine starts the control is pushed back to a suitable fast idle position for driving away. The control should be pushed fully in directly the engine will run without hesitation.

## From Extreme Cold (below −0°C 14°F)

When starting under extremely cold condition **first—fully depress the accelerator pedal three times**. Then follow the procedure previously given for starting from cold.

## Partly Warm

Very slightly depress the accelerator pedal, switch on the ignition, and operate the starter. In most cases the engine will start immediately and idle properly directly the accelerator pedal is released.

If the engine will not start in this way the choke control should be pulled out half way, the ignition switch on, and the starter operated without moving the accelerator pedal. After the engine starts the choke control should be pushed in as soon as the engine will run without the choke.

## When Hot

The choke control should never be used when the engine is hot.

If difficult starting occurs the accelerator pedal should be fully and slowly depressed and the starter operated with the ignition switched on. The engine will then start easily and the accelerator pedal should be released.

The accelerator pedal must not be pumped, or agitated, as this will cause the accelerator pump to inject an excessive quantity of fuel into the inlet manifold. This fuel will vaporize and produce an excessively rich mixture that will prevent the engine from starting.

## DIAGNOSIS OF FAULTS – SOLEX

### Excessive Fuel Consumption

**Causes**
1. Difficult operating conditions such as town driving or very hilly country.
2. Leakage in the fuel system.
3. Partial flooding.
4. Incorrect jets fitted.
5. Choke operating cable incorrectly adjusted.
6. Starter assembly deffective.

**Procedure**
1. Ensure that engine is correctly tuned. Carry out fuel consumption test over known test route to check consumption under normal driving conditions.
2. Check fuel system for leakage starting at the fuel tank, checking all unions, fuel lines, and every possible place at which fuel can leak.
3. Ensure that float needle and seat assembly is properly tightened in carburetor top body and that the single joint washer under the seating is in position and not damaged.

Renew float needle/seat assembly and float if these items are in anyway suspect.

4. Ensure that the correct sizes of air correction jets, emulsion tubes and main jets are fitted. Check that the main jets are tight in their holders and are in their respective throttle barrel.

5. Check that the choke operating cable is correctly adjusted so that the operating lever is against its back stop when the choke control is 1/16 in. from the full in position.

6. Check the face of the disc in the starter assembly and the carburetor body face against which it operates, to ensure that they are free from scoring. This is rather unlikely but if the disc is not seating properly fuel can, if a "passage" exists, pass into the induction manifold through the passage. Normally the disc completely cuts off the passage when the lever is against its back stop.

## Insufficient Top Speed
**Causes:**
1. Primary throttle not opening fully. This will also prevent full opening of the secondary throttle.
2. Secondary throttle spindle sticking.
3. Secondary throttle sticking closed due to incorrect adjustment of its closed position stop screw.
4. Secondary throttle operating unit not opening secondary throttle correctly.
5. Secondary barrel main jet blocked.
6. Main jet sizes incorrect.

**Procedure:**
1. Check that the primary throttle is opened fully when the accelerator pedal is fully depressed

2. Hold the primary throttle fully open. Disconnect the ball joint on the end of the rod from the secondary throttle arm and check that the secondary throttle is perfectly free to open and close against its stops. Close the secondary throttle firmly against its closed position with finger and thumb pressure and check that it is not sticking in its closed position when the carburetor is **cold** and again when it is **hot**.

Reconnect the ball joint and check that the operating unit diaphragm can lift the secondary throttle fully open. This is done by lifting the diaphragm on its connecting rod just below the lock nut above the ball joint with a small pair of pliers.

3. Adjust secondary throttle stop screw as explained under ADJUSTMENTS—Secondary throttle stop.

4. High speed is dependent upon the correct operating of the secondary throttle after the primary throttle lever allows it to open. If its operating unit is deffective the secondary throttle will not open properly.

For this unit to operate correctly there must be:
(a.) An air tight diaphragm.
(b.) An air tight joint between the operating unit and the car-

buretor body. A suitable joint is used between these two faces.
(c.) Clear passage-ways, also between the choke tube and the diaphragm upper face. A small brass dowel with a small restriction drilling is used between the unit face and carburetor body. This must be clear.

The secondary operating unit can be tested, after removing it from the carburetor, by holding a suitable piece of rubber tube over its brass locating dowel and sucking air through the tube by holding the other end of the tube in the mouth. This suction should move the diaphragm over the whole of its operating range. After this the unit should be immersed in water, so that it is just covered, and the diaphragm depressed by finger and thumb pressure while the other first finger blocks off the brass dowel inlet hole. If the diaphragm is faulty air bubbles will be seen.

5. Check that both main jets are clear and are the correct size.

## Faulty Slow Running
**Causes:**
1. Slow running adjustment incorrectly set.
2. Slow running pilot jet blocked.
3. Slow running passage-way partly blocked.
4. Incorrect operation of crankcase ventilation regulator fitted in inlet manifold.
5. Air leak at carburetor flange joint or at induction manifold to cylinder head joint.
6. Secondary throttle closed stop incorrectly set. This allows too much air to pass by the closed secondary throttle when the engine is idling.

**Procedure:**
1. Adjust slow running as described under ADJUSTMENTS.
2. Remove slow running (pilot) jet and blow through its metering orifice, with clean compressed air as it is not possible to see through the actual orifice.
3. Remove slow running volume control screw and slow running jet. Blow through slow running system passage-ways and replace jet and screw. The latter should be screwed onto its seat by finger pressure only and turned back one complete turn before running the engine to adjust the slow running.
4. Remove crankcase ventilation regulator from the inlet manifold. Dismantle, clean and check.
5. Remove carburetor and induction manifold. Check flanges for distortion and carefully reface if necessary.
6. Adjust secondary throttle stop (see ADJUSTMENTS).

## Flat Spot at Small Primary Throttle Opening
**Causes:**
1. Slow running adjustment set too weak.
2. By-pass (progression) holes obstructed in the primary throttle barrel.
3. Secondary throttle closed stop incorrectly set.

**Procedure:**
1. Adjust the slow running to give reliable idling just off of the rich or "hunting" condition.
2. If the flat spot still exists blow through the by-pass (progression) holes in the primary throttle barrel with compressed air. This can be done with the carburetor in position by removing the slow running jet and lightly screwing the volume control screw onto its seal. The compressed air supply nozzle is then applied at the slow running jet location. Readjust volume control screw.
3. Adjust the secondary throttle closed position stop as described under ADJUSTMENTS.

## Flat Spot at Wide Primary Throttle Opening
**Causes:**
1. Secondary throttle stiff in action.
2. By-pass (progression) holes in the secondary throttle barrel partly or fully blocked.
3. Secondary throttle operating unit deffective.

**Procedure:**
1. Check that the secondary throttle is perfectly free to operate over its whole range, particularly from its closed position.
2. Blow through the by-pass orifice (progression) holes in the secondary throttle barrel. This can be done by applying compressed air at the secondary barrel pilot jet position after removing the jet.
3. Check action of the secondary throttle operating unit as described under "Insufficient top speed".

## Poor Acceleration
**Cause:**
Faulty operation of the accelerator pump which prevents the temporary enrichment of the mixture needed when the primary throttle is suddenly opened.

**Procedure:**
1. Check that the small circlips, on the accelerator pump push rod are in place. If the circlip behind the spring is missing the accelerator pump actuating lever will not operate correctly when the primary throttle is opened.

2. Check through the whole of the accelerator pump circuit in the following order.

Remove carburetor top body and float. This requires the removal of the combined screw and discharge ball valve.

Remove the jet and ball valve below the jet in float chamber.

Remove the four corner flat headed brass screws holding the accelerator pump to the carburetor body, and the circlip on the outer end of the accelerator pump operating rod. Lift off pump assembly from carburetor body.

Remove the two brass screws holding the accelerator pump end cover to its body. Remove cover and inspect diaphragm and renew if faulty.

Blow through passages with compressed air. These passages feed and discharge fuel to and from the accelerator pump chamber.

Replace intake ball valve and jet.

Reassemble accelerator pump. When refitting the diaphragm it should be pushed against its back stop on its operating lever side, before tightening the two screws that hold the pump cover plate to the accelerator pump body. This ensures that the diaphragm can move over its whole range and pump effectively.

## Difficult Starting from Cold

**Causes:**
1. Incorrect use of choke control.
2. Choke control not operating starter assembly correctly.
3. Starter jet blocked or partly blocked.
4. Starting air control piston stuck.

**Procedure:**
1. See under STARTING THE ENGINE.
2. Check operating of choke control to ensure that the control is moving the starter assembly operating lever over its whole range of movement. Insufficient movement could be caused by a very stiff or damaged choke control cable.
3. The starter jet can be seen in the float chamber base when the carburetor top body and float are removed. If it is blocked that is an indication that the entire fuel system needs cleaning out particularly the fuel pump fuel sediment chamber.
4. The starter air control piston movement can be checked after removing the carburetor top body. The piston is spring loaded on its under side and should snap back onto its retaining ring that is pressed into the carburetor main body. If the piston is stuck, or stiff in action, it can usually be freed off by using penetrating oil. Should it be necessary the piston retaining

ring can be pried out carefully as it is slightly tapered. The piston and its return spring can then be removed and the piston and its bore in the carburetor body cleaned.

## SOLEX B. 32 P.A.I.A.

### Notes on Dismantling and Reassembly - See Fig. 13

A fully exploded view of the carbureter from which the particular position of any part can be seen is given. Many of these parts can be removed and replaced with the carburetor in position in the engine.

Particular attention should be given to the following:
1. Pilot jets (72) and (75), main jets (28) and (77), and choke tubes (11) and (15) must be fitted to their respective throttle barrels. In some instances they are not interchangeable.
2. The choke tubes (11) and (15) are held in position by the two pointed set screws and lock nuts, (73 and 74). They are located correctly by narrow slots on their lower ends.
3. A gasket (70) is used between the secondary throttle operating unit body (69) and the carburetor main body (16).

The small rubber sealing ring (71) must be used at its location on the vacuum passage between the secondary throttle operating unit cover (83) and body (69).
6. The lever (60) must be assembled to the starter assembly disc valve (58) spindle so that they take the relative positions shown.
7. The lever (42) and items (34) to (45) must be assembled to the primary throttle spindle in the order shown.
8. **The lever (42) must be assembled so that its outer end comes below its roller contact on the secondary throttle shaft lever.**

### To Remove

1. Loosen air cleaner hose connection on the top of the carburetor.
2. Remove top half of clamp holding the air cleaner body to its bracket on the engine valve cover. Remove cleaner.
3. Withdraw fuel line from its connection on the float chamber.
4. Remove vacuum advance line from its connection on the carburetor.
5. Disconnect choke control inner and outer operating cable.
6. Disconnect throttle operating shaft at carburetor end.
7. Remove four ½ in. A.F. nuts and flat washers. Lift off carburetor and blank off flange on inlet manifold.

# SOLEX B. 32 P.A.I.A.

**CARBURETTOR PARTS**

1. Screw and accelerator pump ball valve assembly.
2. Fibre washer.
3. Top body and float chamber cover.
4. Needle valve assembly washer.
5. Float needle valve assembly.
6. Joint—top body to main body.
7. Float pivot pin.
8. Float.
9. Air correction jets.
10. Emulsion tubes.
11. Secondary throttle choke tube.
12. Starter jet.
13. Accelerator pump bleed back jet.
14. Accelerator pump intake ball valve.
15. Primary throttle choke tube.
16. Carburettor main body.
17. Joint—accelerator pump to main body.
18. Accelerator pump body.
19. Accelerator pump diaphragm return spring.
20. Accelerator pump diaphragm. (membrane)
21. Accelerator pump fixing screw.
22. Accelerator pump cover fixing screw.
23. Accelerator pump cover and lever assembly.
24. Wire type circlip.
25. Accelerator pump lever operating spring.
26. Accelerator pump operating rod.
27. Fibre washer.
28. Main jet—primary throttle barrel.
29. Main jet holder.
30. Volume control adjustment spring.
31. Slow running mixture volume control screw.
32. Lever retaining nut.
33. Accelerator pump operating lever.
34. Shoulder spacing washer.
35. Nylon sealing washer.
36. Primary throttle.
37. Primary throttle fixing screws.
38. Primary throttle spindle.
39. Return spring, secondary throttle return lever.
40. Spring positioning plate.
41. Lever bearing.
42. Lever—secondary throttle release and return
43. Lock washer.
44. Nut—primary throttle operating lever.
45. Primary throttle operating lever.
46. Primary throttle abutment plate.
47. Slow running speed adjustment screw spring.
48. Slow running speed adjustment screw.
49. Secondary throttle lever nut.
50. Secondary throttle operating lever.
51. Secondary throttle spindle.
52. Secondary throttle closed position stop screw.
53. Stop screw lock nut.
54. Secondary throttle stop plate.
55. Stop plate fixing nut.
56. Secondary throttle.
57. Secondary throttle fixing screws.
58. Starter assembly disc valve.
59. Starter assembly body.
60. Starter assembly operating lever.
61. Spring washer.
62. Lever fixing nut.
63. Starter assembly fixing screw and spring washer.
64. Choke cable to lever fixing screw.
65. Circlip.
66. Lever pivot—choke inner cable.
67. Fixing screw—choke control outer cable.
68. Fixing screw and spring washer—secondary throttle operating unit.
69. Secondary throttle operating unit body.
70. Joint—secondary throttle operating unit to carburettor main body.
71. Small rubber sealing ring.
72. Pilot jet—primary throttle barrel.
73. Fixing screws for choke tubes.
74. Fixing screw lock nuts.
75. Pilot jet—secondary throttle barrel.
76. Fibre washer.
77. Main jet—secondary throttle barrel.
78. Main jet holder.
79. Ball joint clip.
80. Connecting rod and spring loaded ball joint.
81. Secondary throttle operating diaphragm. (membrane)
82. Diaphragm return spring.
83. Secondary throttle operating unit cover.
84. Cover fixing screw.
85. Fixing screw and spring washer—carburettor top body.
86. Dip tube—starting fuel circuit.

Note—Items 69, 81 and 83.—The secondary throttle operating unit is also known as the depression chamber assembly.

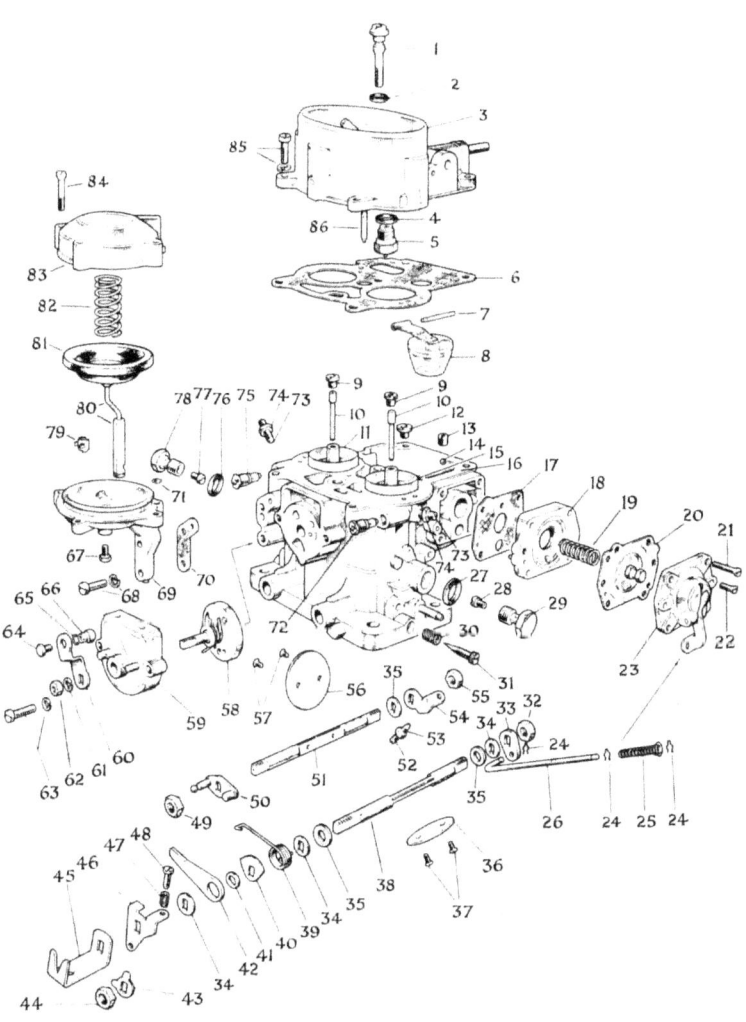

Fig. 13 - Solex B. 32 P.A.I.A. Carburetor—Exploded View

## CLEANING

The jets, passage ways, and float chamber can be cleaned without removing the carburetor if the following procedure is carried out.
1. Remove air cleaner.
2. Remove carburetor top body by taking out the accelerator discharge valve screw assembly and four fixing screws.
3. Lift out float and float lever pivot.
4. Remove accelerator pump bleed back jet in the float chamber. Blow down hole into which the accelerator pump delivery assembly screws. This will blow fuel out of the accelerator pump and its passage system. While doing this a finger should be held over the jet position to prevent possible loss of the non-return ball valve. Replace jet.
5. Remove main jet and slow running (pilot) jet in the primary throttle barrel. This will drain most of the fuel from the float chamber. The remaining fuel can be soaked away with clean lintless rag after which the float chamber should be blown out with clean compressed air.
6. With a suitable nozzle blow compressed air into the slow running jet and main jet position. After this blow down through the air correction jet, and jets which should then be replaced.
7. Remove the main jet and the pilot jet from the secondary throttle barrel and repeat procedure in previous paragraph.
8. With the choke control in the normal fully in position, insert the air nozzle into the upper **brass** end of the starter dip tube well. This will blow air back through the starter jet. Continue blowing air in at the same place and very slowly pull out the choke control. This will allow air to blow through the starter assembly passageways.
9. Blow through fuel intake pipe and dip tube.
10. Replace carburetor top body and fill float chamber with fuel by turning the engine with the starter motor, or by operating the fuel pump primary lever (if fitted). Operate the primary throttle and check that fuel is being discharged from the delivery nozzle.
11. Refit the air cleaner.

## To Refit

Check the carburetor flange face for flatness and carefully reface if necessary. After refacing the flange face must be checked with "marking blue" on a surace plate, or other reliable flat face. The use of a straight edge is not a satisfactory method of checking carburetor flanges for flatness and particularly so on this carburetor.

Remove blank placed over inlet manifold flange.

One gasket is used between each side of the thick heat insulation.

## ADJUSTMENTS – SOLEX B. 32 P.A.I.A.

The only adjustments are:
1. Slow running mixture and slow running speed.
2. Choke control cable.
3. Secondary throttle closed position stop.
4. Secondary throttle operating rod.

### Slow Running – To Adjust

Adjust the slow running speed adjustment screw to give an engine idling speed of 850 r.p.m.

Adjust the slow running volume control screw so that the engine is running evenly with the screw rotated anti-clockwise as far as possible.

Re-adjust the engine speed if necessary with the slow running speed adjustment screw.

When this adjustment is finished the engine should be running evenly at 850 r.p.m. just off the "hunting" or rich idling condition. This is obtained by having the volume control screw rotated anti-clockwise as far as possible consistent with even running at the given idling speed.

### Choke Control Cable

Release set screws holding choke control outer and inner cables on the starter assembly.

Push the outer cable into its fixing abutment as far as possible and tighten its securing set screw.

Push the starter assembly operating lever over against its operating stop farthest from its outer cable fixing.

Position the choke control so that its knob is 1/8 in. from its full in position, and tighten set screw securing outer cable at lever end.

Pull choke control outwards as far as possible and check that starter assembly operating lever comes against the stop nearest to the outer cable fixing position.

Push choke control fully inwards and check that the starter assembly operating lever comes against its stop farthest from its outer cable fixing.

## Secondary Throttle Stop

This is a very important adjustment. It prevents the secondary throttle barrel jet system from supplying fuel when the primary throttle barrel only is needed. It also ensures that the secondary throttle cannot stick closed.

The adjustment needed cannot be made with the carburetor in position because it is necessary to measure the clearance between the secondary throttle and its throttle bore.

1. Remove the carburetor, clean its exterior and carefully scrape away any varnish deposits in both throttle bores.
2. Release the spring loaded ball joint to disconnect the shaft from the secondary throttle ball joint on the secondary throttle spindle lever.

ADJUSTABLE STOP

**Fig. 14 - Secondary Throttle Closed Position Stop**

3. Hold the primary throttle in its fully open position by inserting a short length of ½ in. dia bar between the open primary throttle and its throttle bore.

4. Adjust the secondary throttle stop so that secondary throttle has .002 in. clearance between the throttle plate and its throttle bore, at **each side** of its diameter at right angles to the throttle spindle.

A .002 in. feeler gauge 3/16 in. wide should be used for checking the throttle plate clearance.

If the clearances are uneven the throttle plate fixing screws should be loosened off so that the throttle plate centralizes as its clearance is checked. Retighten the fixing screws when similar clearances are obtained.

5. Refit the carburetor and adjust the slow running as described under ADJUSTMENTS.

## Secondary Throttle Operating Rod

This rod is adjusted in its diaphragm end so that its ball joint end lines up with the ball on the secondary throttle lever when the secondary throttle is closed and the diaphragm is at the bottom of its stroke.

# NOTES

# VOLKSWAGEN 1200 & 1300

Early Volkswagens used Solex 26VFI and VFIS units. The 1192 cc 30 and 36 hp engines were fitted with 28 PCI models. Starting with the 40 hp engine in 1961, the 28 PICT with automatic choke was used. In 1964 the letter I was added to the designation to indicate the substitution of a diaphragm for the vacuum piston in the automatic choke. The 1300 VW uses a 30 PICT which is the same as the 28 with larger venturi and different jets. We will consider the PICT type first and the earlier models subsequently.

The 28 P.I.C.T. carburetor, (Fig. 60), mounts on top of the intake manifold by two studs and takes an oil bath type air cleaner. Fuel is fed from the pump to the needle valve controlled float bowl. The carburetor has idling, normal running, and power and acceleration systems. It consists of the bowl or base piece, (Fig. 61), including float, venturi, accelerator pump and the jet system; and the top part, (Fig. 61A), the bowl cover which includes automatic choke, float needle valve, and pump jets. It is a single barrel down-draft design.

The various systems in the carburetor are designed to allow it to efficiently meter the correct amount of fuel into the air stream on the many different conditions of engine load and speed, and air temperature.

### Pre-Heater

Air enters the air cleaner through a small extension or horn. Coming into the bottom of the horn is a small hose that robs warm air from the car's heating system. A pivoting, weight-loaded flap, (Fig. 62), closes off the open end of the horn. When idling in the winter, there is insufficient vacuum inside the horn to open the flap and most of the air comes into the horn via the air tube. This prevents the jets from icing and the car from stalling. As engine speed increases, vacuum increases, the flap opens and cool air is drawn in. When open all the way, the flap blocks the warm air entrance and only cold air is inhaled. Since warm air is only needed during the winter, the flap should be fixed in its open position when air temperature is regularly above 68°.

### Choke

Starting, (Fig. 63), requires a richer mixture than normal running and this is arranged automatically by the choke. The basic principle of choking, whether manual or automatic, is to restrict

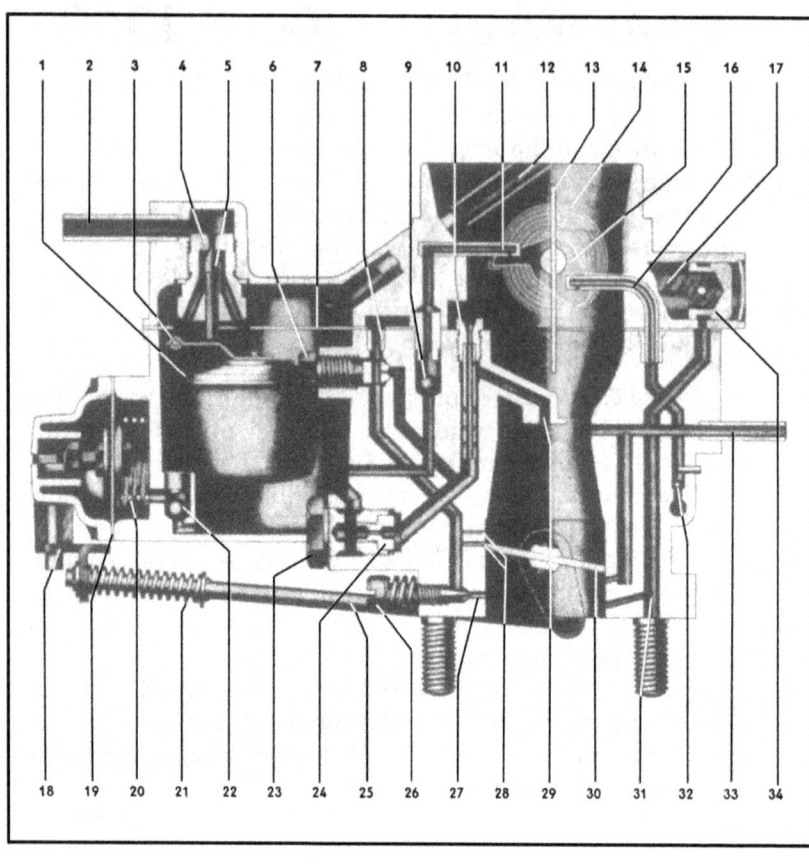

**FIG. 60**

Solex 28 PICT

1 - Float
2 - Fuel line
3 - Float lever
4 - Float needle valve
5 - Float needle
6 - Pilot jet
7 - Gasket
8 - Pilot air drilling
9 - Ball check valve in power fuel system
10 - Air correction jet with emulsion tube
11 - Power fuel tube
12 - Float bowl vent tube
13 - Choke valve
14 - Bi-metal spring
15 - Operating lever
16 - Accelerator pump discharge tube
17 - Piston rod
18 - Pump lever
19 - Pump diaphragm
20 - Diaphragm spring
21 - Spring
22 - Ball check valve for accelerator pump
23 - Main jet carrier
24 - Main jet
25 - Pump connector rod
26 - Volume control screw
27 - Idle port
28 - By-pass port
29 - Discharge arm
30 - Throttle valve
31 - Vacuum drilling
32 - Ball check valve in accelerator pump drilling
33 - Vacuum connection
34 - Vacuum piston

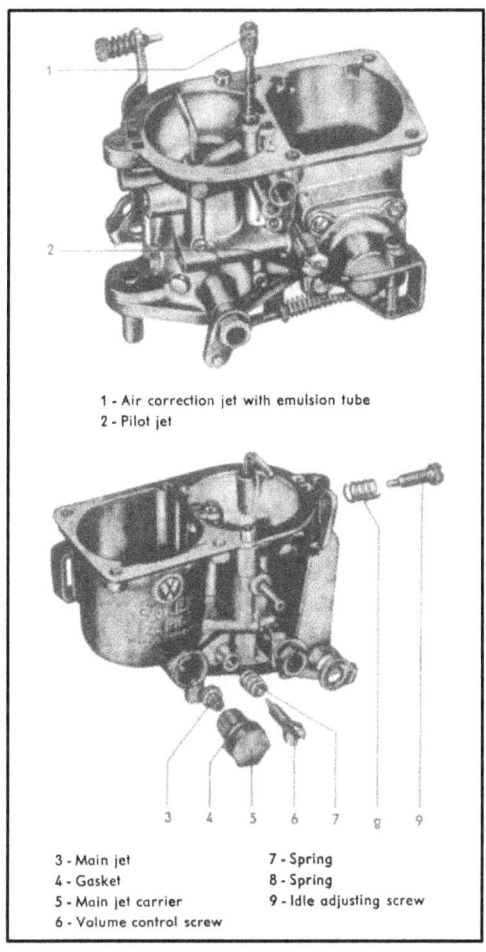

1 - Air correction jet with emulsion tube
2 - Pilot jet

3 - Main jet
4 - Gasket
5 - Main jet carrier
6 - Volume control screw
7 - Spring
8 - Spring
9 - Idle adjusting screw

FIG. 61

the entrance of air between the float bowl vent and the venturi in order to increase the vacuum which then "draws out" more gasoline and enrichens the mixture. The manual choke model had a centrally pivoted butterfly valve with a spring loaded poppet valve to allow the entrance of extra air in order to prevent the mixture from becoming too rich at high speed with the choke closed. With the automatic choke, three devices accomplish this task; the butterfly is pivoted off center so that inrushing air tends to open the valve all by itself. The valve then flutters according to air pressure. The freely pivoting, fast idling cam is a weight that also tends to open the choke. Finally there is a vacuum piston connected by a passage to the underside of the throttle valve that unloads the choke during high vacuum conditions such as over-run when coasting.

All three devices act counter to a spiral-shaped, bi-metallic

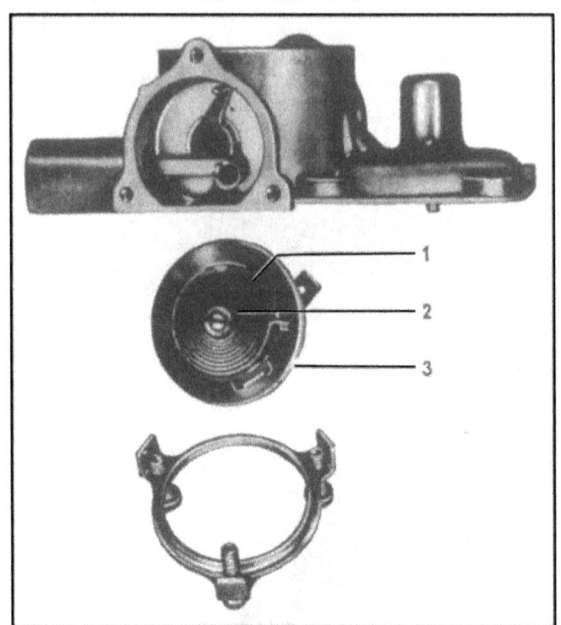

**FIG. 61**A  1 - Heater element  2 - Bi-metal spring  3 - Ceramic plate

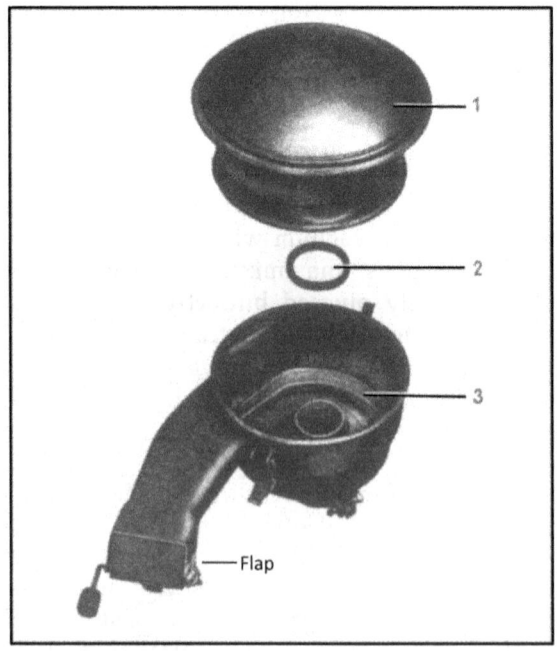

**FIG. 62**  1 - Filter element    2 - Gasket    3 - Oil reservoir

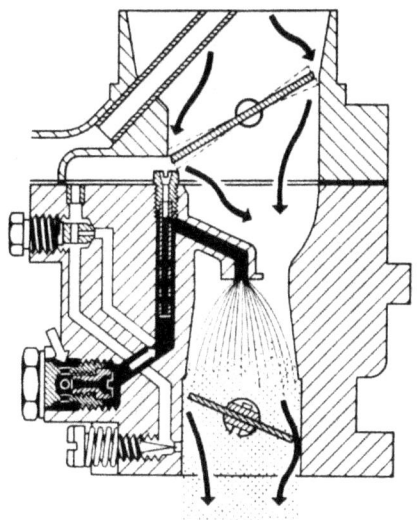

FIG. 63

spring that tries to rotate the choke closed. Next to the spring in a ceramic housing is an electric heater coil that turns on and off with the ignition switch. When cold, the spring holds the choke shut to enrichen the mixture and the three unloading devices balance its action under certain conditions. As the coil heats the bi-metallic spring, the spring unwinds and opens the choke in varying degrees until it is finally held open all the way, according to air temperature and length of time after starting. A lever from the throttle shaft comes up to the stepped cam balance weight on the choke. An adjusting screw (throttle stop) in the end of the lever rests on one of the steps. This has the action of assuring a minimum throttle valve opening when the choke is closed, so that the engine will continue to run at idle when cold. In cold weather, pressing the accelerator pedal to floor before starting frees the cam from the throttle adjusting screw so the choke, which was last positioned fully opened, can then seek its own degree of closing.

When starting, the gas flows from the float chamber through the main jet up through the emulsion tube and out through the main spraying arm into the "waist" of the venturi where it mixes with the slowly moving air drawn past the fluttering choke valve. The venturi is a restriction in the carburetor barrel which increases the speed of the air flow and thus creates a pressure drop or vacuum that "pulls" gas from the jets. If the engine is flooded, turning on the ignition and waiting before starting (with accelerator held to floor) will allow the coil to open choke for easier starting.

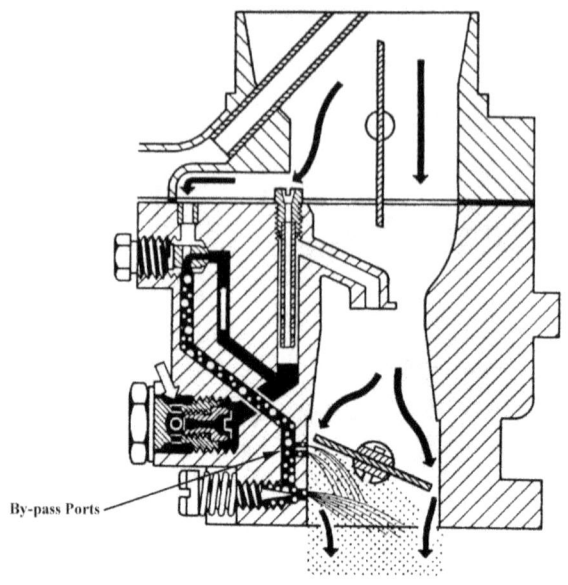

**FIG. 64**

### Idling System

When the engine warms up the choke fully opens, (Fig. 64). When idling, the idling system comes into play. Because the throttle valve is only slightly open, there is little air speed and thus insufficient vacuum to draw gas out through the main spraying arm. Gas then comes through the main jet and up to a pilot jet which restricts gas flow and pre-mixes the gas with correct amount of air coming in through a pilot jet air bleed. From here the "bubbled" gas flows down and out through three by-pass ports below, level with, and just above the throttle valve. Fuel is metered according to the amount of throttle opening. These three ports smooth the transfer to the main jet system during normal running.

The idling mixture is adjusted by turning the volume control screw which moves a tapered needle in or out of the lowest port.

### Normal Running

During normal running speeds, the same spraying arm that squirted the mixture for starting is used again, but now there is sufficient air speed and vacuum in the venturi. The emulsion tube which didn't function during starting is now activated by the increased vacuum. It's function is to pre-mix the gas coming in from the main jet with air entering through an air correction jet before the gas is sprayed. This action helps atomize the fuel for more efficient mixing in the venturi.

The emulsion tube is a small tube with holes along its length. It is situated in the vertical passage between main jet and spraying arm. At its top is the air correction jet. As the throttle opens, the rising vacuum in the venturi increases gas flow from the spraying arm and the gas level around the emulsion tube drops. This exposes more of the holes in the tube to allow more air to mix with fuel to constantly adjust the pre-mixture according to needs.

**Power Fuel System**

The power fuel system adds more fuel to enrichen the mixture at full load and high engine speeds (Fig. 65). It has its own spraying arm, the power fuel tube, which, because it is situated above choke level, is only subject to vacuum at high air speed. The power fuel tube connects directly to the float chamber and a ball check valve assures that it only functions under high vacuum. Once started, its delivery is progressive right up to top engine speed. Since it only passes fuel at high engine speed it aids gas economy during part load conditions.

**Accelerator Pump**

Lastly there is an accelerator pump which is a miniature diaphragm-type pump linked to the throttle valve so that the mixture gets an extra shot of gas during acceleration, (Fig. 66). The system works only while the accelerator is being depressed and stops when speed is attained and the pedal stops moving. A spring on the link between throttle shaft and accelerator pump insures that the accelerator pump functions only during initial accelerator pedal travel. On highways when varying speed between medium and high, the accelerator pump doesn't continually waste gas since vacuum is sufficiently high for the power fuel system to do its job.

The carburetor is thus a form of computer varying mixture and quantity according to road conditions.

**Idling Adjustment**

If the idling mixture is too rich, the engine may stall under braking or when the idling speed is too slow. Adjust with screw on lowest step of cam. Turn idling speed screw, (Fig. 67), for an engine speed of 550 rpm. Turn volume control screw, (Fig. 68), to the right until speed begins to drop and then back to the left $1/4$ to $1/3$ turn. Again regulate the idling speed. Turn volume control screw slowly to avoid damaging tapered needle in fully closed position. (When correctly adjusted, the volume control screw will usually be $1^{1}/_{4}$ to $1^{1}/_{2}$ turns opened from the fully closed position.) Finally, test the adjustment by flipping accel-

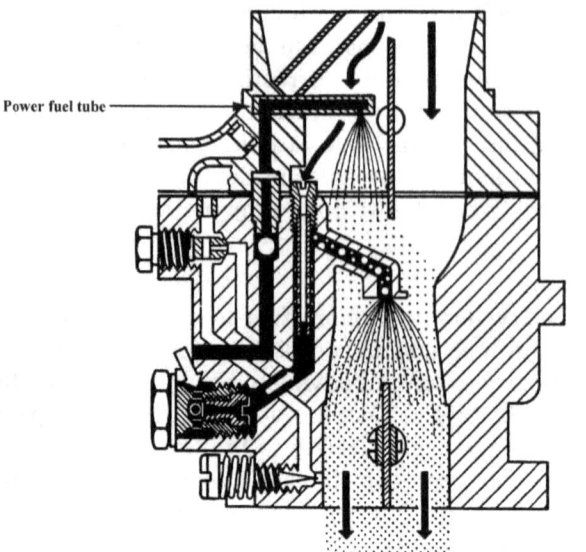

FIG. 65

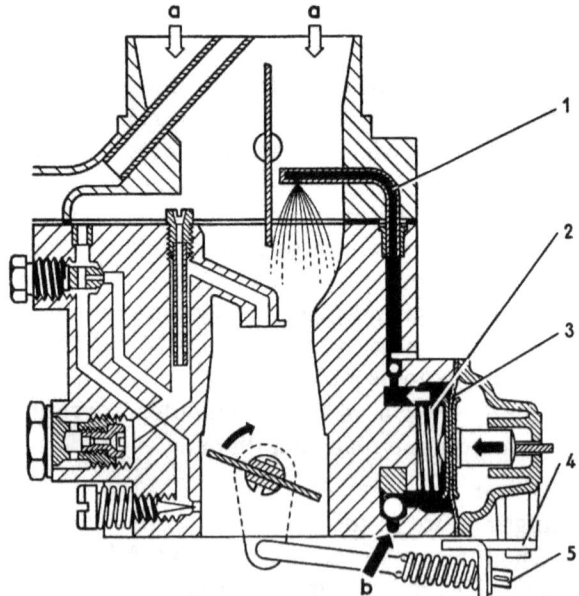

a - Air
b - Fuel from float bowl

1 - Discharge B tube
2 - Diaphragm spring
3 - Pump diaphragm
4 - Pump lever
5 - Pump connector rod

FIG. 66

FIG. 67

erator and by depressing clutch at idle. If engine stalls, the mixture is too weak and the volume control screw should be turned left 1/8 of a turn. The carburetor should only be adjusted with engine warm.

**Cable Adjustment**

The accelerator cable is adjusted at carburetor, (Fig. 69), by loosening the cable swivel-pin and depressing the accelerator all the way to floor, while opening the throttle valve lever so that the clearance between throttle lever and stop at carburetor is .04". Tighten the cable swivel pin in this position. This assures that the accelerator pedal bottoms before the throttle lever, so that foot pressure cannot break the accelerator cable.

| SPECIFICATIONS | 28 PICT | 30 PICT |
|---|---|---|
| Venturi | 22.5 m | 24 mm |
| Main jet | 122.5 | 125 |
| Air correction jet | 130 y* | 125 z |
| Pilot jet | 55 | g 55 |
| Pilot air bleed | 2.0 mm | 2.0 mm |
| Pump jet | 0.5 | 0.5 |
| Power fuel jet | 1.0 | .75 |
| Emulsion tube ... in unit with air correction jet | | in unit |
| Float needle valve | 1.5 mm | 1.5 mm |
| Weight of float | 5.7 g | 5.7 g |
| *Karmann Ghia | 145 y | 170 z |

**Early Model Fuel System**

The fuel system of pre-1962 VW's includes a fuel tap with filter. The front mounted fuel tank has a capacity of 10.5 gallons. The three position fuel tap (shut, open and reserve) is situated underneath the fuel tank and operated from inside the

**FIG. 68**

**FIG. 69**

car. With the tap in the normal position (straight up) approximately 1.3 gallons is reserved which can only flow out after the tap has been turned to the reserve position. Fig. 70 - 71 show tap positions.

**Early Carburetor**

Fig. 72 shows the Solex 28 P.C.I. used on pre-1961 VW's. It is a down draft carburetor with accelerating pump, a fixed main

FIG. 70 —Three-way fuel tap FIG. 71
1-normal position, 2-reserve, 3-shut off

jet, additional air correction, and manual choke.

There is a separate idle system (for idling and low speed range) and a power system (for high speed range). The carburetor float bowl is supplied with fuel by the engine-driven fuel pump. The float and needle assembly keeps a constant level in the float bowl. With normal operation (part load), fuel from the float bowl flows through the main jet into the mixing- (also called spraying-) well, and it is discharged through the radial outlet holes by the depression (partial vacuum) in the choke tube (venturi). This fuel then is mixed with the air drawn in through the carburetor throat. The depression in the venturi is a function of engine speed and throttle opening.

As the throttle is opened wider the fuel level in the mixing well decreases (fuel flow is limited by the size of the main jet) and air is drawn in through the air correction jet (13). This air passes through the holes of the emulsion tube (14) where a "pre-mixing" process takes place with the fuel drawn from the main jet. This rich fuel-air mixture then passes through the discharge holes in the narrowest part of the venturi where it is mixed with the air drawn in through the carburetor throat (primary air) to form a combustible mixture of the correct consistency. Jet and venturi sizes are combined in such a way that the correct fuel-air ratio is maintained throughout the speed range.

## Idling Circuit

At very small throttle openings the depression in the venturi is insufficient to draw fuel out of the mixing well. The carburetor therefore is provided with a separate idle and low speed system. The pilot jet, mixture adjustment screw (12) and pilot

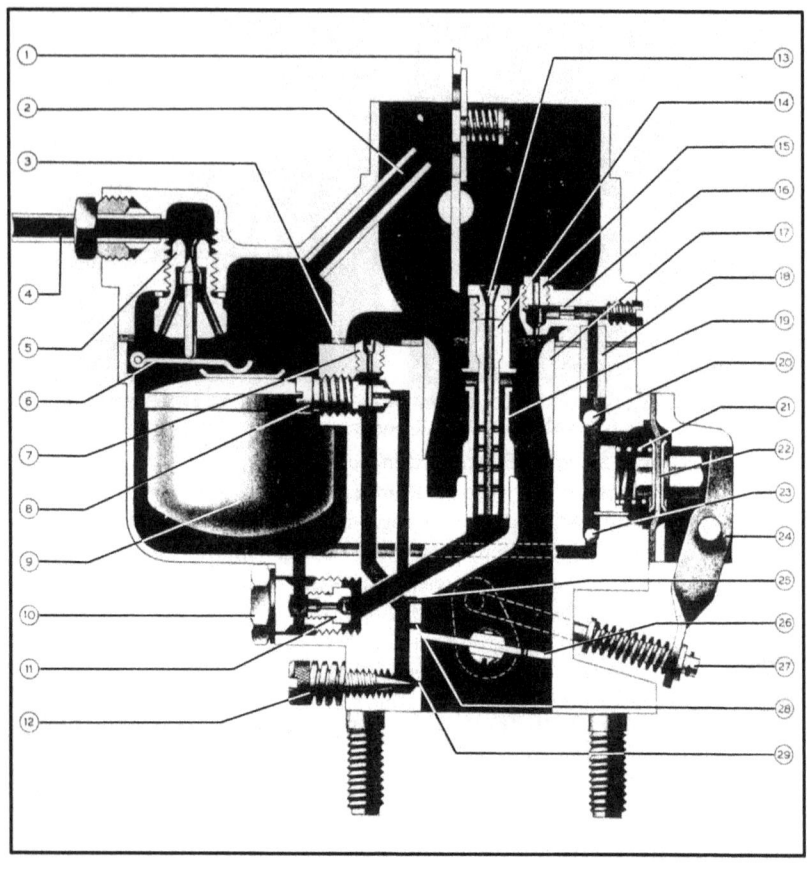

**FIG. 72**

## SOLEX 28 PCI

| | | |
|---|---|---|
| 1-Choke valve | 11-Main jet | 21-Diaphragm spring (pump) |
| 2-Vent tube | 12-Mixture adjusting screw | 22-Diaphragm (pump) |
| 3-Gasket | 13-Air correction jet | 23-Lower ball check valve |
| 4-Fuel line | 14-Emulsion tube | 24-Pump lever |
| 5-Float needle valve | 15-Air correction jet (pump) | 25-Idle air bleed passage |
| 6-Needle valve lever | 16-Pump jet | 26-Throttle valve |
| 7-Pilot jet air bleed | 17-Venturi | 27-Throttle valve link |
| 8-Pilot jet | 18-Fitting tube | 28-Accelerator port |
| 9-Float | 19-Spraying well | 29-Idle port |
| 10-Main jet carrier | 20-Upper ball check valve | |

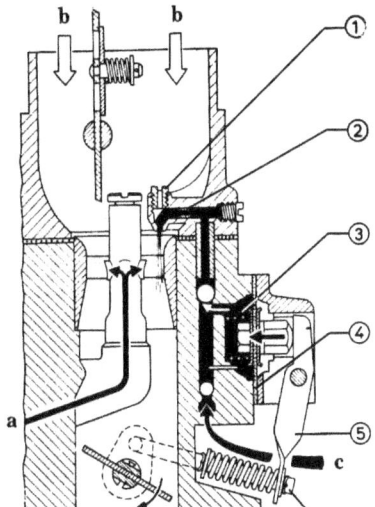

a-Fuel from main jet
b-Primary air
c-Fuel from float bowl

1-Pump discharge nozzle and air correction jet
2-Pump jet
3-Diaphragm spring
4-Diaphragm
5-Pump lever
6-Throttle valve link

**FIG. 73**

jet air bleed combine to supply the correct mixture for this speed range. The depression **under** the throttle valve in the low speed range is considerable and it is here that the idling port discharges its fuel. This rich mixture is mixed with the air flowing past the partially opened throttle valve to give a mixture of the correct consistency. The flow of fuel is regulated by the screw (12). Screwing in weakens the mixture.

To insure smooth take over from idling range to part-load range, two accelerating ports (28) are provided in the carburetor throat. As the throttle is opened wider, the depression above the throttle increases and additional fuel is drawn from these orifices. A little above these ports is an idle air bleed passage (25) the purpose of which is to lean out the mixture when the throttle is snapped shut, thus preventing stalling of the engine.

**Accelerating System**

(Fig. 72 & 73) The carburetor is provided with a diaphragm type accelerating pump as shown in the illustrations. The spring-loaded diaphragm (4) is linked to the throttle. When the throttle valve closes, the diaphragm is pushed back by the spring and fuel is drawn in the suction chamber from the float bowl through the lower ball check valve (23). When the throttle is opened, the pump diaphragm is pushed back and fuel is discharged through the upper ball check valve (20) through the pump jet (2) on out through the discharge nozzle into the ven-

**FIG. 74**

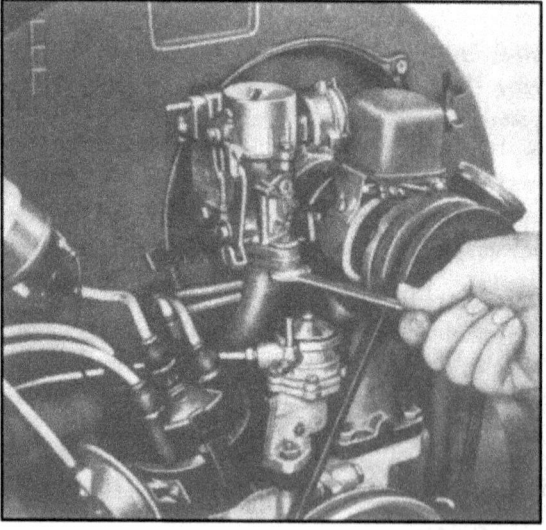

**FIG. 75**

to

turi. This additional fuel prevents "flat spots" and insures instantaneous pick-up when throttle valve is suddenly opened. The pump chamber fills up only when the throttle is near its closing point.

**Power System**

In the higher speed range at wider throttle openings, the accelerator pump system also serves as power system. Under these conditions, additional fuel is supplied through the pump

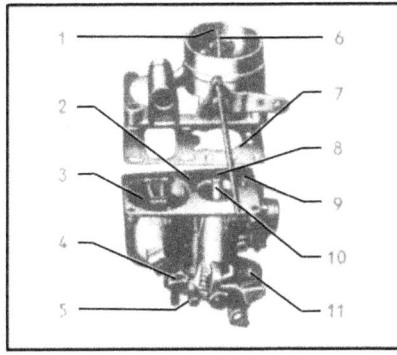 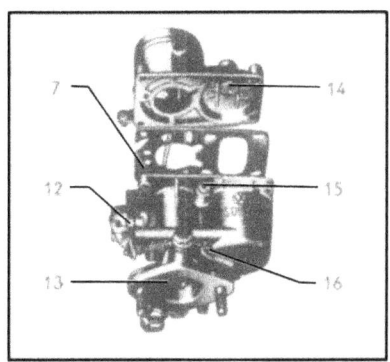

1-Choke valve
2-Pilot jet air bleed
3-Float
4-Main jet
5-Idle mixture adjustment
6-Poppet valve
7-Gasket
8-Air correction jet
9-Fitting tube
10-Emulsion tube
11-Idle adjusting screw
12-Accelerator pump
13-Throttle valve
14-Float needle valve
15-Pilot jet
16-Connection for vacuum line

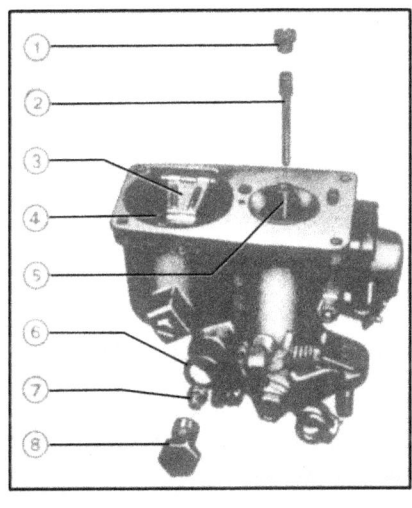 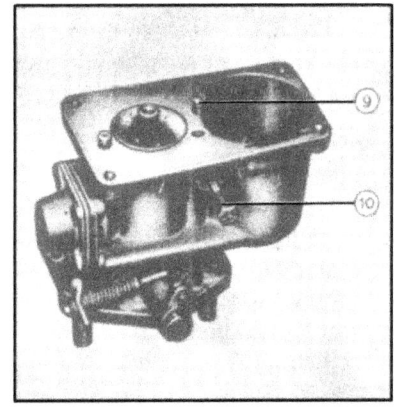

1-Air correction jet
2-Emulsion tube
3-Float toggle lever
4-Float
5-Spraying well
6-Gasket
7-Main jet
8-Main jet carrier
9-Pilot jet air bleed
10-Pilot jet

**FIG. 76 Carburetor disassembled**

discharge nozzle.

## Adjustments

A correctly adjusted idling mixture is very important. Mixture should only be adjusted after engine has attained operating temperature, as described previously.

| VW Engine 1946-1960 | Engine | 1131 c.c. — 25 b.h.p. | | | 1192 c.c. — 30 b.h.p. | | |
|---|---|---|---|---|---|---|---|
| | Carburetor Type | 26 VFI | 26 VFIS | | 28 PCI | | |
| | Up to Eng. No. | 194 695 | 481 712 | 695 281 | 849 904 | 3 919 979 991 589 | 3 919 979 3 538 143 |
| Venturi ................mm dia. | | 21.5 | 21.5 | 20.0 | 21.5 | 21.5 | 21.5 |
| Main jet ............................. | | 120 | 120 | 105 | 122.5 | 117.5 | 117.5 |
| Air correction jet ............... | | 170 | 180 | 190 | 200 | 195 | 180 |
| Pilot jet ............................. | | 45 g | 45 g | 50 g | 50 g | 50 g | 50 g |
| Pilot jet air bleed........mm. dia. | | 1.5 | 1.0 | 0.8 | 0.8 | 0.8 | 0.8 |
| Emulsion tube ..................... | | 0 | 0 | 10 | 29 | 29 | 29 |
| Spraying well..............mm dia. | | 5.3 | 5.3 | 5.5 | 5.0 | 5.0 | 5.0 |
| Float needle valve.............mm | | 1.2 | 1.2/1.5 | 1.5 | 1.5 | 1.5 | 1.5 |

## Removing and Installing Carburetor

Remove air cleaner, disconnect fuel line, accelerator cable, choke cable. Unscrew carburetor flange nuts. When installing always use new manifold flange gasket.

## Cleaning Carburetor

To dismantle carburetor for cleaning: remove air cleaner, disconnect fuel line, remove carburetor bowl cover. If bowl cover has to be removed completely, choke control cable must be disconnected.

Remove float assembly, main jet plug. Clean main jet and float bowl Clean pilot jet air bleed, pilot jet, air correction jet, emulsion tube.

Jets and passages should be cleaned with compressed air. Fig. 76 shows the various parts of the disassembled carburetor. The venturi can be removed after the retaining screw has been taken out. Fig. 77 shows the various parts of the accelerating pump. (Flat spots when pressing on accelerator usually indicate a faulty accelerating pump.)

## Inspection

Check needle valve for correct seating. Check accelerating pump diaphragm. Check float for leaks (dip in hot water and check for air bubbles and if necessary replace). When reinstalling venturi make sure that it is installed correctly (Fig. 78). Do not overtighten retaining screw. Check clearance of throttle shaft. Air leaks at this point will upset the mixture. Inspect

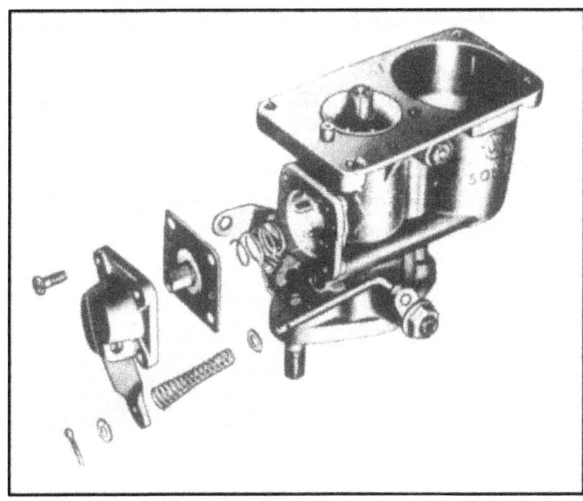

FIG. 77

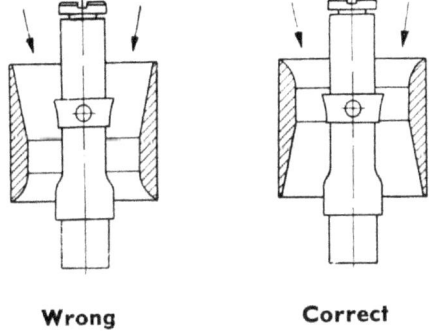

Wrong　　　Correct

FIG. 78

idling mixture control screw for correct seating.

..**NOTE:** This same procedure can be used on the later model carburetor. Do not forget to connect the choke heater element wire.

# VOLKSWAGEN 1500 & 1500 S

The Volkswagen 1500 Variant and the new fast-back are both obtainable in the more powerful "S" model. The difference between the standard and the "S" is that the standard uses a single Solex 32 PHN and the "S" uses two Solex 32 PDSIT carburetors. Use of a Unisyn synchronizing gage to achieve carburetor balance on the "S" model is advised.

### FIG. 1

Carburetor, intake side
1 - Carburetor body
2 - Float chamber cover
3 - Carburetor screws
4 - Body to cover gasket
5 - Air inlet flange
6 - Choke valve
7 - Choke valve shaft
8 - Choke valve lever
9 - Vent passage
10 - Vent space
11 - Discharge arm
12 - Choke control housing
13 - Cylinder for vacuum piston
14 - Cover with bi-metal coil and heater element
15 - Cover retaining ring
16 - Electro-magnetic pilot jet

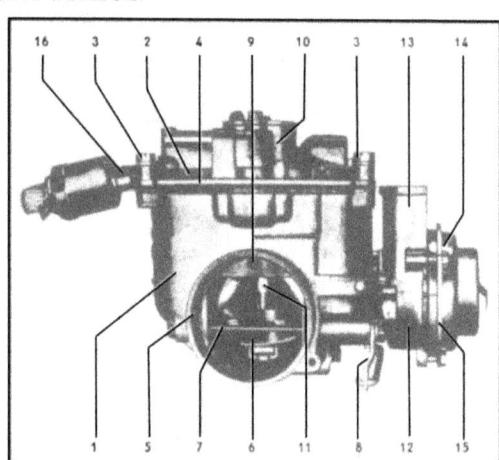

The SOLEX 32 PHN carburetor is a side draft type distinguished by the fact that the induction passage is horizontal and below the float chambers. With this design, the discharge openings for the idling and normal running mixtures are below the level of the fuel which accounts for the unusual internal construction of the carburetor. All the drillings for the individual systems pass up through the carburetor body to the cover and from there down to the various discharge ports in the choke tube.

The carburetor has an automatic choke, an accelerator pump, a power fuel system and a double vacuum drilling for the ignition advance mechanism. The induction tube diameter is 32 mm. The oil bath air cleaner is located near the carburetor and connected by means of an intake elbow.

(Refer to Fig. 1 for the following description)

The carburetor consists of two main parts: the body (1) and the cover (2). A gasket (4) is installed between the two parts and they are held together by four cheese head screws (3).

On the **intake side of the carburetor** is the air intake passage (5) which is opened and closed by the choke valve (6). The choke valve is secured off center on the choke valve shaft (7) by two screws and operated by means of the choke valve lever on the right (8). The air for the mixture and the float chamber ventilation enters the vent space (10) in the cover via the vent passage (9). The oil bath air cleaner reduces the ingress of dirt into the fuel and carburetor to a minimum. The discharge arm (11) projects into the center of the choke tube.

# FIG.2 - SOLEX 32 PHN CARBURETOR

**Float chamber cover, inside**

13 - Cover
14 - Float needle valve
15 - Pilot jet
16 - Emulsion tube
17 - Air jet
18 - Air outlet jet with ball valve

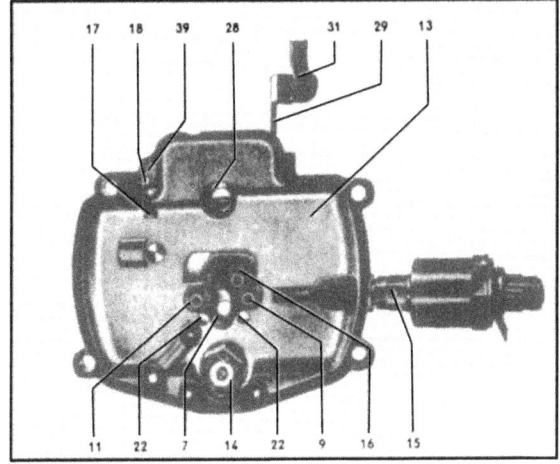

**Float chamber cover, outside**

19 - Adaptor for fuel hose
20 - Vent space
21 - Threaded holes for sealing plate screws
22 - Float chamber vent hole
23 - Air correction jet
24 - Idling passage
25 - Pilot air bleed drilling
26 - Carburetor body to cover screws
27 - Pump plunger
28 - Hole for pump plunger
29 - Pump lever
30 - Balance drilling for float chambers See Carburetor body below
31 - Connecting rod with spring
32 - Throttle valve lever

**Carburetor body**
(Float and accelerator pump removed)

33 - Main jet
34 - Pump chamber
35 - Ball valve for accelerator pump
36 - Fuel outlet on pressure stroke
37 - Drilling with needle valve
38 - Drilling with capacity rod
39 - Transfer chamber for accelerator system - see Cover
40 - Ball valve ⎫ for power fuel
41 - Fuel drilling ⎭ system

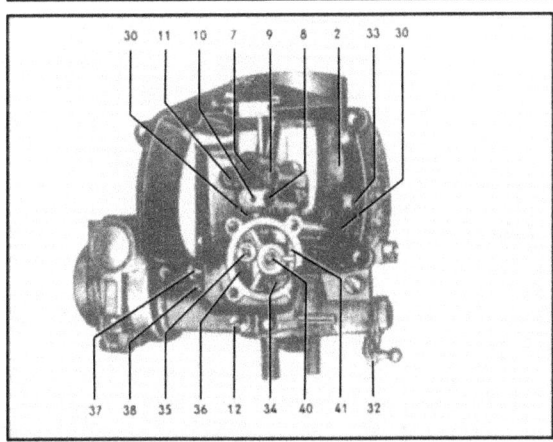

171

On the right-hand side of the carburetor is the choke control housing (12) with the cylinder for the vacuum piston (13) cast onto it. The choke control housing is sealed by a cover (14) with heater element cable connector which is secured by a retaining ring (15) and three screws. On the left side of the carburetor cover is the pilot jet (16) which is combined with a solenoid operated cut-off valve.

(Refer to Fig. 3 & Fig. 4 for the following description)

The **carburetor** is attached to the **intake manifold** by means of two studs in the flange (17). The throttle valve (18) is secured on the throttle valve shaft (19) by two screws and operated by the throttle lever (20) which is connected to the accelerator cable by the relay linkage.

In the induction tube — at the point where the choke tube cross section is smallest — is the opening of the discharge arm (21), and further forward, the accelerator pump injector tube (22).

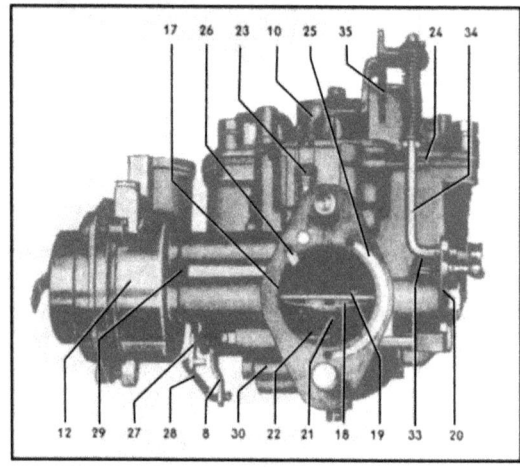

**FIG.3**

**Carburetor, engine side**
17 - Carburetor flange
18 - Throttle valve
19 - Throttle valve shaft
20 - Throttle valve lever
21 - Discharge arm opening
22 - Injector tube for accelerator pump
23 - Volume control screw
24 - Adaptor for vacuum hose to distributor
25 - Drilling for spark advance vacuum
26 - Drilling for choke piston vacuum
27 - Choke lever
28 - Connecting rod
29 - Sealing plate for choke control housing
30 - Balance drilling for float chambers

The volume control screw (23) regulates the volume of the idling mixture. The connecting pipe (24) for the vacuum hose to the distributor is pressed in. Part of the vacuum drilling (25) for the spark advance is milled into the carburetor flange. The vacuum which operates the automatic choke piston is also taken from the carburetor flange (26). The choke valve lever (8) and the choke lever (27) are connected by the rod (28).

The main jet carrier (31) is screwed into the left side of the carburetor body and the seat for the electro-magnetic pilot jet (32) is in the float chamber cover. The throttle valve lever (20) is located on the throttle valve shaft (19). The idling speed is regulated by the idle adjustment screw (33). The throttle valve lever operates the accelerator pump by means of the lever (35) which is mounted on the float chamber cover and the connecting rod and spring (34).

On the right-hand side of the carburetor is the automatic choke. The choke control housing (12) is attached to the carburetor body by two screws (36) and is sealed by the gasket (29). Around the edge of the housing are three lugs with threaded holes for the screws of the retaining ring which secures the automatic choke cover (14). In the cover is the ceramic insert with the heater element (37) and the bi-metal coil (38). A gasket (39) is fitted between cover and choke control housing.

On the intermediate spindle (40) is the freely mounted fast idle cam (41) and the cam return spring (42) which is attached at one end to a vertical pin in the cam. At the outer end of the spindle is the fixed operating lever (43) which has three arms. The arm pointing outwards engages the bi-metal coil and moves the fast idle cam by means of the vertical pin. The second arm is attached to the rod (44) of the vacuum piston (45) which slides in the vertical cylinder (13). The intermediate spindle is secured by a nut at the back of the choke control housing.

On the extended end of the throttle valve shaft (19) in the choke control housing is a stop lever (46) on one arm of which is a stop screw (47). The second-angled arm contacts the third arm of the operating lever.

The movement of the operating lever is transmitted via the choke lever (27), the connecting rod (28) and the choke valve with counterweight arm (8) to the choke valve shaft (7).

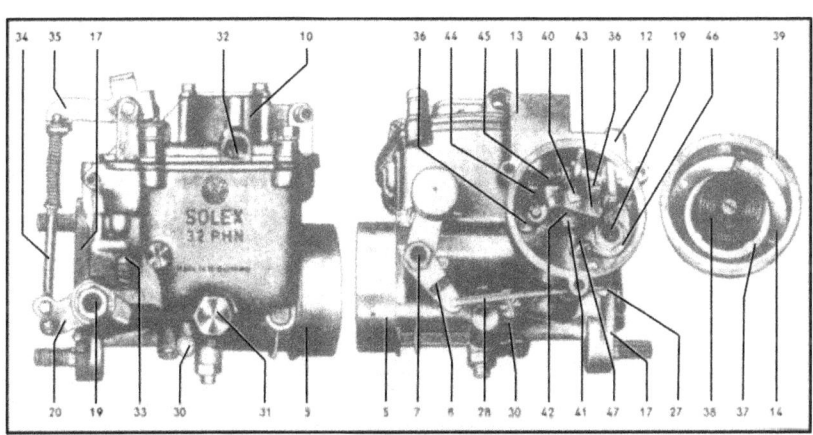

**FIG. 4**

**Carburetor, left side**

31 - Main jet carrier
32 - Seat for electro-magnetic pilot jet
33 - Idle adjustment screw
34 - Connecting rod with spring
35 - Pump lever

**Carburetor (right side), Automatic choke**

36 - Screws for choke control housing
37 - Ceramic insert with heater element
38 - Bi-metal coil
39 - Gasket for cover

40 - Intermediate spindle
41 - Fast idle cam
42 - Cam return spring
43 - Operating lever
44 - Piston rod
45 - Piston
46 - Stop lever
47 - Stop screw

(Refer to Fig. 2 & Fig. 5 for the following description)

The **carburetor body** (1) encloses two float chambers (2) which are separated from each other by the main bore (3). The fuel level is equalized by a balance drilling (30) in the bottom of the body. The float arm (4) with the twin floats is located in a recess in the body wall by means of a pin (5). The accelerator pump (6) is secured in the body by four screws.

The fuel flows into the float chamber through the fuel line adaptor (19) and the float valve (14) which is screwed into the cover (13). Air passes through the vent passage (7) into the vent space (20) which is sealed with a plate and an airtight gasket.

The threaded holes (21) are for the sealing plate screws. The float chamber is ventilated through the two holes (22).

The block cast in the center of the body contains the vent passage and two drillings each for the idling system and normal running. The fuel passes from the main jet (33) through the mixing well (8) to below the air correction jet (23) for normal operation and up through passage (9) and through the float chamber cover (13) to the pilot jet (15) when idling.

The additional air for the normal running mixture is drawn from the vent space (20) through the air correction jet (23) and mixes with the fuel in the emulsion tube (16). The emulsion tube is inserted through the float chamber cover and suspended in the mixing well (8). The mixture passes through passage (10) to the discharge arm. From the pilot jet (15) the fuel flows to the center in the pilot drilling (24) and mixes with the air entering through the pilot air bleed drilling (25). The idling mixture then passes from the float chamber cover through the carburetor body via passage (11) to the volume control screw (12).

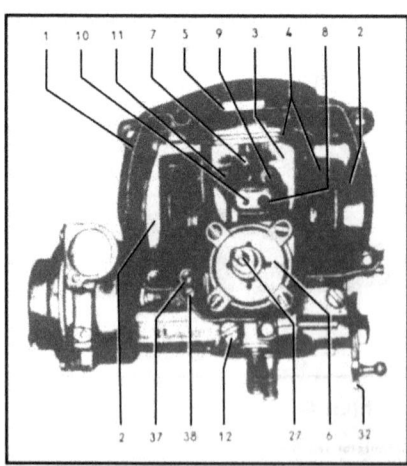

**FIG. 5**

**Carburetor body**

1 - Body
2 - Float chambers
3 - Main bore
4 - Floats with arm
5 - Float pin
6 - Accelerator pump
7 - Vent passage
8 - Mixing well (Reserve)
9 - Pilot jet fuel drilling
10 - Drilling to discharge arm
11 - Drilling for idling mixture
12 - Volume control screw

The float chamber cover is attached to the body with four screws (26) and is sealed with a gasket. The accelerator pump plunger (27) projects through a hole (28) in the cover and is operated by the pump lever (29) which is connected to the throttle valve lever (32) by the rod and spring (31).

The fuel for the accelerator system is drawn past a ball valve (35) into the pump chamber (34) on the suction stroke. On the pressure stroke the fuel is forced through drilling (36) upwards via a drilling with a needle valve (37) to the transfer chamber (39) and then through the drilling with the capacity rod (38) to the injector tube. The transfer chamber is connected to the carburetor body vent space by a passage with an air jet for air inlet (17) and a ball valve for air outlet (18).

At the bottom of the pump chamber is the ball valve for the power fuel system (40) which is operated by the pump plunger so that fuel can flow through passage (41) into the mixing well (8).

**Automatic Choke** - (from cold fully depress accelerator pedal).

The automatic choke has the task of enriching the mixture to suit the temperature when starting a cold engine, weakening it progressively as the engine warms up and increasing the idling speed until the engine has reached its normal temperature. It is fully automatic and facilitates starting and driving until the engine is sufficiently warm to run smoothly.

In the choke control cover is the ceramic insert with heater element and the bi-metal coil which is shaped to form a hook at the outer end. At low temperatures the bi-metal coil uncurls and the hooked end turns the angled arm of the operating lever on the intermediate spindle. This movement is transmitted via the choke lever connecting rod and choke valve lever to the choke valve shaft and so closes the choke. This ensures that the cold engine receives the rich mixture required when starting.

The movement of the bi-metal coil is also transferred by the operating lever to the fast idle cam so that its return spring is tensioned. As the bi-metal coil tightens, the fast idle cam is moved to a position where the stop lever screw rests on the highest step when the accelerator pedal is released. The stop lever on the throttle valve shaft holds the throttle slightly open and so increases the idling speed. Depending on the closing effort of the bi-metal coil, the stop screw will rest on one of the four steps. As the closing effort decreases due to increasing heat, the return spring turns the fast idle cam in the opposite direction until the stop screw rests on the lowest step when the accelerator pedal is released. In this position the engine runs at the normal idling speed.

Several forces work together to open the choke valve. The off-center mounting of the choke valve shaft in the intake opening results in the two parts of the choke valve being of different sizes. The larger flap turns downwards to open so that the stream of induction air tends to open the valve. This effort is assisted by the counterweighted arm of the choke valve lever which also works in the same direction.

As the bi-metal coil warms up it loses its closing effort. Adequate heat is available as soon as the ignition is switched on and the heater element receives current. The current is supplied by a cable from a terminal on the ignition coil to the flat connector on the choke control housing cover. After about 3 or 4 minutes, the closing effort of the bi-metal coil is reduced to such an extent that the choke is fully open.

The choke valve can, however, be opened against the tension of the bi-metal coil by means of the vacuum piston, which is connected to the mixing chamber by a drilling which ends near the idling port. When the throttle is slightly open there is a strong depression at this point which moves the piston up into the cylinder. The piston movement is transmitted by the piston rod to an arm on the operating lever and the choke valve opens. This ensures that the very rich starting mixture is automatically weakened to suit the engine operating conditions.

To equalize pressure, the choke control housing is provided with a drilling which ends in the air intake passage, at the front of the choke valve. The vacuum piston has an annular groove and a drilling which registers with a groove in the cylinder that relieves housing pressure at a specified piston position.

At a fairly large throttle valve opening angle, the choke valve is also opened by the angled arm of the stop lever contacting an arm on the operating lever that rotates the intermediate spindle.

To enable the automatic choke to work properly, the accelerator pedal must be fully depressed before starting the engine from cold. The bi-metal coil can then close the choke valve. The starter should be operated immediately after switching on the ignition so that the choke valve is not opened prematurely by the heater element as it warms up.

During the starting process, the choke valve flutters between the open position — under the influence of the vacuum — and the closed position — due to the tension of the bi-metal coil. The vacuum thus created in the choke tube draws fuel from the mixing well via the discharge arm. In this manner a rich mixture is formed which ensures easy starting even at very low temperatures. The increasing vacuum at the throttle valve becomes effective at the piston which then opens the choke valve slightly and prevents the mixture from becoming excessively rich. The choke valve is now progressively opened by the vacuum piston and the increasing heat at the bi-metal coil, until it is fully open and the mixture automatically weakened to suit the engine operating conditions.

If the accelerator pedal is released while the engine is still cold, the stop lever contacts one of the steps on the fast idle cam and keeps the engine running at a fast idling speed. The engine will not run at the proper idling speed until the stop lever is resting on the lowest step. The carburetor then changes over automatically to the proper idling circuit.

## Removing and Installing Carburetor
### Removal

1 — Unscrew the oil bath air cleaner wing screw far enough to permit the cleaner to be lifted and the elbow pulled off.

2 — Loosen hose clip on carburetor intake flange and take elbow off.

3 — Pull off fuel and vacuum hoses.

4 — Pull off the cables for the heater element, the automatic choke and the cut-off valve solenoid.

5 — Disconnect the throttle valve lever from the connecting link with the aid of a screwdriver.

6 — Unscrew carburetor securing nuts on the intake flange of the pre-heater pipe with a 13 mm cranked wrench and remove carburetor.

FIG. 6

**Installation**

The following points must be observed during installation:

1 — Install a new intake flange gasket.

2 — Slide the elbow carefully onto the oil bath air cleaner adaptor to prevent the entry of secondary air.

3 — Connect the cables for the heater element and cut-off valve.

4 — Adjust the idling when the engine is warm.

**Disassembly and Assembly of Carburetor**
**Disassembly**

1 — Remove carburetor.

2 — Remove the two screws in the upper part of the carburetor and take off vent space cover and gasket.

3 — Remove the four screws securing the float chamber cover.

FIG. 7

4 — Detach the accelerator pump connector rod from the throttle lever by turning the rod until the lug aligns with the groove in the lever.

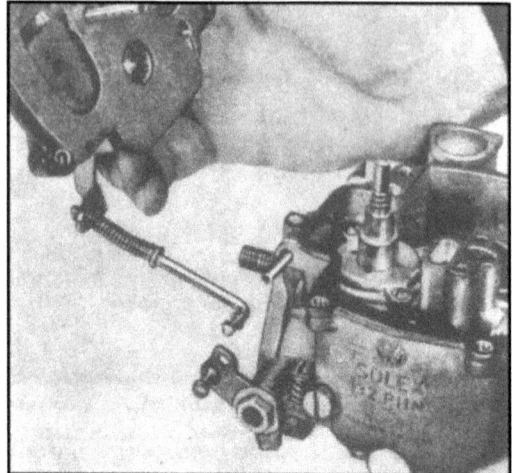

FIG. 8

5 — Lift off float chamber cover and remove the gasket.
6 — Screw the air correction jet and the cut-off valve out of the cover.
7 — Screw out the float needle valve. If it is necessary to remove the emulsion tube, it should be pressed outwards through the cover.
8 — Take the float out of the carburetor body.
9 — Remove the spring on the accelerator pump connector rod. Tip the carburetor up to remove the needle valve and the capacity rod from the accelerator pump system.

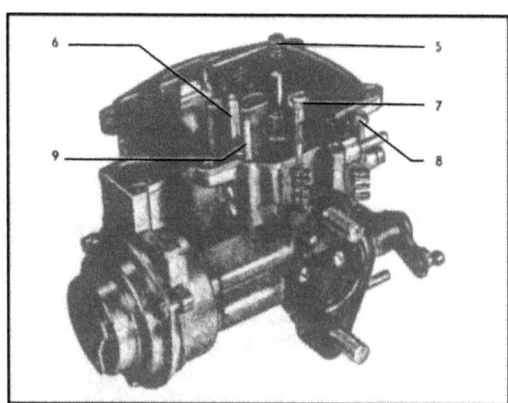

FIG. 9

10 — Screw out the volume control screw and the idle adjusting screw.
11 — Unscrew main jet carrier with main jet.
12 — Remove four accelerator screws and take off the cover with diaphragm and spring.

13 — Unscrew the plug in the power fuel system.

**FIG. 10**

14 — Remove the three screws securing the automatic choke and take off the cover with retaining ring and gasket.

### Cleaning
1 — Clean all the carburetor parts (except the automatic choke), with particular attention to the passages, drillings and corners. Under no circumstances should pins or pieces of wire be used to clean the jets as they will damage or enlarge the calibrated drillings.

2 — All parts, valves and drillings should be blown out with compressed air.

### Checking and Assembly
Assembly takes place in the reverse order. The following points should be observed when checking the parts:

### Float Chamber Cover
1 — Check float needle for ease of movement. If it tends to stick, the float needle valve should be replaced.

2 — Examine the condition of the needle valve gasket and replace if necessary.

3 — Check that the gasket seats properly on installation.

4 — Check the installed needle valve for leaks and correct operation.

### Carburetor body
1 — Check the bi-metal spring (1), heater element (2) and ceramic plate (3) for damage. If necessary, install a new cover assembly as the individual parts must not be replaced.

**FIG. 11**

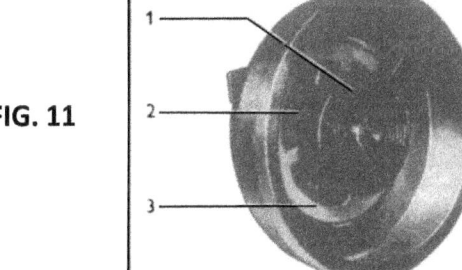

2 — Check the operation of the spring for the fast idle cam lever. Lubricate the steps on the cam.

3 — If the terminal on the cover is damaged, the cover should be replaced.

**Important** - See Fig. 12
When installing the cover, take care that the mark aligns with the mark on the housing.

FIG. 12

4 — Dip the float in hot water. If bubbles appear the float is leaking and must be replaced.

5 — Check all jets for correct sizes as shown in the "Carburetor Data." When replacing jets or valves, only genuine "SOLEX" parts should be used. All these parts are available as spares. Only these parts are accurately calibrated and ensure correct adjustment and low fuel consumption.

6 — Check throttle shaft clearance. Excessive clearance encourages the ingress of secondary air and has a detrimental effect on the starting and idling conditions. If necessary, the holes for the throttle shaft must be bushed.

7 — Examine the tapered portion of the volume control screw and replace if the tip is bent or broken. Only brass volume control screws should be used. Check the tapped hole and seat for the screw in the carburetor lower part and remove the tip of the old screw if it has broken off.

8 — Insert the capacity rod and needle valve.

## Main Jet With High Altitude Corrector - See Fig. 13

As the height above sea level increases the air becomes thinner, that is to say, it contains less oxygen. If the fuel quantity remains constant, the air to fuel ratio of the mixture will change. In order to maintain the proper portions of air and fuel and thus ensure the formation of the correct mixture, a high altitude corrector with a suitable main jet can be installed in place of the main jet carrier.

**Operation**

The main jet (1) of normal size is screwed to one end of the high altitude corrector. The fuel is supplied to the main jet through four oblique holes, and through a small hole between the main jet and the four oblique holes. The fuel also flows into the vacuum element chamber (3).

The vacuum element (4) is supposed axially and fixed in position at one end by means of an adaptor which is screwed into the housing. The conical end of the needle (2) which is mounted at the other end of the vacuum element slides freely in the passage leading to the main jet.

When the vacuum element (4) expands due to the changing atmospheric pressure at high altitudes, the needle progressively throttles the fuel supply for the main jet. The fuel supply through the small hole remains the same.

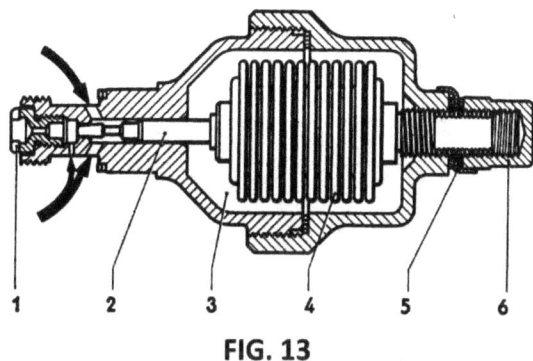

FIG. 13

The vacuum element is set during assembly by means of the adjusting nut (6) which is secured with a lock plate (5). This ensures that at sea level, the needle will be in a position which does not effect the normal fuel consumption.

**Caution**

The adjustment of the vacuum element must not be altered under any circumstances.

**Carburetor Settings**

The carburetor settings have been tested and established at the Volkswagen factory and should not normally be altered. Every carburetor is checked and set for standard fuel. Altering the settings by replacing the jets with non-standard sizes is detrimental under normal operating conditions and should be avoided. Excessive fuel consumption and poor engine performance are generally due to other causes. If the idling mixture is too rich the engine will tend to stall when braking sharply. The prescribed jet combination and a correctly adjusted idling speed are essential requirements for proper carburetor functioning. When changing from ordinary to super fuel it is usually only necessary to adjust the idling setting. This should be done carefully when the engine is warm.

**Specifications**

| | |
|---|---|
| Venturi (integral) | 23.5 mm dia. |
| Main jet | 137.5 |
| Air correction jet | 125 |
| Emulsion tube | 48 |
| Pilot jet | 45 |
| Pilot air bleed | 1.4 mm dia. |
| Pump jet | 0.8 mm dia. |
| Power fuel jet | 1.2 mm dia. |
| Float needle valve | 1.5 mm dia. |
| Pump delivery quantity | 1.2 cm³/stroke |

**Idle Adjustment**

The idle adjustment should be checked regularly and adjusted as required. **This should be carried out when the engine is warm.**

**Important**

Check that the stop screw is not resting on one of the steps of the fast idle cam.

1 — Set the engine idling speed to approximately 550 rpm. with the idle adjusting screw.

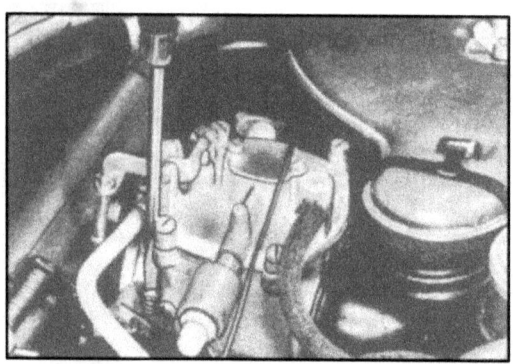

FIG. 14

2 — Turn the volume control screw to the right until the engine speed begins to drop, then give it a quarter to a third of a turn to the left.

FIG. 15

**Note:**

Turn the volume control screw carefully to avoid damaging the screw tip or the idle port.

3 — Regulate the idling speed as required.

The normal idling speed is usually attained with the volume control screw 1¼ to 1½ turns from the fully closed position. Take care when adjusting the screw as careless handling can easily lead to the tip of the screw or the idle port being damaged. Accurate idling adjustment is of great importance as it has a considerable influence on fuel consumption in the low and medium speed ranges. In some cases the consumption can be increased by as much as ½ litre over 100 kms (1 Imp. gallon over 560 miles or 1 U.S. gallon over 470 miles). This effect will be particularly noticeable on vehicles which are already operating under unfavourable conditions.

The adjustment is correct if the warm engine continues to run when the throttle is opened and closed suddenly with the clutch pedal depressed. If the engine stalls, the idling mixture is too weak and the volume control screw can be screwed out ⅛ of a turn. Finally check that the transfer is smooth by opening the throttle slowly and gradually increasing the engine speed. Should the engine stall when the throttle is closed quickly, for instance when braking sharply, the idling mixture is probably too rich. If the engine idles unevenly when all the adjustments have been checked, the fault may lie in a damaged intake manifold flange gasket, a cracked or loose intake manifold or an improperly adjusted fuel pump.

Faults in the ignition system and excessive variations between the compression pressures in the individual cylinders can also have a detrimental effect on the idling.

## 1965 1500 N. CARBURETOR SPECIFICATIONS

Carburetor ............................. SOLEX 32 PHN-1 side draft with accelerator pump and automatic choke
Choke tube ............................................................. 23.5 mm dia. (integral)
Main jet .................................................................................................... 130
Air correction jet ................................................................................... 115
Emulsion tube ......................................................................................... 48
Pilot jet[1]) ........................................ g 50 with electro-magnetic cut-off valve
Pilot jet air bleed ................................................................... 1.4 mm dia.
Pump jet ................................................................................. 0.7 mm dia.
Power fuel jet ....................................................................... 0.7 mm dia.
Float needle valve ............................................................... 1.5 mm dia.
Float weight .................................................... approx. 12.5 grams
Pump capacity ............................. 0.8 to 1.0 cc per stroke (adjustable

## 1500 S CARBURETOR SPECIFICATIONS

Carburetor .................... 2 SOLEX 32 PDSIT-2/-3 (left/right) downdraft carburetors with accelerator pumps and automatic chokes
Choke tube ............................................................................. 23 mm dia.
Main jet ........................................................................................ X 135
Air correction jet ............................................................................ 180
Pilot jet ........................................................................................... g 45
Pilot jet air bleed ................................................................... 2.0 mm dia.
Pump injection tube .............. 0.5 mm dia. (distance from center of tube to carburetor body 15 mm)
Power fuel jet ..................... 0.8 mm dia. (distance from center of tube to carburetor body 10.5)
Float needle valve .................... 1.2 mm dia. (gasket 1.5 mm thick)
Float weight ................................................................................. 7.3 grams
Pump capacity ............................................................. 0.35-0.55 cc per stroke
Air cleaner ................................................. Oil bath type with pre-heating tube
Fuel delivery ...... Mechanical diaphragm type pump with protective cap
Delivery pressure ................................................Maximum 3.0 m WS (4.3 psi.) at 3800 rpm
Quantity delivered via float
needle valve 1.2¹) ................... Min. 24 liters per hour (400 c per minute) at 3800 rpm
Fuel filtering ........................ By strainers in fuel tank and fuel pump
Fuel quantity indication ............ By fuel gauge with electrical sender unit
¹) with damping ball

## 1600 MODEL CARBURETOR SPECIFICATIONS

Carburetor .................... 2 SOLEX 32 PDSIT-2/-3 (left/right) downdraft carburetors with accelerator pumps and automatic chokes
Choke tube ............................................................................. 23 mm dia.
Main jet ........................................................................................ X 130
Air correction jet ............................................................................ 240
Pilot jet .............................. g 45 (with electro-magnetic cut-off valve)
Pilot jet air bleed ................................................................... 2.1 mm dia.
Pump injection tube .............. 0.5 mm dia. (distance from center of tube to carburetor body 16 mm)
Power fuel jet ..................... 0.8 mm dia. (distance from center of tube to carburetor body 14.5 mm)
Float needle valve .................... 1.2 mm dia. (gasket 1.5 mm thick)
Float weight ................................................................................. 7.3 grams
Pump capacity ............................................................. 0.35-0.55 cc per stroke
Air cleaner ................................................. Oil bath type with pre-heating tube
Fuel pump ..................... Diaphragm type, upper part with protective cap and fuel valve
Delivery pressure ................................................Maximum 3.0 m WS (4.3 psi.) at 3800 rpm
Quantity delivered via float
needle valve 1.2¹) ................... Min. 24 liters per hour (400 c per minute) at 3800 rpm

## Carburetor Trouble Checking

| Symptoms | Cause | Remedy |
|---|---|---|
| 1 - Engine will not start (with fuel in tank and ignition in order) | a - Automatic choke not working properly | a - Check the vacuum piston for freedom of movement and, if necessary squirt easing oil through the choke control housing |
| | b - Choke valve sticking | b - Free the choke valve shaft with easing oil (or tapping lightly with a hammer). Check intermediate spindle and free off if necessary |
| | c - Bi-metal spring unhooked or broken | c - Re-connect spring, or if broken, replace complete cover. **Note marks when installing** |
| | d - Float needle valve sticking and carburetor flooding | d - Clean or replace float needle valve |
| | | **Important** If a large quantity of fuel has passed from the flooded carburetor into the engine, switch on the ignition and wait 1 minute before starting and then open throttle fully. |
| 2 - Engine runs continually at a fast idle | a - Automatic choke not switching off | a - Check heater element cable and both connections |
| | b - Heater element defective | b - Replace complete cover. **Note marks when installing** |
| | c - Fast idle cam sticking | c - Free cam with easing oil |
| 3 - Engine idles unevenly or stalls | a - Idling adjustment incorrect | a - Adjust idling correctly (550—600 engine rpm or 1000 generator rpm, with clutch pedal depressed) |
| | b - Pilot jet blocked | b - Clean jet |
| | c - Electro-magnetic cut-off valve defective | c - Check if engine continues to run with valve at "Aus" (round valve) or with knurled nut loosened (elongated valve). If it does, replace cut-off valve |
| 4 - Engine "runs-on" when ignition is switched off | a - Idling mixture too rich | a - Weaken idling mixture |
| | b - Idling speed too fast | b - Regulate idling speed |
| | c - Electro-magnetic cut-off valve switch incorrectly set | c - The thicker part of the switch lever on the valve must be at "Ein" (round valve) or the knurled nut tightened (elongated valve) |

# Carburetor Trouble Checking

| Symptoms | Cause | Remedy |
|---|---|---|
| 5 - Banging in the exhaust when vehicle is over-running the engine | a - Idling mixture slightly weak | a - Enrich mixture by turning the volume control screw approximately $1/8$ of a turn |
| | b - Leakage | b - Push elbow on to the air cleaner adaptor so that it seals properly. Check intake manifold and carburetor for leaks (with fuel in a pressure oil can). Tighten nuts or replace gaskets |
| 6 - Poor transfer from idling to normal running | a - Accelerator system dirty, needle valve sticking | a - Check if the ball valve vent in the float chamber cover is free. Clean accelerator system and check that it is working properly |
| | b - Torn diaphragm | b - Replace diaphragm |
| | c - Idling adjustment incorrect | c - Adjust idling correctly |
| 7 - Engine stalls when accelerator pedal is released suddenly | Idling mixture too rich | Adjust idling correctly |
| 8 - Engine runs unevenly (surges) with black exhaust smoke at low idling speed and smokes badly as idling speed increases. Spark plugs soot-up quickly and mis-fire | a - Excessive pressure on the float needle valve | a - Check fuel pump pressure and reduce if necessary |
| | b - Leaky float | b - Replace float |
| | c - Float needle valve not closing | c - Check needle valve and replace if necessary |
| 9 - Engine runs unevenly at full throttle, misfires and cuts out or loses power | Fuel starvation | a - Clean main jet and power fuel system |
| | | b - Clean float needle valve |
| | | c - Check fuel pump pressure and increase if necessary (max. 4.3 lbs./sq. in.) |
| | | d - Clean fuel tank and strainer |
| 10 - Excessive fuel consumption | a - Jet sizes not properly matched | a - Install correct set of jets. Check spark plug condition |
| | b - Excessive pressure at float needle valve | b - Check fuel pump pressure (max. 4.3 lbs/sq. in.) |
| | c - Leaky float | c - Replace float |
| | d - Float needle valve not closing | d - Check needle valve and replace if necessary |
| | e - Automatic choke not working properly | e - Check heater cable and connections. Replace complete cover if necessary. **Note marks when installing** |

**Note:**

A poor transfer and a tendency to stall when idling can also be caused by insufficient ignition advance, inadequate breaker point gap or dirty spark plugs. Always check ignition system when in doubt.

## AUTOBOOKS WORKSHOP MANUALS

ALFA ROMEO GIULIA 1300, 1600, 1750, 2000 1962-1978 WSM
BMW 1600 1966-1973 WSM
BMW 2000 & 2002 1966-1976 WSM
BMW 2500, 2800, 3.0 & 3.3 1968-1977 WSM
BMW 316, 320, 320i 1975-1977 WSM
BMW 518, 520, 520i 1973-1981 WSM
FIAT 1100, 1100D, 1100R & 1200 1957-1969 WSM
FIAT 124 1966-1974 WSM
FIAT 124 SPORT 1966-1975 WSM
FIAT 125 & 125 SPECIAL 1967-1973 WSM
FIAT 126, 126L, 126 DV, 126/650 & 126/650 DV 1972-1982 WSM
FIAT 127 SALOON, SPECIAL & SPORT, 900, 1050 1971-1981 WSM
FIAT 128 1969-1982 WSM
FIAT 1300, 1500 1961-1967 WSM
FIAT 131 MIRAFIORI 1975-1982 WSM
FIAT 132 1972-1982 WSM
FIAT 500 1957-1973 WSM
FIAT 600, 600D & MULTIPLA 1955-1969 WSM
FIAT 850 1964-1972 WSM
JAGUAR E-TYPE 1961-1972 WSM
JAGUAR MK 1, 2 1955-1969 WSM
JAGUAR S TYPE, 420 1963-1968 WSM
JAGUAR XK 120, 140, 150 MK 7, 8, 9 1948-1961 WSM
LAND ROVER 1, 2 1948-1961 WSM
MERCEDES-BENZ 190 1959-1968 WSM
MERCEDES-BENZ 220/8 1968-1972 WSM
MERCEDES-BENZ 220B 1959-1965 WSM
MERCEDES-BENZ 230 1963-1968 WSM
MERCEDES-BENZ 250 1968-1972 WSM
MERCEDES-BENZ 280 1968-1972 WSM
MG MIDGET TA-TF 1936-1955 WSM
MINI 1959-1980 WSM
MORRIS MINOR 1952-1971 WSM
PEUGEOT 404 1960-1975 WSM
PORSCHE 911 1964-1973 WSM
PORSCHE 911 1970-1977 WSM
RENAULT 16 1965-1979 WSM
RENAULT 8, 10, 1100 1962-1971 WSM
ROVER 3500, 3500S 1968-1976 WSM
SUNBEAM RAPIER, ALPINE 1955-1965 WSM
TRIUMPH SPITFIRE, GT6, VITESSE 1962-1968 WSM
TRIUMPH TR2, TR3, TR3A 1952-1962 WSM
TRIUMPH TR4, TR4A 1961-1967 WSM
VOLKSWAGEN BEETLE 1968-1977 WSM

## VELOCEPRESS AUTOMOBILE BOOKS & MANUALS

ABARTH BUYERS GUIDE
AUSTIN-HEALEY 6-CYLINDER WSM
AUSTIN-HEALEY SPRITE & MG MIDGET 1958-1971 WSM
BMW 600 LIMOUSINE FACTORY WSM
BMW 600 LIMOUSINE OWNERS HAND BOOK & SERVICE MANUAL
BMW ISETTA FACTORY WSM
BOOK OF THE CARRERA PANAMERICANA - MEXICAN ROAD RACE
COMPLETE CATALOG OF JAPANESE MOTOR VEHICLES
CORVAIR 1960-1969 OWNERS WORKSHOP MANUAL
CORVETTE V8 1955-1962 OWNERS WORKSHOP MANUAL
DIALED IN - THE JAN OPPERMAN STORY
FERRARI 250/GT SERVICE AND MAINTENANCE
FERRARI 308 SERIES BUYER'S AND OWNER'S GUIDE
FERRARI BERLINETTA LUSSO
FERRARI BROCHURES AND SALES LITERATURE 1946-1967
FERRARI BROCHURES AND SALES LITERATURE 1968-1989
FERRARI GUIDE TO PERFORMANCE
FERRARI OPP, MAINTENANCE & SERVICE H/BOOKS 1948-1963
FERRARI OWNER'S HANDBOOK
FERRARI SERIAL NUMBERS PART I - ODD NUMBERS TO 21399
FERRARI SERIAL NUMBERS PART II - EVEN NUMBERS TO 1050
FERRARI SPYDER CALIFORNIA
FERRARI TUNING TIPS & MAINTENANCE TECHNIQUES
HENRY'S FABULOUS MODEL "A" FORD
HOW TO BUILD A FIBERGLASS CAR
HOW TO BUILD A RACING CAR
HOW TO RESTORE THE MODEL 'A' FORD
IF HEMINGWAY HAD WRITTEN A RACING NOVEL
JAGUAR E-TYPE 3.8 & 4.2 WSM
LE MANS 24 (THE BOOK THAT THE FILM WAS BASED ON)
MASERATI BROCHURES AND SALES LITERATURE
MASERATI OWNER'S HANDBOOK
METROPOLITAN FACTORY WSM
MGA & MGB OWNERS HANDBOOK & WSM
OBERT'S FIAT GUIDE
PERFORMANCE TUNING THE SUNBEAM TIGER
PORSCHE 356 1948-1965 WSM
PORSCHE 912 WSM
SOUPING THE VOLKSWAGEN
SOLEX CARBURETORS (EMPHASIS ON UK & EU AUTOMOBILES)
SU CARBURETORS (EMPHASIS ON UK AUTOMOBILES)
TRIUMPH TR2, TR3, TR4 1953-1965 WSM
TUNING FOR SPEED (P.E. IRVING)
VEDA ORR'S NEW REVISED HOT ROD PICTORIAL
VOLKSWAGEN TRANSPORTER, TRUCKS, STATION WAGONS WSM
VOLVO 1944-1968 WSM
WEBER CARBURETORS (EMPHASIS ON ALFA & FIAT)

## BROOKLANDS BOOKS & ROAD TEST PORTFOLIOS (RTP)

AC CARS 1904-2009
ALFA ROMEO 1920-1933 ROAD TEST PORTFOLIO
ALFA ROMEO 1934-1940 ROAD TEST PORTFOLIO
BRABHAM RALT HONDA THE RON TAURANAC STORY
BUGATTI TYPE 10 TO TYPE 40 ROAD TEST PORTFOLIO
BUGATTI TYPE 10 TO TYPE 251 ROAD TEST PORTFOLIO
BUGATTI TYPE 41 TO TYPE 55 ROAD TEST PORTFOLIO
BUGATTI TYPE 57 TO TYPE 251 ROAD TEST PORTFOLIO
DELAHAYE ROAD TEST PORTFOLIO
FERRARI ROAD CARS 1946-1956 ROAD TEST PORTFOLIO
FIAT 500 1936-1972 ROAD TEST PORTFOLIO
FIAT DINO ROAD TEST PORTFOLIO
HISPANO SUIZA ROAD TEST PORTFOLIO
HONDA ST1100/ST1300 PAN EUROPEAN 1990-2002 RTP
JAGUAR MK1 & MK2 ROAD TEST PORTFOLIO
LOTUS CORTINA ROAD TEST PORTFOLIO
MV AGUSTA F4 750 & 1000 1997-2007 ROAD TEST PORTFOLIO
TATRA CARS ROAD TEST PORTFOLIO

## VELOCEPRESS MOTORCYCLE BOOKS & MANUALS

AJS SINGLES & TWINS 250cc THRU 1000cc 1932-1948 (BOOK OF)
AJS SINGLES 1955-65 350cc & 500cc (BOOK OF)
AJS SINGLES 1945-60 350cc & 500cc MODELS 16 & 18 (BOOK OF)
ARIEL 1939-1960 4 STROKE SINGLES (BOOK OF)
ARIEL LEADER & ARROW 1958-1964 (BOOK OF)
ARIEL MOTORCYCLES 1933-1951 WSM
ARIEL PREWAR MODELS 1932-1939 (BOOK OF)
BMW M/CYCLES R26 R27 (1956-1967) FACTORY WSM
BMW M/CYCLES R50 R50S R60 R69S (1955-1969) FACTORY WSM
BSA BANTAM (BOOK OF)
BSA ALL FOUR-STROKE SINGLES & V-TWINS 1936-1952 (BOOK OF)
BSA OHV & SV SINGLES - 250cc 1954-1970 (BOOK OF)
BSA OHV & SV SINGLES 1945-54 250-600cc (BOOK OF)
BSA OHV SINGLES 350 & 500cc 1955-1967 (BOOK OF)
BSA PRE-WAR MODELS TO 1939 (BOOK OF)
BSA TWINS 1948-1962 (BOOK OF)
BSA TWINS 1962-1969 (SECOND BOOK OF)
CATALOG OF BRITISH MOTORCYCLES (1951 MODELS)
DOUGLAS PRE-WAR ALL MODELS 1929-1939 (BOOK OF)
DOUGLAS POST-WAR ALL MODELS 1948-1957 FACTORY WSM
DUCATI 160cc, 250cc & 350cc OHC MODELS FACTORY WSM
HONDA 50 ALL MODELS UP TO 1970 INC MONKEY & TRAIL (BOOK OF)
HONDA 90 ALL MODELS UP TO 1966 (BOOK OF)
HONDA MOTORCYCLES 125-150 TWINS C/CS/CB/CA WSM
HONDA MOTORCYCLES 250-305 TWINS C/CS/CB WSM
HONDA MOTORCYCLES C100 SUPER CUB WSM
HONDA MOTORCYCLES C110 SPORT CUB 1962-1969 WSM
HONDA TWINS & SINGLES 50cc THRU 305cc 1960-1966 (BOOK OF)
HONDA TWINS ALL MODELS 125cc THRU 450cc UP TO 1968 (BOOK OF)
INDIAN PONYBIKE, BOY RACER & PAPOOSE ILL PARTS LIST & SALES LIT
J.A.P. ENGINES 1927-1952 & MOTORCYCLES 1934-1952 (BOOK OF)
LAMBRETTA ALL 125 & 150cc MODELS 1947-1957 (BOOK OF)
LAMBRETTA LI & TV MODELS 1957-1970 (SECOND BOOK OF)
MATCHLESS 350 & 500cc SINGLES 1945-1956 (BOOK OF)
MATCHLESS 350 & 500cc SINGLES 1955-1966 (BOOK OF)
NORTON 1932-1947 (BOOK OF)
NORTON 1938-1956 (BOOK OF)
NORTON DOMINATOR TWINS 1955-1965 (BOOK OF)
NORTON MODELS 19, 50 & ES2 1955-1963 (BOOK OF)
NORTON MOTORCYCLES 1957-1970 FACTORY WSM
NORTON PREWAR MODELS 1932-1939 (BOOK OF)
NSU PRIMA ALL MODELS 1956-1964 (BOOK OF)
NSU QUICKLY ALL MODELS 1953-1963 (BOOK OF)
RALEIGH MOPEDS 1960-1969 (BOOK OF)
ROYAL ENFIELD SINGLES & V TWINS 1937-1953 (BOOK OF)
ROYAL ENFIELD SINGLES 1946-1962 (BOOK OF)
ROYAL ENFIELD 736cc INTERCEPTOR FACTORY WSM
ROYAL ENFIELD 250cc & 350cc SINGLES 1958-1966 (SECOND BOOK OF)
SUNBEAM MOTORCYCLES 1928-1939 (BOOK OF)
SUNBEAM S7 & S8 1946-1957 (BOOK OF)
SUZUKI 50cc & 80cc UP TO 1966 (BOOK OF)
SUZUKI T10 1963-1967 FACTORY WSM
SUZUKI T20 & T200 1965-1969 FACTORY WSM
TRIUMPH PRE-WAR MOTORCYCLE 1935-1939 (BOOK OF)
TRIUMPH MOTORCYCLES 1935-1949 (BOOK OF)
TRIUMPH MOTORCYCLES 1937-1951 WSM
TRIUMPH MOTORCYCLES 1945-1955 FACTORY WSM
TRIUMPH TWINS 1945-1958 (BOOK OF)
TRIUMPH TWINS 1956-1969 (BOOK OF)
VELOCETTE ALL SINGLES & TWINS 1925-1970 (BOOK OF)
VESPA 1951-1961 (BOOK OF)
VESPA 125 & 150cc & GS MODELS 1955-1963 (SECOND BOOK OF)
VESPA 90, 125 & 150cc 1963-1972 (THIRD BOOK OF)
VESPA 65 & 35 1955 1968 (BOOK OF)
VILLIERS ENGINE (BOOK OF)
VINCENT MOTORCYCLES 1935-1955 WSM

**PLEASE VISIT OUR WEBSITE
www.VelocePress.com
FOR A DETAILED DESCRIPTION
OF ANY OF THESE TITLES**

Other books in this same series
of 'Floyd Clymer' carburetor
manuals are available from:

www.VelocePress.com

Please visit our website for a complete list of our automobile and motorcycle titles

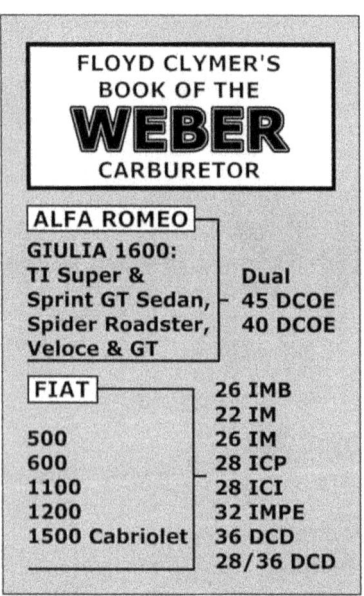

Floyd Clymer's
Book Of The
Weber
Carburetor

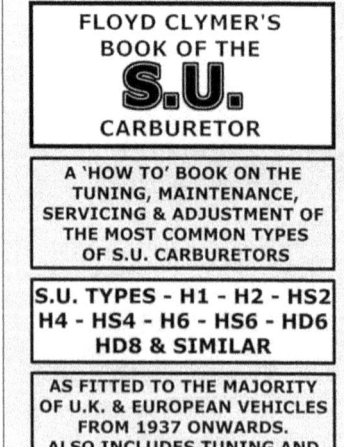

Floyd Clymer's
Book Of The
S.U.
Carburetor

www.ingramcontent.com/pod-product-compliance
Lightning Source LLC
Chambersburg PA
CBHW060347190426
43201CB00043B/1759